MATTHEW

Readings: A New Biblical Commentary

MATTHEW

Margaret Davies

JSOT PRESS

In memory of my mother, Gwynneth Davies, and in gratitude to
my stepmother, Renie Davies, and to my aunt, Betty Cleeves.

Copyright © 1993 Sheffield Academic Press

Published by JSOT Press
JSOT Press is an imprint of
Sheffield Academic Press Ltd
343 Fulwood Road
Sheffield S10 3BP
England

Typeset by Sheffield Academic Press
and
Printed on acid-free paper in Great Britain
by Bookcraft (Bath) Limited
Bath

British Library Cataloguing in Publication Data

Davies, Margaret
    Matthew.—(Readings: A New Biblical
    Commentary, ISSN 0952-7656)
    I. Title II. Series
    226.2

ISBN 1-85075-392-x
ISBN 1-85075-432-2 pa

Contents

Acknowledgments

I would like to express my indebtedness not only to the many academic studies that have informed my own, but also to the undergraduate and postgraduate students whose questions and comments have helped me to develop my interpretation of the Gospel according to Matthew. In addition, I am very grateful for the help and support of the editor of the *Readings* series, Professor David Clines, and of the desk editor, Ms Helen Tookey. Mrs Audrey Newton and Mrs Gillian Fogg kindly prepared the indexes. They deserve my sincere thanks.

Introduction

The Gospel according to Matthew was written in Hellenistic Greek nearly two thousand years ago. How are we to read and understand it at the end of the twentieth century? We have no reliable external evidence about who wrote it, for whom or in what particular circumstances. In the late second century, Christians speculated about the identity of the author, and some attributed the work to the apostle Matthew in an attempt to give it apostolic authority. The attribution, however, cannot be traced to an earlier period, and, even if it were correct, we know next to nothing about the apostle Matthew. In particular, we have no external information about why the author wrote the narrative, from which Greek sources he worked, or for what situation he wrote. But we do have the text itself, or rather, we have handwritten copies of the text from the third, fourth and subsequent centuries, the earliest written on either papyrus or vellum. From these it is possible to reconstruct, to a very large extent, what the original work must have contained. I shall use, and translate into English, the critically reconstructed text, edited by Kurt Aland, Matthew Black, Carlo Martini, Bruce Metzger and Allen Wikren, in the third (corrected) edition of *The Greek New Testament*[1] and I shall notice and interpret variant readings provided in the critical apparatus.

The text is written in Hellenistic Greek, a language which no one speaks or writes today. Moreover, it differs from many other Hellenistic Greek works in that it contains stylistic peculiarities which seem to reflect idioms from another language group, the Semitic languages. Some of these peculiarities are to be explained by the fact that the text quotes other texts, the Jewish Scriptures, most of which were originally written in Hebrew. Translations of these Hebrew Scriptures into Greek (for example, the Septuagint) sometimes reflect the original Hebrew constructions, hence creating new Greek idioms. For example, the use of a double negative in a prohibition is found in the quotation in Mt. 13.14 and is typical of the Septuagint. It is also found in the Gospel outside quotations (e.g. 16.22, 21.19). Similarly, the use of the verb 'to take' as an auxiliary is found in the quotation in 27.9 and outside of quotations (e.g. 17.27; 25.1; 27.24, 48, 59). Other Semitic idioms in the Greek of the Gospel seem to reflect the Aramaic language spoken in the Near East during the first century CE; for example, 'the son of the human being' or 'the son of

---

1   United Bible Societies, 1983.

man' is an Aramaic idiom for 'the human being' (e.g. 8.20; 9.6). Similarly, 'sons of the kingdom' is an Aramaism for those who were to inherit the kingdom (8.12; 13.38), 'sons of the evil one' is an Aramaism for human agents of the evil one (13.38), and 'sons of your Father who is in heaven' is an Aramaism for human agents of your heavenly Father (5.45). The text also contains transliterations of Hebrew or Aramaic words: 'amen' (5.18, 26); 'gehenna' (5.22); 'rabbi' (23.7, 8); 'Golgotha' (27.33); 'Satan' (4.10; 12.26). It is clear that one answer to the question 'how are we to read and understand the Gospel according to Matthew?' is that we must be conversant with the kind of Hellenistic Greek in which the text is written. Those who do not read this Greek will have to rely on translations provided by others, and to recognize that translations are always interpretive approximations, whether they are mine or those of printed English editions.

Not only is the language of the First Gospel no longer spoken or written, but the cultural, political and economic world in which it was written or to which it refers no longer exists. We are fortunate in having a mass of information from archaeology and from other works of the period from which a general reconstruction of Jewish life in Palestine and Christian life in the eastern Mediterranean under the Roman imperial system in the first century CE may be attempted. But we lack particulars, and, even on the general level, there is room for debate because of the inevitable limitations of the evidence. Moreover, the text itself is a creative interpretation, not only of anthropological, political, economic and ethical realities, but also of theological realities. The world which the text creates may never have existed in history. The narrative also includes references to future events which it recognizes as not yet existing (e.g. chs. 24–25). It will be necessary to elucidate the human and theological world which the narrative creates, both through a sympathetic absorption into that narrative world, and by a critical discussion of its anthropological, historical, ethical and theological references.

Is it possible, however, for any twentieth-century reader to become absorbed into, or moved and enlightened by, a narrative, whether an ancient or a modern work? What powers can a narrative exert over a reader? These are questions which have exercised many modern literary critics who are linked together under the collective description 'reader-response critics'. They all recognize, of course, that a text can exert no power over a reader unless that reader decides to read the text. They also notice that a reader can decide to read a text for a variety of reasons which affect the reading. For example, a reader may read a text to while away a few hours. Even such a purpose would fail, however, unless the reader were to make enough sense of the text to continue the task. Or readers may read a text because they wish to appear well-read in the social group to which they belong. Just which texts are available for reading, and which of them are accorded relative importance, depends on the cultural and social interests of the readers' societies. The easy availability of texts and translations of the Gospel according to Matthew depends, not only on the cultural and social interests of groups within modern Western societies, but also on the cultural and social interests of some groups over a period of nearly two thousand years. The text attained and retained the status of a 'classic', eventually forming part of the Christian church's sacred Scriptures. But can even an ideal reader, who reads the text to understand and appreciate its meanings, and who is prepared to take a lot of time and trouble to do so, really understand the text itself?

Readers come to a text with varieties of experience in reading, and their experience will affect their appreciation of the new narrative. Readers who come to the First Gospel after reading modern philosophical texts will be dissatisfied with its presentation of philosophical, anthropological and theological assumptions for which no philosophical arguments are offered. Readers familiar with modern forms of historical writing will be puzzled by the Gospel's narrative focus, which tells the story through the eyes of an omniscient and omnipresent narrator, without citing or assessing sources, and without reflection on the causal connections between events which the narrative implies. Readers who enjoy nineteenth-century historical novels will immediately recognize the convention of the omniscient and omnipresent narrator, but may understand the First Gospel as fiction rather than as some form of history. Readers of modern detective fiction will find that the many predictions of what would happen to Jesus before the events are described create a different form of suspense. Readers who like modern biographies will miss descriptions of the social setting, the subject's upbringing and education and the continuing influences these may exercise. Even readers of ancient Hellenistic biographies may be affronted by the subject's low social status, by the narrow and provincial scope of his ministry, and by the strange theological, anthropological and eschatological elements in the narrative world.

The reading experience which would best prepare people who want to make sense of the First Gospel would include the whole of Jewish Scriptures, and especially those narratives about the prophets Moses (Exodus–Deuteronomy), Elijah (1 Kings 17–2 Kings 2) and Elisha (1 Kings 19–2 Kings 13), and the eschatological predictions in the books of Isaiah, Ezekiel and Daniel, and in other Jewish works, such as *1 Enoch* and *2 Baruch*, which never became part of Jewish or Christian Scriptures. In addition, familiarity with other Gospels, those according to Mark, Luke and John within the New Testament, as well as the Gospels according to Thomas and Peter, and the *Protevangelium of James*, which did not become part of Christian Scriptures, would help to situate the Gospel within a broad genre or kind of writing. Reading modern scholarly reconstructions of people's lives in the first-century eastern Mediterranean would help modern readers of the Gospel to concretize some aspects of the narrative world while wide reading in theology and ethics would introduce them to the narrative's central concerns. Nevertheless, can even such experienced readers really understand the text? Since all readers have to *make* sense of the text, is not every reading an idiosyncratic creation?

The initial answer to this question must be 'yes'. Every reader brings to a reading his or her own unique experience, experience both of living and of reflecting on life. Each reading is therefore limited by the individual's experience. But how much of a constraint is this obvious limitation? Norman Holland argues that,

> all of us, as we read, use the literary work to symbolise and finally to replicate ourselves. We work out through the text our own characteristic patterns of desire and adaptation. We interact with the work, making it part of our own psychic economy and making ourselves part of the literary work—as we interpret it.[1]

He goes on to specify three modalities in which our identity recreates itself as we read:

> First, adaptations must be matched; and, therefore, we interpret the new experience in such a way as to cast it in terms of our characteristic ways of coping with the world.[2]

In more detail:

> The individual can accept the literary work only to the extent he exactly recreates with it a verbal form of his particular pattern of defense mechanisms and, in a broader sense, the particular system of adaptive strategies that he keeps between himself and the world.[3]

Once this is achieved, the reader,

> derives from it [the work so adapted] fantasies of the particular kind that yield him pleasure ...The fantasy content we conventionally locate in the literary work is really created by the reader from the literary work to express his own desires.[4]

Moreover,

> different readers can all gain pleasure from the same fantasy and one reader can gain pleasure from many different fantasies because

---

    1   'Unity Identity Text Self', in J.P. Tompkins (ed.), *Reader-Response Criticism* (Baltimore: Johns Hopkins University Press, 1980), p. 124.
    2   Holland, 'Unity Identity Text Self', p. 124.
    3   Holland, 'Unity Identity Text Self', p. 125.
    4   Holland, 'Unity Identity Text Self', p. 125.

all readers create from the fantasy seemingly 'in' the work fantasies to suit their several character structures.[1]

Finally,

> a third modality completes the individual's re-creation of his identity or life-style from the literary work…We seek our own particular version of the aesthetic unity Plato and Aristotle first described, but we use other ways as well: comparing this experience with others, associating to it, bringing one's knowledge or expertise to bear, evaluating it, placing it in a tradition, treating it as an encoded message to be decoded, and all the other strategies of professional, amateur and vulgar literary criticism. All serve to synthesise the experience and make it part of the mind's continuing effort to balance the pressures of the drives for gratification, the restraints of conscience and reality, and one's inner need to avoid emotional and cognitive dissonance.[2]

Holland's description of the reading process leads me to recognize, albeit dimly, my own desire to avoid emotional and cognitive dissonance, and readers of the following narrative will perceive my strategies of avoidance more clearly than I do. But I do not accept that my defences are impregnable or that I am isolated in the prison of my own ego. Were that picture true, I should never have learned to speak, to read or to write, since all communication would have been impossible. Nor should I have related to other people and to the world in non-linguistic ways. In fact, Holland denies that he is positing an isolated, solipsistic self. Rather, he concludes:

> Every time a human being reaches out, across or by means of symbols, to the world, he re-enacts the principles that define that mingling of self and other, the creative and relational quality of all our experience, not least the writing and reading of literature.[3]

But Holland does not go on to explore in more detail the creative and relational quality of all our experience.

Other reader-response critics have elucidated various aspects of that relational quality. For example, Stanley Fish has drawn attention to the important fact that readers belong to interpretive communities.[4] He asks the following questions:

> Why should two or more readers ever agree, and why should regular, that is, habitual, differences in the career of a single reader ever occur? What is the explanation on the one hand of the

1   Holland, 'Unity Identity Text Self', p. 126.
2   Holland, 'Unity Identity Text Self', p. 126.
3   Holland, 'Unity Identity Text Self', pp. 131-32.
4   'Interpreting the Variorum', in Tompkins (ed.) *Reader-Response Criticism*.

stability of interpretation (at least among certain groups at certain times) and on the other of the orderly variety of interpretations if it is not the stability and variety of texts?[1]

And he suggests the following answer: 'The answer to all these questions is to be found in ...the notion of interpretive communities'.[2] He defines interpretive communities as communities

> made up of those who share interpretive strategies not for reading (in the conventional sense) but for writing texts, for constituting their properties and assigning their intentions. In other words these strategies exist prior to the act of reading and therefore determine the shape of what is read rather than, as is usually assumed, the other way round ...This, then, is the explanation both for the stability of interpretation among different readers (they belong to the same community) and for the regularity with which a single reader will employ different interpretive strategies and thus make different texts (he belongs to different communities).[3]

Moreover, this perception helps to account for changes from one period to another:

> Interpretive communities grow larger and decline, and individuals move from one to another; thus while the alignments are not permanent, they are always there, providing just enough stability for the interpretive battles to go on, and just enough shift and slippage to ensure that they will never be settled.[4]

The changes highlight the fact that 'interpretive communities are no more stable than texts because interpretive communities are not natural and universal, but learned'.[5] Nevertheless,

> this does not mean that there is a point at which an individual has not yet learned any. The ability to interpret is not acquired; it is constitutive of being human. What is acquired are the ways of interpreting and those same ways can be forgotten or supplanted, or complicated or dropped from favour.[6]

People who are familiar with the history of biblical interpretation will recognize the force of Fish's argument. Modern commentaries do not employ the same strategies as their mediaeval predecessors, for example, and, in Fish's sense, do not write (rather than read) the same texts. Modern commentaries are far less interested in theology and far more interested in history. Moreover, even amongst modern commentaries, it is possible to distinguish, on the basis of the writings alone, without any

1   Fish, 'Interpreting the Variorum', p. 182.
2   Fish, 'Interpreting the Variorum', p. 182.
3   Fish, 'Interpreting the Variorum', p. 182.
4   Fish, 'Interpreting the Variorum', p. 182.
5   Fish, 'Interpreting the Variorum', p. 183.
6   Fish, 'Interpreting the Variorum', p. 183.

prior knowledge of the authors' biographies, to which interpretive communities they belong. Academic commentaries differ from pastoral, Catholic from Protestant, evangelical from liberal. Every commentary highlights some matters while obscuring others through its interpretive strategies. My commentary will be no exception, so let me tell the reader to which interpretive communities I belong. I am a British, female academic, a member of the Anglican church, but not of its evangelical wing, a member of the Labour Party and of several civil liberty groups.

Nevertheless, Fish's account of the reading process considers only one side of it, the conserving and confirming side. It entirely overlooks its disconcerting and undermining aspects. Were Fish's account correct, it would be impossible to explain why oppressive political regimes have found it necessary to ban particular books. 'Interpretive communities' cannot immunize people against finding new and unexpected insights in narratives, any more than they can entirely obscure the invalidity of arguments. Fish supposes that truth and 'belief acceptable to an interpretive community' are one and the same. His understanding of rhetoric is too narrow, recognizing its persuasive force but failing to notice its cognitive force.[1] It is manifestly the case that rationality is relative to the standards of some particular tradition, and that truths claimed at one time may come to seem inadequate in the future, but these observations do not provide support for Fish's relativist view. On the contrary, when interpretive communities recognize that they can no longer assert the truths that they once found persuasive, they have to meet the crisis, either by discovering what they lack in other traditions, or by linguistic innovation. If the crisis cannot be met, the interpretive community disappears.[2] In *After Virtue*,[3] MacIntyre makes an essential distinction between practices and institutions, which Fish fails to see. A practice is a coherent and complex form of socially established co-operative human activity by which goods internal to that activity are achieved: standards of excellence appropriate to and partially definitive of the activity. So, there are practices appropriate to, for example, the arts, including theology, the sciences, games, politics and family life. Practices systematically extend human conceptions of the ends and goods involved, but these ends and goods are always internal to the practice. The practice of medicine, for example, systematically extends knowledge of human physical and mental well-being and the effective prevention and treatment of illness, by doctors entering into a relationship with fellow practitioners of the past and present. The virtues of justice, courage and

1 See C. Norris, *What's Wrong with Postmodernism?* (London: Harvester Wheatsheaf, 1990), ch. 2.
2 See A. MacIntyre, *Whose Justice? Which Rationality?* (London: Duckworth, 1988).
3 London: Duckworth, 1981.

honesty are internal to the practice. The pursuit of money or fame are not internal to the practice and if they become the ends, the practice is undermined. Social institutions should facilitate practices, but we can ask how far they do so. How far do particular health services facilitate the practice of medicine? How far do particular church and university institutions facilitate the practice of theology? Recent government policies in Britain have attempted to replace goals internal to these practices with 'market forces', that is, the pursuit of financial objectives. How far do these ends undermine the practices which the institutions are supposed to facilitate?

I shall attempt to make sense of the Gospel according to Matthew in its own terms, as an expression of theological and ethical practice in the first-century church. I shall try to do justice to its insights and not to use the text to justify twentieth-century Anglican practice or the activities of Amnesty International. Reading and reflecting on the text has given me surprises and uncomfortable challenges. The text has not always confirmed what I already believed, nor has it always expressed what I wanted it to express.

One of the interpretive strategies which will be used in my interpretation of the Gospel according to Matthew is that described by another reader-response critic, Wolfgang Iser.[1] Iser, like his fellow reader-response critics, recognizes that texts themselves are indeterminate and that it is the reader who makes them determinate. He admits that literary works initiate 'performances' of meaning, while denying that the texts determine that meaning. Nevertheless, he distinguishes actual readers from 'implied readers'. A history of responses or interpretations would have the actual readers in view, whereas concentration on the potential effects of a literary text has the 'implied reader' in view. The 'implied reader' embodies all those predispositions necessary for a literary work to have its effect, predispositions which are laid down in the text itself and which trigger the re-creative response of the 'implied reader'. The text's structure pre-structures the 'implied reader's response. Each actualization by a real reader represents a selective realization of the 'implied reader'.

For Iser, literature is not a depiction of reality, it does not provide a window on the world, but relates rather to models or concepts of reality. The repertoire of the text, with its references to earlier works, to social and historical norms, to the whole culture from which the text has emerged, reduces contingencies and complexities to a meaningful structure. The text can therefore stand over against contingent reality by forming new patterns of meaning, which the 'implied reader' is encouraged to experience. The literary repertoire supplies guidelines for

1   W. Iser, *The Act of Reading: A Theory of Aesthetic Response* (ET; Baltimore: Johns Hopkins University Press, 1978).

a dialogue between text and reader, offering possibilities of comprehension. Four perspectives interact: the perspective of the narrator, the perspectives of characters, the perspective of the plot, and the perspective of the 'implied reader'. Ultimate meanings transcend each of the more determinate elements of the text through their interplay.

Hence, text and reader are not related as object and observer, because the reader is 'in' the text, moving with it. And the text is not just denotive. Readers do not simply find out whether the text gives an accurate or inaccurate depiction of an object; rather, they have to build up the object for themselves, sometimes in a manner running counter to the familiar world. And the shifting viewpoint of the text, for example the shift from the narrator's to the character's viewpoint, forces the reader to synthesize. Consistency is the product of the interaction of text and reader, meanings are dependent on groupings. What is meant can be the opposite of what is said, as when irony is used. The selection of which possibility dominates the grouping is the reader's and is dependent on her or his dispositions and experiences. Naturally, we can only bring another person's thoughts into our foreground if they are in some way related to the background of our own orientations. Otherwise they would be totally incomprehensible. Nevertheless, our assimilation of the alien experience has retroactive effects on our own store of experience.

Iser, however, notes that some texts are more indeterminate than others. Modern novels which are focused through an unreliable narrator or through several narrators, or which try to abandon the narrator altogether, are far more indeterminate than didactic texts. The techniques of didactic narratives like the First Gospel attempt to manoeuvre readers into the right position so that all they have to do is adopt the attitude mapped out for them. 'The right position' is that of the narrator's and hero's perspective, which coincide and reinforce one another, and other perspectives function as contrasts to bring about acceptance of the hero's values. Nevertheless, readers' participation is still essential for the text to become a reality, and the decision to accept or reject 'the right position', however closely guided, is still that of the readers.

The reading which follows will attempt, on the one hand, to appreciate the force of the Gospel's rhetoric, creatively responding to its strategies and conventions, and playing the role mapped out for the 'implied reader'. On the other hand, it will recognize the gap which exists between this 'implied reader' and modern Western readers, and will discuss ethical, social, historical and theological issues which arise from this difference in perspectives.

Before I begin, however, it may be helpful for me to draw attention to the major conventions and strategies through which the Gospel according to Matthew guides readers' responses. The First Gospel purports to give an account of past events, centring on the life, death and resurrection of Jesus of Nazareth, and reactions to him. In some sense, it is, then, a historical narrative. But it is different from modern historical narratives in a number of respects, which will be discussed one by one.

1. The Gospel provides no extended descriptions of the political, social and economic environment in which Jesus lived. It mentions some contemporary officials: Herod the king, in connection with Jesus' birth (Mt. 2.1-19. Herod the Great died in 4 BCE); Archelaus, his son, who ruled Judaea (2.22. He also ruled Samaria, and was deposed in 6 CE); Herod the tetrarch's execution of John the Baptist at the request of the daughter of Herodias, who is described as his brother's wife, whom he had subsequently married (14.1-12. Herod Antipas, the tetrarch, another of Herod the Great's sons, ruled Galilee and Peraea from 4 BCE until he was deposed in 39 CE. Josephus, the first-century Jewish historian, mentions that Herod Antipas married Herodias, and calls her the wife of his half-brother Herod [*Ant.* 18.110, 148]); Pilate, the governor in Jerusalem (27.2-26. Rome ruled Judaea through its own Roman appointee after Archelaus was deposed, and Pontius Pilate was prefect from 26–36 CE. He normally resided at Caesarea, but moved to Jerusalem during Jewish pilgrimage festivals); Caesar (22.17. Tiberius was the Roman emperor, that is, Caesar, from 14–37 CE. Anyone who lived in Palestine was subject to Roman taxation); Caiaphas the high priest (26.3-5, 57-68. According to Jewish law, the high priest was appointed for life, but Rome deposed those high priests whom it found unsatisfactory and another member of the chief priestly families became high priest. Caiaphas was high priest from about 18–36 CE). The Matthaean text provides no dates, but the names of these officials imply a date for Jesus' life between about 4 BCE and about 36 CE. We have to use other sources, especially the works of Josephus, to fill in historical details and to gain an understanding of Rome's political control of the area. Herod Antipas and other descendents of Herod the Great inherited sections of his empire over which they ruled as clients of Rome, but, as practising Jews, they could regulate internal affairs as long as taxes were paid to Rome and peace was maintained. Judaea and Samaria were ruled by a Roman prefect, subject to the Roman legate of Syria, but Jewish interests in Judaea were safeguarded by the high priest and his advisors. In fact, Jews had gained important concessions from Rome during the first century BCE, which allowed them to keep the sabbath and to offer sacrifices in the Jerusalem temple for the emperor rather than to Roman gods. They also had the right to assemble in their synagogues, both in Palestine and throughout the Roman world (see Josephus, *Ant.* 14.190-267).

The Gospel also refers to some social groups among the Jewish population of Palestine—Pharisees, scribes, Sadducees, chief priests and Herodians—but without indicating their number or relative influence. Again more details can be gained from Josephus's works. He numbers the Pharisees at about 6000 (*Ant.* 17.42) whereas the number of priests seems to have been about 20,000 (*Apion* 2.108). From among the priests, a much smaller group constituted the chief priestly families. It is surprising that none of the Gospels mentions the important Jewish sect, the Essenes, which Josephus numbers at 4000 (*Ant.* 18.20).

Incidental references in the Gospel assume a social situation in which there were soldiers of the occupying power (Mt. 5.41; 27.27-50); there were tax collectors (9.9-11. Taxes were collected by a system of farming them out. At each stage, the tax collector could take his cut from the proceeds); there were divisions between rich and poor (e.g. 19.16-23), there were debtors (e.g. 18.23-35), there were absentee landlords (e.g. 25.14-30), servants and masters (e.g. 24.45-51). Apparently, society allowed men to divorce their wives but not vice versa (5.31-32; 19.3-10). This fits into the general picture of a patriarchal society. Agricultural and pastoral concerns seem to predominate, but merchants appear in 13.45 and 25.14-30, and fishermen in 4.18-22 and 13.47-50. Illness of all kinds, some of it understood as demon possession, is pictured as pervasive.

2. The Gospel contains no extended descriptions of geography and many of the incidents related are not exactly located. Readers gain a general impression of Galilean hill country near the lake, and some small Galilean settlements are named and even called, inappropriately, cities. Nazareth was the place where Jesus grew up (2.21-23), but as an adult he moved to Capernaum on the lake (4.13), where most of his ministry was centred. There are general references to Jesus' visits to other Galilean settlements (e.g. 9.35), but the only other one to be named is Chorazin (11.21), and what happened there is not depicted. It is surprising that neither Antipas's old capital, Sepphoris, nor his new capital, Tiberias, is mentioned. Bethsaida and Caesarea-Philippi were in Philip the tetrarch's territory (11.21; 16.13. Philip, half-brother to Antipas, ruled Iturea and Trachonitis from 4 BCE until 34 CE). Jesus' activities are said to have attracted crowds from a much wider area—Syria, the Decapolis, Jerusalem, Judaea and beyond the Jordan river (presumably Peraea [4.23-25])—and one incident is set across the Galilean lake in the country of the Gadarenes (8.28-34). The incidents in 15.21-39 are placed in the district of Tyre and Sidon, two important Gentile ports on the Mediterranean coast. John the Baptist's ministry is located in the wilderness of Judaea near the river Jordan (3.1, 5, 13) but since he was imprisoned and executed by Herod Antipas, readers have to infer that he was sometimes active in the latter's territory. The wilderness in which Jesus was put to the test is not specified (4.1-11).

Jesus is described leaving Galilee for Judaea (19.1) and Jerusalem (20.17), via Jericho (20.29), and some places around Jerusalem are mentioned: the Mount of Olives (21.1; 24.3), Bethphage (21.1), Bethany (21.17; 26.6), Gethsemane (26.36-56) and Golgotha (27.33). Of these, only the Mount of Olives and Bethany can be exactly located today. Most of the incidents related in chs. 21–25 are set in or just outside the Jerusalem temple, but there is only an incidental reference to its buildings (24.1) and no indication of its magnificence. The text assumes its centrally important role in Jewish religious life, and the setting of the final days of Jesus' life is at one of the three annual pilgrim festivals, Passover. Otherwise, there are references to sacrifices which were offered at the temple (5.23-24; 8.4), to the temple tax which all Jews paid for its upkeep (17.24-27), and to tithes, which Palestinian Jews also gave to the temple (23.23-24). The temple personnel, the high priest Caiaphas, the chief priests (other priests are mentioned only in 8.4 and 12.4-5) and their officers play important roles in the passion narrative (chs. 26–27). Perhaps readers are to assume that Jesus was first taken after his arrest to the high priest's house, with a courtyard (26.57-75). Such large houses with courtyards have been excavated in the upper city, near the temple. The praetorium, where Pilate stayed when he visited Jerusalem, could refer either to Herod's palace in the upper city or to the Antonia fortress which overlooked the temple, and where Roman troops were stationed (27.27). The judgment seat (27.19) would have been in the square outside. No precise location in or outside of Jerusalem is indicated for the house in which Jesus ate his last supper (26.17-29), or for the site of his burial (27.60-61; 28.1-8).

Insofar as archaeology and other literature allow us to locate the named places, they fit into the historical period encompassed by the narrative.

3. Historical narratives recount a series of events which imply a system of cause and effect. In modern histories, geographical, political, economic, ethnic, social and individual factors are woven into such a system. The religious convictions of groups are described when they are pertinent to developments. The system of cause and effect which the Matthaean series of events imply is, however, different. Its account of historical events is set within a theological framework, according to which the transcendent God, the Creator of all things, is the first and final cause. The theological perceptions of the Jewish Scriptures are taken over, and those Scriptures are quoted and alluded to as authoritative oracles of God which indicate both his nature and his purpose for human beings.

Although the world is seen as God's creation and is, therefore, good, Scripture's view of human beings is also assumed: they are mortal creatures who are understood to have lived lives which are unjust and violent, and, in doing so, to have rebelled against God, become sinners, failed to conform to God's purpose, and acted disobediently. Scripture had depicted the violence of human society as abhorrent to the Creator God (Gen. 6.5-8, 11), but had also described God's mercy towards people whom he sought to save, first through Noah, and then through

God's covenant with Abraham and his descendents (Genesis 12–50). Scripture had emphasized God's patient care and his inspiration of human agents, priests, judges, kings, and especially prophets, whom God 'sent' to Israel in order to save the people from the consequences of their disobedience and infidelity. In both Scripture and the First Gospel, ethics is understood, not as an autonomous human endeavour, but as the expression of religious commitment. Moreover, both the social and the physical world are seen to express the corruption which disobedience had caused. Human life is lived amidst the dangers of illness, war, famine and oppression. But the Gospel according to Matthew also posits a spiritual dimension to evil. Satan, the tester or the slanderer, is a spiritual power, opposed to the Creator God, who slanders God and uses people as his agents in the social world to oppose and betray God and his agents, and whose minions, evil spirits or demons, take possession of people, making them ill or mad.

Yet the Gospel does not present people as mere puppets of these spiritual powers, whether the Creator God's, whose inspiration prompts people to live just and merciful lives, whose minions, the angels, bring saving insight or reassurance, and whose power brings wholeness and life, even after death; or the slanderer's, whose inspiration prompts people to live unjust and merciless lives, and whose power brings physical corruption. Rather, people are depicted as responsible religious and ethical agents, who deserve praise or blame for their spiritual allegiance. Moreover, since only God is conceived as the Creator and sustainer of their lives, those people who become agents of the slanderer are presented as foolish, people who despise genuine insight. Nevertheless, while obedience and fidelity to God are understood to be 'easy and light' (Mt. 11.30), they are only so if people refuse the forms of security which an alienated world seems to offer them, whether wealth, political power, social status or family devotion, and who live self-consciously in dependence solely on the Creator God.

The narrative, therefore, implies a system of cause and effect. The transcendent God is the cause of all existence, the Creator and sustainer of human life, the merciful inspirer of all goodness, the restorer of wholeness, whether ethical or physical, who gives life, even to the dead. The slanderer is the cause of destructive evil, whether ethical or physical, but his power is circumscribed by God's creative mercy. On the other hand, people are responsible for their agency, their allegiance to God or to the slanderer. In an ultimate sense, they are free to choose, but their choice is obscured by the world into which they are born, in which power and wealth are attained and retained by violence and oppression. If they are to resist a life of injustice and extortion, they must also refuse wealth and worldly power. In doing so, they become the victims of human injustice and suffer persecution, even martyrdom, at the hands of the powerful. The Gospel according to Matthew, however, does not reflect philosophically and systematically on the implications of this view of causality. Its insights are pragmatic rather than systematic. It was not until Augustine wrote his *City of God* in the fifth century that Christians seriously wrestled with the problem of evil in a systematic way.

It is in this theological and anthropological context that the story of Jesus' life, death and resurrection is told. Scripture's promises to Abraham and his descendants and to David and his descendants are said to be fulfilled in their descendant, Jesus of Nazareth, the first person completely to fulfil God's purpose in obedience through the inspiration of God's spirit. Jesus' life, death and resurrection are recounted, there-fore, not just out of interest in his personal biography, but because his life as God's agent is taken to be exemplary for all people, whether Jews or Gentiles, including the readers of the narrative. Moreover, it is not just Jesus' teaching which is important but the whole of his story, which instantiates the teaching and shows the way to remain faithful to God. Furthermore, the narrative looks forward to a time in the imminent future when history would be brought to an end at God's eschatologi-cal judgment, when all forms of evil would be destroyed, and when followers of Jesus would share with him an immortal existence in a transformed world.

From a modern perspective, what is missing from the narrative is sociological analysis. I have already mentioned that, although reference is made to social groups and to rulers, their relative influence is not described, and nor are the effects of the Roman imperial system in Palestine. No sociological account of tensions between either Jesus' followers and Jewish groups or Jesus' followers and Roman officials is provided when such tensions are intimated, for example, in Mt. 10.16-25. Religious and ethical interests are foregrounded to the exclusion of sociological interests. This is not surprising in a work which was written in the first century CE, but modern readers cannot ignore the insights of sociology when they read social history, and they cannot avoid pon-dering the sociological implications of the picture of reality the narrative creates.

4. I have already mentioned that, unlike modern historical narratives, the Matthaean narrative is focused through an omniscient and omnipresent narrator. This narrator can describe not only people's actions but also their emotions and thoughts (e.g. 1.19; 2.3; 7.28-29; 9.3, 8, 36). More than that, however, he knows when God's oracles are fulfilled, records angelic messages and even the voice of God, and recognizes the activities of Satan and his minions. This convention too is adopted from the historical narratives of Jewish Scripture, although the Gospel is more reticent in recording God's speech than some of them are. The convention implies the narrator's absolute reliability and prophetic insight, and hence claims authority. It also gives the narrator

power to select, associate, give and withhold information in a manner which creates the kind of understanding in the 'implied reader' which the author wished to instil. In doing this, however, the narrator does not draw attention to himself. He is covert, self-effacing and unobtrusive, but all the more influential for being so. He sometimes supplies information for 'implied readers' which suggests that the original readers were unfamiliar with beliefs or customs (e.g. 22.23; 27.15). He interprets some implications of the narrative to make them clear: that Jesus' teaching was authoritative (7.29), that his disciples understood him (16.12; 17.13), that some of Jesus' parables were directed against Jewish leaders and that they perceived this (21.45). He sometimes evaluates characters' activities: Pharisees and Sadducees tested him (16.1; 19.3), the chief priest and the whole council sought false testimony against Jesus (26.59), and even Pilate knew that it was out of envy that the Jewish leaders delivered up Jesus (27.18).

Rhetorical strategies also draw readers into the narrative. Rhetorical and other questions on Jesus' lips encourage readers to supply answers which mould their understanding (e.g. 5.13, 46-47; 6.25-31; 7.3-4, 9-10, 16; 12.26-27, 29, 34; 16.26; 18.12; 23.17, 19), while the general pronouns in Jesus' exhortations and predictions—whoever, everyone, no-one, many, all—include the readers (e.g. 5.19; 6.24; 7.24, 26; 8.11; 19.30; 20.28; 26.28). The narrator's use of the direct, rather than indirect, speech of characters, especially the discourses of Jesus which take up so much of the narrative, create the sense that the characters directly address the readers, as well as the crowds and disciples within the story. Further, some of the questions raised by characters within the story could be answered by the 'implied readers' whose knowledge is greater than theirs (e.g. 8.27, 29; 12.23; 13.54-56).

The convention of the narrator's omniscience and omnipresence does not imply, however, that the author claimed to be omniscient or omnipresent. The author was limited by his historical, social and cultural situation, and by his insights.

It is the narrator's omniscience which encompasses the omniscience of God, but even this narrator is not omnipotent. His only power is the power of persuasion, whereas the Creator God whom the narrative acknowledges, who sends angelic and human agents to persuade people, is conceived as ultimately omnipotent in that his creative activity keeps all things in being.

5. The Gospel according to Matthew is a short narrative and it clearly provides an incomplete account of Jesus' life. Although infancy stories are included, nothing is recounted of his upbringing in Nazareth, of family influence or education. There is an obvious gap of many years between the end of ch. 2 and the account of Jesus' baptism in 3.13-17. Other gaps become clear as readers continue to read. For example, Jesus' woes against Chorazin and Bethsaida (11.21) imply that he

performed miracles in those places, but none is related. In general, the text omits matters which would allow readers to concretize particulars about Jesus, what he looked like, how he dressed, how old he was, what he ate, where he slept, how he financed his ministry. Moreover, the only story which gives some sense of Jesus' struggle to understand the nature of his mission is the narrative of his testing which is presented as a confrontation between Jesus and the slanderer (4.1-11). In chs. 4–25 his ministry is recounted in a series of episodes, each of which exemplifies an aspect of the total picture for readers' comprehension, rather than an earlier or later embodiment of the ministry's aims and objectives. There are no false starts or wrong moves in the account. Furthermore, in comparison with the other Gospels, much of Jesus' teaching seems to have been brought together into a series of five or six discourses (chs. 5–7, 10, 13, 18, 23, 24–25), and his healing activity is at first presented as a series (chs. 8–9). Clearly the order of the narrative is sometimes determined by subject matter rather than chronology. The plot is constructed in terms of reactions to Jesus, acceptance or rejection, and the rejection which led to Jesus' crucifixion is ascribed to people who were unjust dissemblers, the kind of people whose views the narrative discourages readers from accepting.

If the portrait of Jesus, the central character, is far from complete, the portraits of other characters and groups are even more partial. Many characters are not named, and readers learn nothing of their lives before and after their meetings with Jesus. Very little can be gathered even about the named disciples of Jesus, although in their cases readers are told that four had been fishermen and one a tax collector before following Jesus, that Judas committed suicide after his betrayal, and that the resurrected Jesus commissioned the remaining eleven to engage in a world-wide mission. Peter often appears as spokesman for the other disciples, and readers are told the significance of his nickname (16.18-19), but they learn only incidentally that he was married (8.14). Two stories illustrate his impetuosity which led to disaster (14.28-31; 26.58, 69-75). Women are occasionally mentioned and some of them are named, but there is none among the disciples, and Jesus' teaching is often orientated towards men (e.g. 5.27-32; 12.41). Even when the Greek word for a human being (*anthrōpos*) is used, the context sometimes limits the reference to men (e.g. 12.11; 13.31; 18.12; 19.5). In other words the narrative, like the society in which it was written, is androcentric. Moreover, groups and individuals are often characterized by evaluative epithets. The scribes and Pharisees are dissemblers (e.g. 15.7; 23.13-36) and blind guides (15.14; 23.19, 24, 26), the disciples are people of little faith (e.g. 8.26; 14.31), Judas is the betrayer (10.4; 26.14-16), Simon is Peter, the Rock (16.18) or Satan (16.23). Their stories provide negative or inadequate examples of relations with God over against which Jesus appears genuine and faithful. In fact, the people depicted are not so much characters as character-types.

The historical narrative, therefore, lacks the particulars and fullness that we expect from modern historical narratives. Nevertheless, these very limitations serve a didactic purpose. The generality of the portrait of Jesus and his associates and opponents makes it easier for people from a variety of social situations to understand Jesus' life as exemplary. The caricatures highlight the central concern, fidelity to God.

But it is a problem for interpreters to decide how far symbolism has replaced historical particularity in the narrative. It is noticeable, for example, that the reference to wilderness in 4.1 is given no exact location, and that none of the mountains mentioned, except the Mount of Olives, is exactly located either (4.8; 5.1; 8.1; 14.23; 15.29; 17.1; 28.16). The references to wilderness and mountain in these passages seem to carry symbolic significance. It is also noticeable that none of the so-called nature miracles (stilling the storm, walking on the water, feeding the five thousand and four thousand, withering the fig tree) is mentioned in the summaries of Jesus' miraculous actions (4.23-24; 8.16; 9.35; 11.5; 14.14, 35-36; 15.30-31; 19.2; 21.14). Are these stories to be understood as symbolic rather than as depictions of particular events? It will be argued in the commentary that they are.

6. The authority of Jewish Scriptures within the rhetoric of the narrative has already been noted. It is these Scriptures which provide the vocabulary and the theological and anthropological presuppositions. God is transcendent Spirit, human creatures are flesh, are mortal. Some Classical and Hellenistic Greek literature explained the exceptional character of some people, successful military leaders and emperors, philosophers and religious leaders, by depicting them as the offspring of a god's union with a human being, as people who were semi-divine and therefore immortal. Even the first-century Jewish philosopher Philo adopted a Platonic view of human beings and reinterpreted the Torah in the light of Platonic conceptions. But the Gospel according to Matthew retains the theology and anthropology of its Scriptures. Jesus, like scriptural prophets and kings, was endowed with God's spirit (3.16), but this inspiration expressed itself in his human fidelity and obedience to the transcendent God; it did not make him divine. Rather, he was mortal like all other human beings, not eternal and transcendent like God. His resurrection after death was God's vindication of his obedient human life, but it was not a divinization. Jesus was resurrected to an individual bodily immortal existence, and other human beings, who are encouraged by the narrative to follow his example, though they would suffer persecution and even martyrdom as he did, would do so in the hope of the same vindication by God.

The First Gospel's use of Scripture is, however, interpretive. On the one hand, Scripture has provided vocabulary and the general ethos. In particular, Jesus is presented as a prophetic type, like Moses, Elijah,

Elisha and Jeremiah. But Jesus is also called Christ, son of David. His portrait, however, is quite unlike that of David in 1 Samuel 16–1 Kings 2. He is not understood as a successful military leader who was to conquer Israel's enemies through military campaigns to establish an empire. On the contrary, he was to be crucified by his enemies. Jesus as a messianic type is much more like the depiction of an ideal king in Deut. 17.14-20, chosen by God from amongst Jewish brethren, someone who would not exercise power by multiplying horses or wives or silver and gold, but who had learned to fear the Lord his God by keeping the words of the law and the statutes, and whose heart would not be lifted up above his brethren.

Scriptural depictions of Israelites have also influenced the Matthaean portrait of Jews. Jewish Scriptures are remarkable in containing trenchant criticisms of the covenant people. They are usually described as people who disregarded or even persecuted God's prophets (e.g. Jer. 7.25; 26.5; Lam. 2.20; 1 Kgs 18.4, 13; 1 Chron. 16.22; 2 Chron. 36.14-16; Neh. 9.26; Ps. 105.15; Jer. 26.20-23). Depictions of the lives of leading prophetic figures, Moses, Elijah and Jeremiah, include references to their suffering rejection and persecution. Moreover, the destruction of Jerusalem and its temple in the sixth century BCE and the exile of Jews in Babylon were interpreted as God's punishment of his unfaithful covenant people, who had ignored prophetic warnings (e.g. Neh. 9.26-37). The Gospel according to Matthew explains the rejection of Jesus in similar terms. It depicts his opponents as people who acted as their forebears had acted, in persecuting and killing the prophets (e.g. 23.29-36), and it even seems to interpret the destruction of Jerusalem and its temple in 70 CE as punishment from God for their rejection of Jesus (22.7; 23.37-39). The Gospel goes out of its way to place the entire blame for Jesus' execution on Jewish shoulders (e.g. 27.24-25), without, however, being entirely successful in obscuring Roman responsibility (e.g. 27.27-38, 58).

Moreover, the narrative seems, at first, not to be entirely consistent in its elucidation of the significance of suffering. On the one hand, it teaches that those who remained faithful to God, the prophets and their successors, John, Jesus and Jesus' followers, would suffer persecution from violent and sinful human opponents. These sufferings are not interpreted as punishments from God (e.g. 24.3-28). On the other hand, the destruction of Jerusalem by its enemies and the sufferings of the Jewish people who were killed, crucified or enslaved seems to be inter-preted as God's punishment for Jewish infidelity. Nevertheless, the Matthaean teaching is consistent if a distinction is made. The war in 66–74 CE, which included the destruction of Jerusalem, was a war against Roman oppression, fought by Jews at a time when there was chaos in the Roman Empire. An incompetent emperor, Nero, was forced to commit suicide, and there were then three claimants to the emperor's throne. It was waged in the hope of gaining Jewish political freedom, as the Maccabees had done in the second century BCE. But the Gospel according to Matthew insists that meeting violence with violence involves infidelity to God (5.38-48). The suffering of prophetic figures was the suffering of people who did not meet violence with violence, whereas the suffering of people who had been defeated in war could be seen as the perpetuation of the violence which God abhorred.

In adopting scriptural conceptions of the Creator God, the First Gospel also adopts some scriptural metaphors which elucidate relations between God and human beings. The dominant metaphor in the Gospel is that which calls God 'Father' and human beings 'sons' (e.g. 5.45, 48; 7.11); just as Scripture had called God the Father of Israel, his son (e.g. Exod. 4.22; Deut. 32.6, 8; Ps. 103.13). God is sometimes distinguished from human fathers in the Matthaean narrative by calling him 'Father in heaven' or 'heavenly Father' (e.g. 5.45, 48). It is an appropriate metaphor since all life was understood to come from God. Moreover, it intimates something of the character of the relationship: God's care for people, people's obedience to God. But the relationship of fathers and sons reflected in Scripture's and the First Gospel's use of the metaphor was different from that in modern Western societies. First-century society was patriarchal, like Israelite society in preceding centuries. Josephus, the first-century Jewish historian, claimed that, 'If a son does not respond to the benefits received from them [his parents]—for the slightest failure in his duty towards them—it hands him over to be stoned' (*Apion* 2.206). A little later in the same work, he made an even more startling claim: 'The mere intention of doing wrong to one's parents or of impiety against God is followed by instant death' (*Apion* 2.217). Even allowing for exaggerations appropriate to an apologetic work, the first-century attitude is markedly different from the Western twentieth-century attitude. Moreover, Ecclesiasticus offers the following advice to fathers: 'Do you have sons? Discipline them and break them in from their earliest years' (7.23). Similarly, in the First Gospel, the heavenly Father is not conceived in sentimental terms. He requires obedience (e.g. 21.28-31), and he does not save his children from difficulties. Obedience is demanded even if it results in the son's suffering torture and death (e.g. 26.36-46). He is the kind of father who rules like a king or landlord, another common metaphor for God adopted from Scripture (e.g. Psalms 93, 97, 99; Mt. 20.1-18; 21.33-41; 22.1-14). These metaphors encourage human obedience to the God who gives life without absolving people from responsibility for their behaviour. Moreover, obedience is stimulated by highlighting God's benevolent mercy (e.g. Exodus 12–40; Mt. 5.45; 18.23-25).

This language also reflects the importance of men in patriarchal societies. It is not balanced by metaphors of God as mother or human beings as daughters. The Gospel is egalitarian in calling human beings brothers (e.g. 5.22; 7.3), but only once does it include sisters (12.50).

Finally, the Gospel foregrounds perceptions which are found only in the later books of Jewish Scripture. According to most of Scripture, God is the one who tests human beings (e.g. Gen. 22.1; Exod. 16.4; see Mt. 6.13; 4.1), and Satan, as the tester, acts as God's agent in Job 1.6-12. Only in 1 Chron. 21.1 does Satan's testing provoke David to sin. But the Gospel identifies the idol Beelzebul (2 Kgs 1.2, 6) with Satan or the slanderer (e.g. 9.34; 12.24-32), as a spiritual power opposed to God, and makes him the prince of demons. Deut. 32.17 and Isa. 65.11 in the Septuagint version call idol-worship sacrificing to demons. Hence, in the First Gospel, some of Jesus' miracles, unlike those attributed to prophets in Scripture, are described as exorcisms of demons (e.g. 8.28-34). In fact, the Gospel's narrative world is much more like that of some extrabiblical Jewish writings like *1 Enoch*, in this respect.

We can see this similarity in another respect also. The eschatological expectation of the Matthaean narrative, the imminent final judgment, is shared with Daniel and *1 Enoch*. The classical prophetic books of Scripture envisage future judgment in political and historical terms, but the Jewish experience of the persecution and martyrdom of faithful and righteous Jews under Antiochus Epiphanes in the second century BCE prompted the kind of eschatological developments which are expressed in 2 Maccabees 7 and the Jewish apocalypses, developments adopted by New Testament Gospels and epistles. Differences, however, should be noted. The Jewish apocalypses express their beliefs through accounts of visions and heavenly journeys. The Gospel according to Matthew expresses its belief through an account of the historical ministry of Jesus, who lived, died and was resurrected. The vision of the future eschatological judgment is expressed through Jesus' prophetic discourse in chs. 24–25, and is justified by recounting past events in Jesus' life.

The Implied Reader
Like other historical narratives, the First Gospel recounts events in the past tense, but offsets the distancing effect which this would otherwise have on readers in a number of ways. I have noted the absence of many historical particulars and the use of direct rather than indirect discourse, which creates an immediacy of impact on the reader. Moreover the promise of the resurrected Jesus' continuing presence in the community of his followers (18.20; 25.40, 45; 28.20) encourages not only disciples in the story but also readers of the narrative to discern his presence in their midst. Furthermore, the rhetoric of history differs from the rhetoric of fiction in this respect: readers can enjoy the rhetoric of fiction no matter how exotic or alien its ethos, without feeling that they themselves are defined by the narrative, whereas a historical narrative like the First Gospel seeks to define who the actual readers are and what their place in history is.

The implied reader created by the rhetorical strategies of the First Gospel is someone who is a follower of Jesus. He or she is probably a second generation Christian rather than a convert from Judaism or from a Gentile religion. The denigration of the Jewish leadership (e.g. 19.30; 20.1-16; 21.28-23, 43) suggests that Judaism is a separate and alien religious group. The denigration of non-Christian Gentiles (e.g. 6.7; 18.17) suggests that Gentile religious traditions are equally alien. The implied reader, however, has accepted the authority of Jewish Scriptures, adopted their theology and anthropology, and has become wholly dedicated to the transcendent God whose spirit inspires human justice and mercy. He or she is prepared to meet persecution and martyrdom in the hope of God's final vindication. He or she lives in a period after Jesus' resurrection (27.8; 28.15) and expects God's imminent eschatological transformation (e.g. 16.28; 24.29-31), while continuing as a member of the church which Jesus' ministry brought into being (16.18; 18.17-20), a member of God's covenant community (26.28). The implied reader is directly addressed only once (24.15) but is indirectly incorporated into the whole narrative. The ordered rhetorical structure of the Gospel, with its dramatic simplicity and its repetitions, implies that an audience could listen to the narrative at a public reading, but the text includes no information about the circumstances in which this might happen. The simple and didactic style, however, should not mislead us into supposing that the audience it creates was to receive its insights and exhortations in a merely passive manner. Rather, the narrative encourages and requires both understanding and active faith in God the Creator and Jesus, God's agent, to be expressed in merciful and reflective lives.

The actual first-century Christian readers, like their successors, may have recognized themselves more easily in the depictions of negative and inadequate responses, but the persuasive power of the work allows them to experience and be moved by the world which the narrative creates, at least while they are reading.

Matthew 1–2: The Conception and Infancy of Jesus

When modern readers pick out a book from a library shelf or buy a book from a shop, they are given a number of clues about the kind of literature they look forward to reading. Shops and libraries display books in an ordered series, so that cookery books are in a different section from philosophy books, histories and biographies from novels and science fiction. The books themselves also provide readers with information which helps to orientate their reading, noting the author, sometimes with a brief biographical sketch, the title, and often a list of contents, as well as some excerpts from reviews. It is unlikely that first-century readers of the Gospel according to Matthew would have acquired a copy from a library or bookshop, although both facilities existed in large cities. It is more likely that a copy was kept by the Christian community which accorded it value. That community may have known or known about the author and the circumstances in which the text was written, but the information has not been passed down through the centuries. Nevertheless, the first sentence and the first chapters of the narrative orientate readers and help them to understand what to expect in the rest of the work.

Jesus' Genealogy: 1.1-17

Like the book of Chronicles in Scripture, the Gospel begins with a genealogy, a 'book of the origin [in Greek *genesis*, genealogy; see Gen. 5.1] of Jesus Christ, son of David, son of Abraham' (1.1). This introduction to the genealogy, and its conclusion in 1.17, which specifies the fourteen generations from Abraham to David, from David to the Babylonian exile and from the exile to Christ, intimates who Jesus was and what roles he was to play. He was a descendant of Abraham, the forefather of all Jews, whom God called so that by him all the families of the earth would be blessed (Gen. 12.4). He was a descendant of David, the king through whom God had given Israel unity and security (1 Samuel 16–1 Kings 2). He was the Christ, the person anointed with God's spirit to become his royal agent (e.g. Deuteronomy 17; 2 Samuel 7; Isaiah 9; 11). The genealogy recalls Israel's history in a manner which makes it appear to lead to fulfilment in Jesus' life.

Modern readers, who may be aware of an alternative genealogy of Jesus in Lk. 3.23-37, cannot help wondering about the sources and historical accuracy of the Matthaean genealogy. The first fourteen generations from Abraham to David seem to be derived from the Septuagint of Ruth 4.18-22 and 1 Chron. 2.5-15. The fourteen generations found in these references may have set the pattern for the following two sets of fourteen. Perhaps the fourteen generations represent the waxing and waning of the moon in its 28-day cycle: waxing to David, waning to the Babylonian exile, and waxing to Jesus. An alternative explanation of the numbers' significance, that fourteen is the sum of the numerical value of the three Hebrew consonants of David's name ($4 + 6 + 4 = 14$), is less convincing, since there is no reason to suppose that the author or original readers of the Gospel knew Hebrew.

Scripture also contains the names of David's descendants to the exile (1 and 2 Kings), although the Matthaean genealogy achieves its structure of fourteen generations by omitting the names of four kings, Ahaziah, Jehoash, Amaziah and Jehoiachim. Scripture, however, does not contain a list of Davidic descendants after the exile. A comparison of the Matthaean genealogy with the Lukan shows marked differences.

Not only does Luke's go back from Abraham to Adam, but even within parallel sections, the two genealogies disagree, especially in the postexilic period. The two fail to agree even over the name of Jesus' grandfather (Jacob, Mt. 1.16; Heli, Lk. 3.23). We do not know what sources were available to the evangelists for the postexilic period and have no way of judging their relative historical reliability.

The general pattern of the Matthaean genealogy, father begetting son, is occasionally broken by the mention of a mother's name. The four women named are Tamar (Genesis 28), Rahab (Josh. 2.2-21; 6.22-25), Ruth (Ruth 3), and the wife of Uriah (2 Samuel 11–12). What do these women have in common? It is possible that they were all understood to be Gentiles. Scripture does not tell whether Bathsheba was a Gentile, but she is described as the wife of Uriah who was a Hittite. If readers are meant to notice their Gentile origins, this would intimate the importance of Gentiles, and women, in the fulfilment of God's purpose. But it is more likely that readers are intended to notice that each of them behaved in a sexually scandalous way while fulfilling God's purpose. Tamar disguised herself as a prostitute to become pregnant by Judah, Rahab was a professional prostitute, Ruth seems to have slept with Boaz before they were married, and Bathsheba committed adultery with David and became his wife only after David had contrived her husband's death in battle. Recalling their stories would help prepare readers for the potentially scandalous story about Mary, who became pregnant before she was married.

The final statement of the genealogy, that 'Joseph was the husband of Mary from whom was born Jesus who is called Christ', again breaks the established pattern of the genealogy, this time in a new way. It implies that Joseph was not the physical father of Jesus. But if Joseph was not his physical father, how was Joseph's genealogy relevant to Jesus? This is the question which the next section will answer.

His Miraculous Conception: 1.18-25

It was common in Hellenistic biographies of great men to recount a miraculous birth which explained the exceptional nature of their achievements (e.g. Dionysius by Zeus [Diodorus Siculus 4.2.1]; Romulus by Mars [Plutarch, Lives, Romulus 2]; Alexander the Great by a god [Plutarch, Lives, Alexander 2]; Plato by Apollo [Diogenes Laertius 3.2]). The pantheon of the ancient Greek or Roman gods pictured them as male or female individuals, whose sexual unions resulted in the birth of offspring. Specially talented heroes, therefore, could be presented as the offspring of a human mother and a god, as semi-divine individuals. If the Matthaean text had taken over this form of story, readers would have to understand Jesus as a semi-divine hero. The Matthaean text, however, does not draw on this tradition, but on Scripture. According to Scripture, God is transcendent Creator, not an individual. God creates and sustains his creation through his spirit (Genesis 1). Human beings are created material individuals, either male or female. Divine and human natures are therefore unmixable. The Matthaean story of Jesus' miraculous conception by the holy spirit is like the story of God's creation of Adam in Genesis 1–2, but whereas God miraculously created Adam without parents, God miraculously created Jesus without one parent, the father. Since all life was understood ultimately to come from God (Gen. 6.3), even ordinary births through the sexual union of parents were understood as blessings from God. Scripture recounts the miraculous births of some of the patriarchs in unusual circumstances, when Sarah was already past child-bearing (Genesis 16–18, 21) or when Rachel was barren (Genesis 30). There are, however, no accounts in Scripture of a virgin conception in the sense of a conception by a woman who had never experienced sexual intercourse ('before they came together', Mt. 1.18). Moreover, there was no expectation that the Christ or messiah would be born miraculously.

The Matthaean story of Jesus' miraculous conception, unlike the Lukan story, is told from the perspective of Joseph's reactions. After the introductory statement that Mary conceived by the Holy Spirit while she was betrothed to Joseph, it is Joseph's response which is noted: he decided to put her away quietly. In this he showed himself to be a just person (1.19). Betrothal was a formal agreement between families, which had to be annulled if marriage did not follow. Readers infer that Joseph regarded Mary's pregnancy as evidence of her union with another man, and his quiet release of her from the betrothal would have left her free to marry her child's father. If this had happened, Joseph's genealogy would not have applied to Jesus, and the narrative goes on to relate how Joseph was dissuaded from his purpose. Like his famous forebear, the patriarch Joseph (Gen. 37.5-11), this Joseph received a message from God through an angel in a dream. As in scriptural passages like Gen. 16.7-13 or Judg. 13.3-5 this angelic messenger intervened to affect the course of history in order to achieve God's purpose. The angel is depicted addressing Joseph in the dream as son of David, and telling him not to be afraid of taking Mary as his wife, since the child was conceived not by another man but by God's spirit. The angel's announcement also contains information about the child: he would be a son whom Joseph should call Jesus (compare Gen. 16.11; 17.19; Isa. 7.14) because he would save his people from their sins. Jesus is the Greek form of the name Joshua, and this Jesus is to be a saviour like his famous forebear (the book of Joshua). But the narrative understands the salvation which this Jesus would bring as a saving of the Jewish people not from their military opponents but from their sins. Readers are encouraged to accept the veracity of this depiction of Jesus' role, provided by God's messenger.

The notion that an angelic messenger from God can appear in a dream to supply someone with vital information which would affect the course of history is not something which comes readily to modern Westerners' minds. We may wish that things could be so, but we accord dreams significance only as expressions of a person's psychological and physical welfare. We recognize that occasionally a person's powerful dream can affect what they do or refrain from doing, but we do not privilege dreams as forms of divine communication. It is even possible for a Westerner to look back on his or her life and see the importance of a dream in helping him or her to understand what should be done in a particular situation, and in this sense he or she might call the dream providential. But to which of his or her many hundreds of dreams he or she would give that significance would depend on his or her ethical and religious insight. The Gospel, however, does not tell the story in this form. It does not describe how the author came to learn of Joseph's according to his dream this particular significance. Rather it tells a story similar in form to those in Scripture on the assumption that the dream had that significance.

Either the angel or the narrator goes on to interpret the conception as a fulfilment of a scriptural prophecy from God (1.22-23). The introductory formula to the quotation is like those in 2 Chron. 36.21 and 22, and is a common feature of the Matthaean narrative (e.g. 2.15, 17; 3.14; 8.17), as elsewhere in the New Testament (e.g. Jn 12.38; 19.24; Acts 2.16). The quotation comes from Isa. 7.14 and the interpretation of the name Emmanuel from Isa. 8.10, although the prophet is not named. The Matthaean quotation conforms to the Septuagint in most particulars, but varies from all the manuscripts of the Septuagint which have survived in substituting 'they will call' for 'you (or she) will call', a change which was probably occasioned by the new context in the Gospel. Unusually, the Septuagint rendered the Hebrew word for 'young woman' with the more definite 'virgin'. This use of 'virgin' means that the child to be born would be the first-born. But no miraculous conception is implied by the Isaiah prophecy in its context in Isaiah 7. On the contrary, the virgin would conceive in the normal way. The prophecy in Isaiah 7 is addressed to Ahaz, king of Judah, at a time when Judah was in danger of attack from Israel and Syria. It gave Ahaz assurance that within a short time the threat would disappear: 'Before the child knows how to refuse the evil and choose the good, the land before whose two kings you are in dread will be deserted' (Isa. 7.16). Moreover, even the greater threat which would come from the king of Assyria would assure the people that 'God is with us' (Isa. 8.5-10). The Matthaean text reinterprets the prophecies in Isa. 7.14 and 8.10 to apply to Jesus, both because the reference to a virgin conceiving applies in a new way to Jesus' conception, and because Jesus' birth, as a miracle brought about by God, would assure people that 'God is with us'. This Matthaean interpretation does not imply that Jesus was divine, but that he was

God's human agent, born miraculously as an indication that 'God is with us', not against us. According to the narrative, God would save people from their sins through this human agent, Jesus. The story concludes by noting that Joseph obeyed the command of the angel of the Lord and received Mary as his wife, without however consummating the marriage ('know' is a euphemism for sexual intercourse; compare Gen. 4.1), and named the child Jesus. Thus Joseph became the legal father of Jesus and Joseph's genealogy became Jesus'.

In view of later developments and controversies in Christian doctrine, it is well to note that the doctrine of the virgin conception has no logical connection with the doctrine of Christ's two natures which was formulated in the Chalcedonian Definition of the Faith in 451 CE. Had the story of the virgin conception taught that Jesus was half human and half divine, after the manner of some Hellenistic stories, it would have precluded the doctrine of Christ's two natures, which teaches, on the contrary, that Jesus is both fully God and fully human. But the story of the virgin conception teaches that the birth of the human being Jesus was brought about miraculously by God as an assurance that 'God is with us'. This left the way open for later Christians to attempt an explanation of how the life of a human being could give knowledge of the transcendent God. The Gospel according to Matthew presupposes the scriptural understanding that human beings are made in the image and likeness of God (Gen. 1.26) and that they should therefore act as God's agents in lives of justice and mercy. Nearly four hundred years of discussions and controversies led to the Chalcedonian Definition which seeks to safeguard both the transcendent nature of God and the creaturely nature of human beings. It safeguards Matthaean insights but develops them further, in order to answer new questions.

It has sometimes been suggested that the birth and infancy stories about Jesus arose from scriptural quotations. In this case, however, the scriptural quotations seems to be appended to the story, and the Isaiah prophecies themselves, read in their own context, could hardly have given rise to an expectation of a miraculous conception. Once a belief that Jesus was miraculously conceived was established, however, the Isaiah prophecies could take on this new meaning.

But what are modern readers to make of the Matthaean citations of short passages from Scripture which are said to be fulfilled in Jesus' life? The Gospel often formally cites and also alludes to Scripture in order to demonstrate that God's promises in Scripture were fulfilled by aspects of Jesus' life and work. The implied reader of the narrative is encouraged to accept both the prophetic authority of Scriptures and the Matthaean insights about their fulfilment. But modern readers are more inclined to read and understand the prophetic oracles of Isaiah, and other passages in Scripture, in the historical and literary contexts in which they were written. We often quote literary texts when they seem appropriate to our present situation, but this is not the same as suggesting that a particular text prophesied that our present situation would come about. Moreover, even modern Christians who argue that Jesus' life, death and resurrection did fulfil hopes engendered by Jewish Scriptures do not do so by citing a few passages out of context. Modern readers, therefore, cannot feel the force of this rhetoric as implied readers are directed to do. For modern readers, the quotation from Isaiah cannot provide a final, clinching argument. Rather, they accept or reject the suggestion that Jesus' life gives them reassurance of God's saving purpose on different grounds, for example, on the basis of other people's experiences and their own.

Some commentators make the suggestion that the story of Jesus' miraculous conception was invented to counter a charge that Jesus was illegitimate. But for a story to effectively counter such a charge, it would need to show that Jesus' parents were properly married before Jesus was conceived, and the Matthaean story signally fails to do that. Rather the Matthaean story about the virgin conception would prompt a charge of illegitimacy by people who rejected the view that Jesus acted as God's agent.

The Visit of the Magi: 2.1-12

The story of Jesus' miraculous conception and birth emphasizes God's initiative in sending his human agent to save people from their sins, and Joseph's acceptance of Jesus as his legal son, in response to the divine message, makes Jesus a descendant of David. Davidic descent is also a feature of the next story but, in addition, it intimates something of what the genealogy had implied by calling Jesus son of Abraham (by whom all the families of the earth would be blessed). The Magi are depicted as Gentiles who received their revelation from nature, from a star. Their arrival in Jerusalem and the explanation of their mission, to 'do obeisance to the king of the Jews', is said to have alarmed Herod, the king of the Jews, and the people of Jerusalem. (Herod the Great ruled Palestine as king and client of Rome between 40 and 4 BCE.) The story tells that the chief priests and scribes, whom Herod assembled and questioned, confirmed the natural revelation by naming Bethlehem, David's birthplace, as the birthplace of the king of the Jews, on the basis of Micah's prophecy (Mic. 5.2, together with 2 Sam. 5.2). The composite quotation omits Ephratha and alters the original reference to Bethlehem's insignificance into its opposite, 'by no means least', as well as differing from the Hebrew and Greek versions in other minor details. These changes serve to fit the quotation into its context in the Gospel. The addition of the text from 2 Sam. 5.2 pictures the king as a shepherd, a common metaphor in Scripture (e.g. Ezek. 34.23).

In the narrative, this is the first mention of chief priests and scribes.

Chief priests were members of the leading priestly families from amongst whom the high priest was chosen. There were many thousands of other priests who took turns to officiate at the sacrifices in the Jerusalem temple. Priesthood was hereditary in Judaism. Levites, another heredi-tary group, also served in the temple but did not officiate at sacrifices. The First Gospel never mentions Levites. In Greek literature, the word for 'scribes' refers to secretaries and clerks who were able to read and to write official documents in a neat and legible script. In the context of first-century Judaism, however, the word refers to people who were knowledgable about Jewish Scriptures and their interpretation. No doubt, like the priests, they could read and write, but their function was that of expert interpreters, advisors and teachers (see Ecclus 38.24–39.11).

The composite quotation from Micah and 2 Samuel makes explicit reference to Scripture, but other passages from Scripture may have influenced the form of the story, especially Psalm 72 which prays for the establishment of justice under a righteous king, and includes the request: 'May the kings of Tarshish and the isles render him tribute, may the kings of Sheba and Seba bring gifts. May all kings fall down before him, all nations serve him' (Ps. 72.10-11, and see Isa. 60.3, 6). Whether an allusion to Balaam's prophecy, 'A star shall come forth out of Jacob and a sceptre shall rise out of Israel' (Num. 24.17) is also intended is more doubtful since the Matthaean narrative does not identify Jesus as the star. Rather the Magi's interest in astrology allowed them to recognize the star as a guide to the king's birthplace.

The narrative goes on to relate that Herod arranged a secret meeting with the Magi to ascertain particulars and to urge them to report back to him when they had found the child in Bethlehem, giving as his reason his own desire to offer this king obeisance. Led once more by the star, in a manner which is difficult to visualize, the Magi discovered the child's home, found him with his mother (Joseph is never mentioned in this episode) and made their appropriate obeisance to the king (compare the obeisance offered to King David, e.g. 2 Sam. 1.2; 18.28; 24.20). The gifts which they are depicted offering, gold, frankincense and myrrh, are appropriate both as gifts to the Christ (Isa. 60.6; Ps. 45.8) and as gifts from the Magi, since frankincense and myrrh were used by magi and were products of Arabia. The departure of the Magi, without reporting back to Herod, is explained as a response to a warning in a dream. This time, no angel of the Lord is said to appear, presumably because the Magi were Gentiles and not Jews.

The story is a powerfully dramatic representation of the significance of Jesus, the king of the Jews, for Gentiles. That significance will be hinted at again in the narrative depiction of Jesus' responses to individual Gentiles and groups of Gentiles during his ministry, but will be fully explained only in the resurrection narrative. The Gospel assumes that the Gentile mission was the responsibility of Jesus' followers after his death and resurrection. Gentile Christian readers and listeners, however, could recognize themselves in stories like that of the Magi's visit.

Has the story been invented to dramatize the fulfilment of scriptural expectations? In this case, the most likely answer is yes. Scripture required that the messianic descendant of David should be born in Bethlehem, but it was well known that Jesus came from Nazareth in Galilee. The Gospels according to Matthew and Luke explain Jesus' birth in Bethlehem and his connection with Nazareth in completely different and contradictory ways, neither of which is convincing. Luke's depiction of a journey to an ancestral home in order to comply with Roman demands for a world-wide census is historically unbelievable—why should Rome require such an unsettling movement through the empire, and why has it left no trace in any other record of the period? Matthew explains the family's return from Egypt not to Judaea but to Galilee by pointing out that Herod's son Archelaus ruled Judaea, but another of Herod's sons, Herod Antipas, ruled Galilee. The Fourth Gospel, more convincingly, denies any connection between Jesus and Bethlehem and never calls Jesus son of David. Rather, it presents Jesus as the Christ not because of physical descent from David but because God had chosen and sent him, in line with the scriptural expectation about the righteous king in Deut. 17.14-20. The Synoptic Gospels depict Jesus as the Christ, son of David, but in doing so they also highlight differences between Jesus and David, since Jesus did not kill his enemies but was killed by them. Jesus' fate is foreshadowed by the next episode of the Matthaean birth narrative.

The Family's Flight into Egypt: 2.13-15
The mention of an appearance of an angel of the Lord in Joseph's dream recalls the story in 1.18-25. This time the angel commanded Joseph to flee to Egypt in order to escape from Herod's efforts to kill the child, and once more Joseph is described obeying the command, and readers are told that the family remained in Egypt until Herod's death. Again, as in 1.18-20, the events are described as a fulfilment of God's oracle in Scripture, this time citing Hos. 11.1, but the Hosean reference to 'his children' is replaced by 'my son'. The change is appropriate for two reasons. The prophecy is said to be fulfilled by an individual, Jesus, and Israel is elsewhere in Scripture called God's son (e.g. Exod. 4.22). This story of Jesus' stay in Egypt and his later return to Palestine, therefore, allows readers to recognize that Jesus was God's son as Israel was God's son. Later in the narrative, Jesus' sonship will be distinguished from Israel's in one respect: Israel was God's disobedient son but Jesus was God's obedient son (4.1-11) The depiction of Joseph's journey to Egypt also reminds readers of the patriarch Joseph's journey to Egypt.

If we ask about the historical accuracy of the story, however, the most we can say is that it is extremely unlikely. People who wished to escape from Herod could have taken to the hills in Galilee or to the desert in Judaea, or could have travelled east out of Herod's kingdom. Fleeing as far as Egypt would have been unnecessary. Nevertheless, the story admirably captures what the Gospel encourages readers to understand about Jesus' significance: Jesus fulfilled Israel's destiny as God's son.

Herod's Killing of Infants: 2.16-18

The narrative relates that Herod was fooled by the Magi, who did not report back to him, but that he was not powerless. He could enforce the massacre of young children in Bethlehem. The mention of the age of the children, from two years and under, suggests the passing of time since Jesus' birth. Again, the events are interpreted as a fulfilment of God's oracle in Scripture, this time through Jeremiah who is named in the formulaic introduction. The Matthaean wording of Jer. 31.15, however, corresponds neither to the Hebrew nor to the Septuagint versions as we have them. It is possible that the text quotes an alternative Greek version, since lost, or that the author quoted from memory. In the context of Jeremiah 31 the image of Rachel weeping for her descendants as they gathered at Ramah to go into exile is negated by the following oracle in which God forbade weeping because he would bring the people back from exile. The Matthaean use of the quotation in its context also suggests that the suffering of the people would be the prelude to God's deliverance.

Anyone who reads about the great events of Israel's history in Scripture soon discerns a pattern. The sufferings of the enslaved Hebrews in Egypt were the prelude to God's deliverance through Moses (Exodus), the sufferings of exiles were the prelude to God's deliverance through Cyrus (Isaiah 40–55), the sufferings of faithful Jews under Antiochus Epiphanes were the prelude to God's deliverance through the Maccabees (1 Maccabees). The First Gospel seems to allude to the experience of Israel in Egypt: Pharaoh killed Hebrew children but Moses, the future deliverer, escaped (Exod. 1.8–2.10). But the Matthaean text explicitly refers to Jeremiah's depiction of the people's suffering at the exile (some of the people, who took Jeremiah with them against his will, fled to Egypt to avoid exile in Babylon). All these echoes of Scripture help to communicate to the Gospel's readers that Herod was Israel's enemy and that Jesus was Israel's deliverer.

It seems likely, moreover, that the story was invented to serve this purpose. The first-century Jewish historian Josephus provides us with detailed accounts of Herod the Great's reign (both in *The Jewish War* and in *Jewish Antiquities*) which include references to Herod's killing his sons, when he suspected them of plotting against him (*War* 1.445–551). We may surmise, then, that had Herod suspected of a child born in Bethlehem that he would become a messianic leader with a following, Herod would have tried to kill the child. Had he wished to do so, however, he could have sent an assassin. Moreover, had Herod really massacred children in Bethlehem, it is impossible to explain why Josephus fails to mention the fact or to describe disturbances which would have followed from it. We have already seen reason to doubt the historical veracity of the story about the Magi's visit and the setting of Jesus' birth in Bethlehem. Likewise we should see this story of Herod's massacre as a fictional dramatization which indicates something of Jesus' significance. Jesus' kingship will be described in terms which are antithetical to those of Herod's kingship: Jesus will not kill to preserve his own life and power. Moreover, the story foreshadows Jesus' fate: this time he is shown to have escaped from a ruler's destructive power, but later he will be shown to have been executed by a ruler's destructive power.

The Family's Move from Egypt to Nazareth: 2.19-23

Once again, Joseph's action is said to be prompted by a divine message in a dream. The message reproduces that to Moses in Midian, where he had fled to escape Pharaoh (Exod. 4.19). The fact of Herod's death is given as a reason for the family's return from Egypt to 'the land of Israel' but no more specific destination is given. Joseph's obedience brought about the fulfilment of Hosea's prophecy quoted in 2.15. The narrative continues by noting that Herod's son Archelaus ruled Judaea, and a further warning in a dream, like that to the Magi, is seen to prompt Joseph to take the family to Galilee, where they settled in Nazareth. (Nazareth was a small settlement, rather off the beaten track.) A reference to the fulfilment of God's oracle again concludes the story, but this time reference is made to the prophets (plural) and 'he shall be called a Nazarene' is not a quotation from Scripture. It is possible that it echoes the descriptions of Samson (Judg. 13.5, 7; 16.17) who was a Nazirite, dedicated from birth to God's service. If so, the parallel is not exact, not only because the two words, Nazarene and Nazirite, are spelt slightly differently, but also because Nazirites drank no alcohol (Num. 6.2) and the narrative will depict Jesus' drinking wine (11.19; 26.27-29). Another suggestion, that Nazarene echoes the Hebrew word for branch in Isaiah's prophecy, 'There shall come forth a shoot from the stump of Jesse [David's father] and a branch shall grow out of his roots' (Isa. 11.1), is even less compelling, both because Nazarene and *neser* (branch) are spelt differently, and because the author and readers of the Gospel are unlikely to have known classical Hebrew. The further suggestion by Davies and Allison[1] that Isa. 4.3, 'he shall be called

---

1   W.D. Davies and D. Allison, *Matthew* (ICC; Edinburgh: T. & T. Clark, 1988).

holy' could also be rendered 'he shall be called a Nazirite', since the Septuagint sometimes translates Nazirite by the word 'holy', meets with a number of difficulties. First of all, the Septuagint reads 'they shall be called holy'. Secondly, Matthew, unlike Mark (1.24), never calls Jesus the 'holy one of God'. Thirdly, the author and readers would have needed to be able to make the substitution on the basis of a knowledge of classical Hebrew or of an alternative Greek version, which is improbable. Of the three possible scriptural allusions suggested, therefore, none is completely convincing, but the first, the echo of Nazirite, offers the least difficulties because Jesus, like Nazirites, lived a life dedicated to God's service, according to the First Gospel.

At this point, a detail of the Matthaean presentation should be noted. Jesus is called a *Nazaraios*, which is understood as a description of someone who came from Nazareth. The more appropriate term in Greek, however, would be *Nazarēnos*. Nevertheless, and in spite of the odd form, which could have been influenced by the term *Naziraios* (Nazirite), *Nazaraios* is best understood as an indication of Jesus' home town, and not, as has sometimes been suggested, as the name of a sect.

This final story in the birth narrative interprets Jesus' residence at Nazareth as part of God's providential purpose and prepares the way for the account of Jesus' Galilean ministry.

Looking back over the birth and infancy narrative, the stories serve the purpose of introducing the reader to the roles that Jesus would play in the rest of the narrative: he was God's son as Israel was God's son; he was David's son, the Christ, but not a king like Herod; he was Abraham's son, a Jew who would bring God's blessings to Gentiles; and he was a prophet like Moses, rescued by God, dedicated to God's service, who would save God's people from their sins. Already his life is seen to be threatened by a ruler. The miraculous conception, the quotations from and allusions to Scripture, and God's guidance through dreams and a star, serve to highlight God's providential care in sending Jesus; they show that God is with his people and not against them.

These first two chapters prefigure what will be explained and illustrated in more detail later in the narrative. I have suggested reasons for doubting the historical accuracy of some particulars, but, as stories, these chapters dramatically communicate a sense of Jesus' destiny and significance. In contrast to modern biographies, no interest is taken in the child's psychological and educational developments, but, as in ancient biographies, the birth and infancy stories provide a clear indication of the character-type to which Jesus would conform in the account which follows.

Matthew 3–4: Introduction to Jesus' Ministry

The birth and infancy narrative had told readers that Jesus was a Jew and the Christ, that he was God's son in the sense that Israel was God's son. The next two chapters, 3 and 4, will elucidate this typology: like Israel after the escape from Egypt, Jesus would pass through water and would be tested in the desert.

John the Baptist: 3.1-12[1]
A new character, John, is introduced, and his activity is dated vaguely 'in those days'. His connection with Jesus is unexplained until later in the narrative. Then it will become clear that years have elapsed since the end of ch. 2, because Jesus will appear as an adult. John is immediately described as 'the Baptist' as if he were already well known to readers. But at first he is depicted as a preacher and his preaching is summarized: 'Repent for the kingdom of heaven has drawn near'. John was an agent of repentance in view of the imminence of the eschatological kingdom which God would soon establish. The imminence of the kingdom of heaven is a key concern of the Gospel and refers to the eschatological kingdom which God would bring into existence after the final judgment, as the rest of the Gospel will make clear. John's role is then further defined as a fulfilment of God's oracle through Isaiah. The usual introductory formula which relates to events, 'that which was spoken', is modified to refer to a person, 'he of whom it was said'. The quotation from Isa. 40.3, which conforms to the Septuagint version, explains why John was preaching in the wilderness of Judaea as a preparation for the way of the Lord, 'way' functioning metaphorically to suggest the way of life which God requires, as in other parts of Scripture (e.g. Deut. 28.9). The description of John's diet is appropriate to his place in the desert and to his ascetic lifestyle (see later 11.18). The description of his clothes (3.4) echoes the description of Elijah's in 2 Kgs 1.8, indicating that John was a prophet like Elijah, a connection made explicit later in the Gospel (11.14; 17.12). The depiction of John's ministry, however, shares only some features with that of Elijah: he was a prophet who was persecuted by a ruler when he declared God's purpose. Miracles are not attributed to John's agency as they are to Elijah's. And John was a baptist. But because Elijah was taken up into heaven (1 Kings 2), he was expected to return in order to herald the eschatological events (Mal. 3.1 quoted with reference to John in Mt. 11.10).

The account, however, represents John's performance of this role in a new way. Not only was he a prophetic preacher, but also a baptist, and the baptism in the river Jordan, undergone by people from

---

1   See Mk 1.3-8; Lk. 3.1-9, 15-17.

Jerusalem, Judaea and the region around the Jordan, is understood as an expression of their repentance, accompanied by their confession of sins, an appropriate preparation for God's judgment. The Jewish historian Josephus also gives an account of John's preaching, baptism and execution (*Ant.* 18.116-19). It seems that scriptural purity washings for the removal of uncleanness were adapted by John to express repentance for sins.

At this point, John's preaching to two groups among the crowds, Pharisees and Sadducees, is recounted in detail (3.7-12; contrast Mark). In the first century, Pharisees were a small group of mostly lay people dedicated to the fulfilment of God's purpose for his people. Josephus numbers them at 6000 (*Ant.* 17.42). The Sadducees were also a small but a very influential group, including aristocratic priests. Both groups will appear later in the Gospel and are associated in 16.1, 6, 11, 12 and 22.34. John is represented as a fierce preacher who did not mince his words, addressing his audience as a brood of vipers (that is, poisonous by nature), warning about the coming wrath (of God), urging that they bear fruit worthy of repentance instead of relying on their status as children of Abraham, since God could raise up descendants of Abraham from stones, and picturing an imminent judgment in terms of an axe placed against a tree, ready to chop it down and throw it into fire if it did not bear good fruit. The image of people as trees bearing good or bad fruit is taken up from Scripture (Psalm 1; Isa. 10.33-34; Ezekiel 31) and will be used again in the Gospel's account of Jesus' preaching (e.g. 7.16-20).

After this recounting of John's preaching, the narrative relates his characterization of his baptism of repentance and his prophecy about someone greater who would follow him. This person would be so much mightier than John that John would be unworthy even to carry his sandals (see Isa. 11.1-2 and contrast Mark and Luke). In distinction from John's baptism of repentance, his baptism would be with the Holy Spirit and with fire, taking up again the image of judgment. Through the metaphor of a person's separating his wheat into his granary and burning the chaff with unquenchable fire (see Mal. 4.1), this coming one is depicted as a judge. John's prophecy introduces a new note in comparison with the birth and infancy narrative: as God's agent, Jesus' ministry (for it soon becomes clear that Jesus is the one about whom John prophesied) would herald God's eschatological judgment, the division of the good from the dross. People could look forward to endowment with God's spirit, but also to the eschatological destruction. This note of judgment is repeated in the Matthaean account of Jesus' teaching (e.g. 7.15-27; 13.37-43, 47-50). The narrative also makes it clear that John, in spite of the importance of his activity and his widespread influence, was inferior to Jesus, the main subject of the narrative, whose partial fulfilment of John's prophecy is recounted in the next section.

John's Baptism of Jesus: 3.13-17[1]

Jesus' arrival at the Jordan from Galilee links with the last mention of him, at 2.22, but from now on he will be described as an adult who would take an active part in what transpired. The Matthaean version of the story of his baptism by John seems to be designed to answer a question: if Jesus was superior to John, why did he submit to John's baptism? Hence John is described trying to prevent Jesus from undergoing baptism: 'I have need to be baptized by you and do you come to me?' (contrast Mark and Luke). The question implies that John had already recognized Jesus as his superior successor, whose baptism would be with the holy spirit and with fire. That Jesus had been baptized by John, however, was part of the historical tradition the evangelist had inherited, and it is skilfully employed to recall Jesus' identity to the reader. Jesus' behaviour is explained as appropriate to the time, in that it fulfilled all righteousness or justice. Justice or righteousness would be a theme of the Matthaean Jesus' preaching (5.6, 10, 20; 6.33), and later Jesus would acknowledge that John had come in the way of justice (21.32). Jesus, therefore, is depicted as endorsing John's preparatory ministry. The narrative then shows that Jesus' own action was endorsed by God through the descent of God's spirit, like a dove, upon him. The dove seems to have symbolized purity (10.16). The story makes clear that Jesus was both prophet and Christ, endowed with God's spirit (e.g. Isa. 61.1; 1 Sam. 16.13). As the bearer of God's spirit, Jesus could baptize with the Holy Spirit (see 28.19). Further, the narrative includes a reference to the voice from heaven, that is God's voice, announcing to the crowds and to the readers (contrast Mark and Luke) that Jesus was God's beloved son in whom he was well pleased, an echo of Isaiah's description of Israel as God's servant (Isa. 42.1; see Mt. 12.18; Isa. 44.2; Ps. 2.7). In some parts of the Gospel's Scripture, God's speech is recorded directly, as in the Pentateuch, or through prophets, as in the prophetic books. In the Gospel, however, God's purpose is made known through the preaching and activities of John, Jesus and Jesus' followers, but the preaching does not take the form of oracles introduced by 'thus says the Lord'. Only on two occasions is the heavenly voice represented addressing Jesus' companions, in the stories of Jesus' baptism and transfiguration (17.5), where the same statement is made about Jesus' sonship. The form of the story is similar to that of the angel of the Lord's address from heaven to Abraham (Gen. 22.11-12, 15-18), of God's instruction to Moses and the people (Deut. 4.10-12), of God's address to Elijah (1 Kgs 19.13-18), or of the voice from heaven's pronouncement of judgment against Nebuchadnezzar (Dan. 4.13-17). A similar story is recounted in rabbinic literature about the first-century Galilean healer Hanina ben Dosa, according to which the voice from

1   See Mk 1.9-11; Lk. 3.21-22.

heaven declared: 'The whole world is sustained on account of my son Hanina' (*b. Ta'an.* 24b). The Matthaean voice from heaven acknowledged Jesus' sonship at two crucial moments in his ministry, at its inception and immediately after the first prediction that his destiny would involve persecution and execution (16.21–17.8).

The reminder to the reader that Jesus was God's son serves to introduce the theme of the next section: sonship.

Jesus Put to the Test: 4.1-11[1]

Jesus' departure into the desert is not depicted as a personal whim but as a response to the Spirit's guidance, to serve a particular purpose: to be tested by the slanderer. This is the first mention of the slanderer in the Gospel, and he is introduced as a familiar figure. The 'slanderer' is the Septuagint translation of the Hebrew 'Satan', who sometimes figures in scriptural stories. In the introductory verses of the book of Job, for example, the slanderer is a member of God's heavenly court, whom God allowed to test Job. This is the role he plays in this story about Jesus. Later in the narrative he will be called the 'prince of demons' (9.34), and named Beelzebul (12.24-32). Beelzebul was the god of Ekron whose worship Elijah had opposed (2 Kgs 1.2, 6), and Scripture interpreted idol-worship as sacrificing to demons (Deut. 32.17; Isa. 65.11) and associated unclean spirits with idol-worship (Zech. 13.2).

The testing of Jesus in the wilderness is reminiscent of the testing of Israel in the wilderness, after Israel had been rescued by God from slavery in Egypt and had passed through the sea. The baptism and testing of Jesus picture him as God's son in the metaphorical sense that Israel was God's son. Unlike Israel, however, Jesus would remain obedient and would not be provoked into putting God to the test (compare Israel, e.g. Exod. 14.10-17, 16; Deut. 8.2).

Jesus' fast for forty days and forty nights both recalls Israel's wanderings in the wilderness for forty years (Deut. 8.2) and explains his hunger which provided the occasion for the first test (compare Israel, Exod. 16; Num. 11). The narrative now calls the slanderer the tester and his suggestion that Jesus tell stones to become bread is introduced by 'If you are a son of God', picking up the words of God's declaration in the previous scene. The tests, then, involve the provocation of God's son to put God to the test, as Israel had done in the wilderness. Jesus' response is a quotation from Scripture (Deut. 8.3). It does not deny the role of miracle worker to God's son, and the Gospel will later describe Jesus' miracles, but it asserts that whatever a son does should be done in obedience to the God in whom he trusts (compare 6.24-34). This trust excludes putting God to the test. Later in the narrative, during the Beelzebul controversy, when Jesus' opponents would accuse him of

---

1   See Mk 1.12-13; Lk. 4.1-13.

performing miracles by the agency of the prince of demons, Jesus would again assert his allegiance to God (12.24-32 and see 16.1).

The second test is set on the pinnacle of the temple in the holy city (that is, Jerusalem, 27.53; see Isa. 48.2; 52.1). Readers have to assume that this setting was imagined by Jesus while he remained in the desert. Once again the test is introduced by the slanderer with 'If you are a son of God', but this time it continues with a quotation from Ps. 91.11-12, part of a psalm which praised God for his fidelity in rescuing Israel. Jesus' counter-quotation from Deut. 6.16, however, excludes the possibility of presuming on God's bounty by putting him to the test. This was the mistake which Israel had made in the wilderness (Deut. 8.1-10). Later in the narrative the account will depict further tests of Jesus' fidelity, for example, by his disciple:

> Jesus began to show his disciples that he must go to Jerusalem and suffer many things ... and be killed ... And Peter took him and began to rebuke him saying, 'Let God be merciful, Lord. This shall never happen to you'. But he turned and said to Peter, 'Get behind me Satan. You are a stumbling block to me; for you are not on the side of God but of people' (16.21-23).

Later, in the description of Jesus' arrest, he would be depicted rebuking the disciple who used a sword and explaining that he refused to call on the help of angels (26.51-54). Even at the scene of Jesus' crucifixion, passers-by will be depicted challenging him: 'If you are a son of God, come down from the cross' (27.40, 43). The whole narrative emphasizes that Jesus remained a faithful and obedient son of God.

The third test is set on an imaginary mountain with a view of all the kingdoms of the world and their splendour. No longer is the slanderer's test introduced by 'If you are a son of God' but by the promise to give Jesus the kingdoms if he would fall down before the tester in obeisance. Israel had succumbed to idolatry in the wilderness (Exodus 32). The Matthaean narrative sees worldly power as evil. Jesus' reply, however, is a command of dismissal, like that to Peter (16.23), and an allusion to Deut. 6.13 which commands exclusive worship of God. At the end of the account of Jesus' ministry, the crucified and resurrected Jesus would claim that God had appointed him as lord of the world (28.18), but only after he had died by public torture in obedience to God's purpose (26.36-46).

The conclusion of the story—'Then the slanderer left him, and behold angels came and began to minister to him'—serves to indicate God's endorsement of Jesus' fidelity and to demonstrate God's care (see 6.24-34). The story, through its stark presentation of a series of tests by the slanderer, orientates the reader to understand the following account of Jesus' ministry. As an epitome, it sums up the significance of Jesus' individual decisions and actions, construing them as expressions of fidelity to God. In particular it prepares readers for an understanding of Jesus' execution in Jerusalem: it is not to be understood as a tragic accident but as Jesus' faithful expression of sonship in refusing to meet the evil of violence with violence, in refusing to put God to the test.

Introduction to Jesus' Galilean Ministry and Summary of his Teaching: 4.12-17[1]

Jesus' return to Galilee is explained as a withdrawal because John had been arrested. The Gospel had set John's ministry in Judaea (3.1) and 4.12 seems to assume that his arrest took place there, and that Galilee was therefore a safer place for his associates. But, in fact, John was imprisoned by Herod Antipas who ruled Galilee and Peraea (14.1-12). Author and readers of the Gospel seem to have been ignorant of these political details.

The narrative relates that Jesus left his home in Nazareth (2.23) and dwelt in Capernaum, a fishing village on the lake of Galilee. Later the narrative will refer to a house in Capernaum as a base for his Galilean ministry (8.5; 9.1; 13.1, 36; 17.24-25). But here Capernaum is introduced because it was in the region of Zebulun and Naphtali and Jesus' presence there is construed as a fulfilment of God's oracle through Isaiah (Isa. 8.23; 9.1-2). The quotation omits some of the wording of the Septuagint in order to bring together the geographical references. The oracle refers to Galilee as 'Galilee of the Gentiles' and to a people who had sat in darkness and the shadow of death but who would see a great light. At its outset, therefore, Jesus' ministry is conceived as bringing light to Gentiles. Like Israel, God's servant, Jesus would bring enlightenment to the peoples of the world (Isa. 42.6). It will be necessary for readers to remember this perspective, since most of the account of Jesus' ministry will centre on his relations with fellow Jews.

Historically, Galilee was Jewish territory, ruled by the son of Herod the Great, Herod Antipas, who was a practising Jew. The area had become part of the Jewish empire during the period of the preceding Hasmonean dynasty, the descendants of the Maccabees who had gained independence from Syria. Some Gentiles could have lived there, especially in cities like Sepphoris and Tiberias, but the ethos was Jewish. Hence there were Jewish synagogues in Galilean towns, Galileans attended the pilgrim festivals at the temple in Jerusalem (26.1-2), and contributed to the functioning of the temple by paying the temple tax (17.24-27) and by tithing their produce (23.23). While reflecting this historical situation in the Galilean episodes which the Gospel will recount, this introductory section uses 'Galilee of the Gentiles' to indicate the wider significance of Jesus' ministry.

The Gospel's introduction is now complete. Readers should be

1   See Mk 1.14-15; Lk. 4.14-15.

prepared to understand the account of Jesus' life which will follow in terms of its theological significance. They know that Jesus was a Jew, a descendant of Abraham, the Christ, descendant of David, God's son, endowed with God's spirit like kings and prophets. The story of Jesus' life is to be told as an assurance that God is with his people, saving them from their sins through his human agent who would bring light to all the peoples of the world, but who was to accomplish this task without putting God to the test and without gaining power by evil means. All these theological perceptions will be illustrated in the narrative which follows, through a series of episodes and discourses.

First of all Jesus' teaching is summarized: 'Repent, for the kingdom of heaven has drawn near' (4.17). Thus, Jesus' teaching is summarized in exactly the same words as John's (3.2). The disciples' teaching will also be summarized in the same way later in the narrative (10.7). The context of all their preaching is the imminence of God's heavenly kingdom, and the appropriate response to its announcement is return to God and a new lifestyle. Later, the Gospel will distinguish Jesus' lifestyle from John's (11.16-19) and will encourage Jesus' followers to conform their lives to his (e.g. 8.19-22).

Jesus' Call of Four Fishermen to Follow Him: 4.18-22[1]

At the very outset of the description of Jesus' ministry, he is depicted calling others to follow him (compare Elijah's call of Elisha, 1 Kgs 19.19-21). This is the point of the narrative. It is not written as a biography of a unique individual for the entertainment of the curious. Rather it is written as a declaration of God's purpose for human beings and Jesus is described as a type or example of human fidelity to God. Jesus' call to his first followers, therefore, involves in his mission not only them but also the readers of the Gospel. They, too, are encouraged to follow Jesus.

Simon, called Peter (the explanation of his nickname will be given later in 16.18, but it seems to be mentioned at his first appearance in the narrative because it was familiar to readers), and his brother Andrew are described as fishermen, which allowed Jesus to interpret their calling metaphorically to become 'fishers of people', that is, missionaries (compare 13.47-50). More briefly, the call of two other fishermen, James and John the sons of Zebedee, is appended. The Gospel contains only one other account of Jesus' summoning a named disciple, that concerning Matthew the tax collector in 9.9-13, although the names of the twelve whom he sent out on a mission would be given later (10.2-4). This first account must therefore be taken as typical, and stress is placed on both the men's immediate response to the summons, their leaving occupation, family and possessions (see 10.25-39; 19.27-30), and their

1   See Mk 1.16-20; Lk. 5.1-11.

acceptance of responsibility for a mission to others (see ch. 10 and 28.16-20). Counter-examples of people who were called but did not follow will be given in chs. 8 and 9 and in 19.16-22.

Summary of Jesus' Activity: Teaching and Healing: 4.23-25[1]

The twin aspects of Jesus' ministry are highlighted in this brief summary. He travelled throughout Galilee, teaching in the synagogues and proclaiming the good news about the kingdom, and he healed every disease and every weakness among the people. The summary emphasizes the completeness of his ministry. This is the first indication that Jesus, like the prophets Elijah and Elisha, would heal people. These twin aspects of teaching and healing will be exemplified in the following sections: preaching in chs. 5–7 and healing in chs. 8–9. Moreover, following Jesus will also become a theme of chs. 8 and 9. In ch. 4 the narrative notes that a report of his activity reached outside of the Jewish environment to the whole of Gentile Syria. His healing attracted crowds, therefore, not only from Galilee, Jerusalem and Judaea, but also from the Gentile cities of the Decapolis.

Matthew 5–7: Jesus' Sermon on the Mount

Up to this point in the narrative, Jesus' preaching had been summarized as 'Repent, for the kingdom of heaven has drawn near' (4.17). Now Jesus is depicted explaining the significance of this eschatological perspective for the present return to God. The setting on the mountain (5.1) and the quotations from the law given on Mount Sinai in ch. 5 suggest that Jesus' teaching role is understood as that of a second Moses. Already in the birth and infancy narrative there had been allusions to Moses' experience. And Deut. 18.15, 18 contains God's promise to Moses: 'I will raise up for them a prophet like you from among their brethren; and I will put my words into his mouth, and he shall speak to them all that I command him'. According to the Gospel, this is what Jesus did. But Jesus' message, unlike Moses', was given in a context in which God's establishment of his eschatological kingdom was expected in the near future. This is not, however, understood to mean that people should wait passively for God's action but that they should respond to Jesus' summons by living in dedication to the God whose judgment was imminent. In the story, Jesus' teaching is addressed to the crowds in the presence of his disciples (5.1-2; 7.28-29). This is the first use of the term 'disciple' in the Gospel. Jesus' summons to the fishermen and their following him to become 'fishers of people' (4.18-22), it now

1   See Lk. 6.17-19.

appears, made them disciples. The word means 'learner' or 'pupil'. The disciples, then, were apprentices to Jesus, who were to follow his example, not just in learning a skill but in learning a way of life. The word is found only twice in Codex A of the Septuagint (Jer. 13.21; 20.11), but in Hellenistic literature, the word was frequently used for followers of philosophers or for members of a philosophical school which practised a particular lifestyle. Josephus applied it to Joshua, Elisha and Baruch when he retold scriptural stories (*Ant.* 6.84; 9.28, 33; 10.158, 178) implying that Joshua was a follower of Moses, Elisha of Elijah and Baruch of Jeremiah. The Gospel will also mention disciples of John the Baptist (9.14) and disciples of the Pharisees (22.16), but all the other references are to Jesus' disciples, and after 10.1-4 to the twelve named disciples, apart from Joseph of Arimathea, who is called a disciple in 27.57. The Gospel distinguishes Jesus' disciples both from the crowds and from the Jewish leadership.

The direct address of Jesus, in the story to crowds and disciples, becomes in the narrative the direct address of Jesus to the readers and listeners. It creates the illusion of immediacy.

Beatitudes: 5.3-12[1]

The sermon opens with Jesus' pronouncement of God's blessings upon those whose present life was far from enviable (compare Ecclus 14.1-2; Dan. 12.12). Nevertheless, they were blessed because to them belonged the kingdom of heaven which God would soon establish (5.3, 10). The 'poor in spirit' (compare Luke 'you poor' and see Isa. 61.1) are not to be understood as the faint-hearted but as those whose economic poverty made them dependent solely on God (see Ps. 12.5). Those that mourn would be comforted, as Isaiah had predicted (Isa. 61.2-3). The humble, not the strong, would inherit the land, as the psalmist had predicted (Ps. 37.11 and see Isa. 61.7; Deut. 4.1). Later, Jesus would be called humble (11.29; 21.6), like Moses (Num. 12.3). Those who hunger and thirst for justice (Luke 'you that hunger now') would be satisfied (see Isa. 61.3, 8, 11). Jesus' followers would be told to show God's justice (5.20; 6.1, 33). Those who show mercy, as Jesus and his followers were to do (6.2-4; 9.13; 12.7 and see 6.12, 14-15; 18.15-35), would receive mercy. The pure in heart (see Ps. 24.4-5), that is, people single-mindedly devoted to God (6.19-24), would see God. Peacemakers would be called sons of God as Jesus was (see Isa. 9.6; Mt. 5.24-26). Those persecuted on account of (their) justice are those to whom the kingdom of heaven would belong. These statements are made in general terms, in the third person plural, but 5.11-12 then addresses the audience directly by changing to the second person plural, and blessing is pronounced on those who would suffer reproach, persecution and

1   See Lk. 6.20-23.

reviling on Jesus' account; that is, the teaching applies to those who would follow Jesus. They could rejoice and be glad now because they would receive a great reward in heaven, at the eschatological judgment (see chs. 24 and 25). Moreover, their experience of persecution is said to mirror that of prophets in the past. The Gospel repeatedly mentions that prophets of the past were persecuted (e.g. 23.31-37) and that those who shared a prophetic calling, John, Jesus and Jesus' followers, could expect the same fate. Not all the prophets mentioned in Scripture are said to have suffered persecution, but there are frequent complaints about Israelites ignoring their messages (e.g. Jer. 7.25; 26.5; Lam. 2.20). Moreover, Scripture depicts some of the major prophets—Moses, Elijah and Jeremiah, with whom the Gospel closely associates John and Jesus (16.14; 17.3, 12)—as suffering persecution, and mentions that prophets were mocked, abused and sometimes killed (1 Kgs 18.4, 13; 1 Chron. 16.22; 2 Chron. 36.14-16; Ps. 105.15; Jer. 26.20-23).

In the light of the eschatological reversal which God was about to effect, Jesus' teaching is structured to encourage people to behave justly and mercifully by living a humble lifestyle and by accepting the inevitable persecution that this would entail.

Salt and Light: 5.13-16[1]

The persecuted, the subject of the previous blessing, are addressed: 'You are the salt of the earth'. The metaphor affirms the irreplaceable importance of those who suffered persecution on Jesus' account. Salt is a basic necessity of life (Ecclus 39.26). The question, 'If the salt has lost its savour, with what will it be salted?' draws the audience into providing the answer 'nothing' which is immediately confirmed.

Similarly, they are addressed with, 'You are the light of the world'. Jesus had been introduced as a light to the nations (4.16), and his followers are to enlighten all peoples by living, as he lived, a humble and persecuted existence. The teaching goes on to encourage them to become conspicuous in good works in order that other people might see them and honour their heavenly Father. The 'good works' must be those mentioned in the beatitudes. Like its Scripture, the Gospel assumes that ethics is the expression of fidelity to God. There is no suggestion that followers of Jesus should form a sect separate from the world. Rather they exist as a light to the world.

These introductory blessings and exhortations encourage people to live humble lives and to accept the rejections and persecutions that would follow, both as their expression of devotion to God in the present and in the hope of God's eschatological reversal in the near future. The story of Jesus' ministry and what happened to him will show his putting this teaching into practice.

1   See Mk 4.21; 9.50; Lk. 8.16; 14.34-35.

Justice or Righteousness and the Law: 5.17-20

Jesus' exposition is introduced by countering a possible misinterpretation: 'Don't think that I came to destroy the law and the prophets; I did not come to destroy but to fulfil'. 'The law and the prophets' encompasses the whole of Matthaean Scripture inherited from Judaism. The Gospel alludes to and quotes psalms (e.g. Mt. 27.46, 48) but does not describe them as a separate part of Scripture, 'writings'. In the first four chapters, the narrative had already indicated that Jesus' life was to be understood as a fulfilment of scriptural expectations, and the instances of Jesus' teaching which will follow in 5.21-48 will show how his teaching is a fulfilment too. Looking at the whole narrative, however, it seems to suppose that 'fulfil' can include change. Circumcision, for example, which is commanded in the law as a mark of the covenant (Genesis 17), is never mentioned in the Gospel, even when the Gentile mission is in view (28.19-20). It is replaced by baptism. Payment of the temple tax, also commanded in the law (Exod. 30.13; 38.26), is advocated only so that offence may not be caused (17.27). The temple sacrifices, which the law required as expressions of thanksgiving or repentance, or for the removal of uncleanness (Leviticus), are advocated in 5.23-24 and 8.4, but may have seemed peripheral, since Jesus' death is understood metaphorically as a covenant sacrifice which also assured people that their sins were forgiven (26.26-29). These instances suggest that the Gospel included such development in its understanding of 'fulfil'. But there are some instances of Jesus' teaching which seem to abrogate commands in the law. Honouring parents, which is required in the Decalogue (Exod. 20.12; Deut. 5.16), is set aside (8.21-22; 10.35-37). Also marriage and child-bearing, commanded in Gen. 1.28, are no longer necessary (19.12). These are, however, the only instances in which the law is abrogated rather than fulfilled, albeit sometimes through change. The abrogations may be deemed necessary in view of the extraordinary circumstances: the nearness of the eschatological kingdom. Family commitments, which were essential for a continuing world, became marginal in view of the eschaton.

Nevertheless, Jesus' assertion in 5.18 is that, while heaven and earth continue to exist, not even the smallest letter or accent would pass from the law until all were accomplished. Hence the audience is warned that 'whoever relaxes one of the least of these commandments and teaches people so, will be called least in the kingdom of heaven, whereas whoever does them and teaches them will be called great in the kingdom of heaven'. 'Whoever' includes the readers as well as the audience in the story. Finally, the point is summarized in an extreme warning: 'unless your justice or righteousness exceeds that of the scribes and Pharisees, you will never enter the kingdom of heaven'. Entry into the coming eschatological kingdom is conditional on the practice of justice which even exceeds that of the scribes and Pharisees, two groups who tried

to put the law's requirements into effect. The Pharisees had already
been criticized, however, by John (3.7-10). The scribes had been mentioned in 2.7. They were lay interpreters and teachers of the law, some
of the most eminent among whom were older contemporaries of Jesus,
Hillel and Shammai. Much of what Jesus is represented as teaching in
the sermon would have met with their approval. Where Jesus' teaching
in the sermon differs from theirs is in his emphasis on the imminence of
the eschatological judgment.

Illustrations of Jesus' Teaching about Fulfilling the Law and the Prophets: 5.21-48

Murder and Anger: 5.21-26.[1] The introductory formula, used at the
beginning of each example, 'you have heard that it was said [implied by
God] to people of old... and/but I say to you ... has often been construed by Christians as antithetical, and the Greek *de* has been translated 'but'. Jesus' teaching in this section, however, is not the antithesis
of the older teaching. It does not teach that his followers should murder
whenever they feel like it, nor commit adultery, nor divorce at their
convenience, nor abrogate oaths, nor retaliate excessively, nor hate
other people. The formula is therefore best translated '*and* I say to you',
since the new teaching is an elaboration of the older teaching.

'You shall not kill' is a quotation from the Decalogue (Exod. 20.13;
Deut. 5.17). Hence, whoever kills is liable to judgment (in a human court
as well as at God's judgment). The sermon adds to this accepted
requirement a further and extreme requirement, that anyone who is
angry with his brother would also be liable to judgment. The term
'brother' means that all human beings devoted to their heavenly Father
are related to one another as brothers. It is a pity that here and elsewhere in the Gospel sisters are not explicitly included. The proposition
is exemplified in two parallel ways: someone who calls his brother by a
foul epithet, 'empty headed', is liable to the council, that is a human
court, and someone who calls him 'fool' is liable to the Gehenna of fire,
a metaphor for eschatological destruction. In precluding angry actions
which lead to murder, the teaching safeguards the original command.
The obvious difficulty of avoiding anger, however, is not discussed.
Later, people would be encouraged to show mercy because they had
received mercy from God (18.23-35). The teaching separates neither
religion and ethics nor attitude and action.

Not only are those addressed to avoid anger themselves, however,
but they are also to avoid provoking others to anger by injuring them.
Two particular examples illustrate the teaching. The first depicts a situation in which someone is offering a gift on the altar (in the temple) and
there remembers that his brother has something against him. In such a

---

1   See Lk. 12.57-59.

case, the audience is admonished to leave the gift before the altar, to first go and be reconciled with the brother, and then come and offer the gift. The sacrifice involved seems to be one of thanksgiving to God, since sacrifices made after, for example, defrauding others required restitution to be made to those defrauded before sacrifice could be offered (Exod. 21.33-36; 22.1, 5-15). The teaching implies that even offering thanks to God is inappropriate for a person who had wronged another human being, suggesting once more that religion and ethics cannot be separated.

The second example depicts a situation in which a person is being taken to court by his adversary in order that a debt may be reclaimed. Making friends quickly with the adversary is recommended, lest the adversary hand the debtor to a judge, the judge to an officer and he be thrown into prison. In Jewish society, unlike in modern Western society, imprisonment was not a punishment for debt, but a means of forcing a debtor to arrange a repayment. If this could not be done, debts had to be worked off by the debtor and his family (see 18.34). No advice is given about how the debtor could secure his adversary's good opinion if repayment were impossible. The teaching assumes that arrangements could have been made before the debtor was brought to a judge.

Adultery and Lust: 5.27-30. 'You shall not commit adultery' is a quotation from the Decalogue (Exod. 20.14; Deut. 5.18). Jesus' teaching then describes lust which leads to adultery: 'everyone who looks at a wife to desire her has already committed adultery with her in his heart' (see Exod. 20.17). As so often in the Gospel, the teaching is addressed to men, not to women. That lust is to be avoided is explained in a striking metaphor: pluck out or cut off the right eye or right hand (those members which catch the wife for adulterous purposes) and cast them away, since it is better to live with a defective body than to be cast into Gehenna at the final judgment. The metaphor makes concrete the activity of lustful behaviour which leads to adultery, and hence makes it avoidable.

Divorce and Remarriage: 5.31-32.[1] The citation is an allusion to Deut. 24.1. According to Deuteronomy and Matthew only a man can divorce. The Markan passage also countenances women's divorcing men, which was possible in Roman law but not in Jewish or Greek law. Divorce was a formal procedure which required a man to give his wife an appropriate written document. The passage in Deuteronomy also suggests a reason for divorce: 'if she finds no favour in his eyes because he has found some indecency in her' (24.1). Just how 'some indecency'

1   See 19.3-9; Mk 10.2-9; Lk. 16.18.

should be construed was a matter of debate among Jewish interpreters. The Matthaean passage interprets it: 'for the reason of unchastity'. This could refer to unchastity before the marriage which would then make its discovery a reason for invalidating the marriage, or it could refer to the wife's adultery during the marriage. Everyone who divorces his wife except for this reason is said 'to make her commit adultery'. Since most divorced women would remarry, if the divorce were invalid the second marriage would be adulterous. Further, the man who married an invalidly divorced woman would also commit adultery. If the married woman had already behaved unchastely, however, the divorce would be valid and the woman could not be said to be forced into an adulterous relationship. The teaching does not encompass the case of a married man who had sexual intercourse with an unmarried woman, presumably because this did not count as adultery according to scriptural law, which applied in a society in which men could marry more than one wife at the same time. By the first century CE, however, most Jewish men were monogamous. The teaching of this section helps to safeguard female security by excluding divorce for offences less serious than unchastity. Later, more positive teaching about the nature of marriage will be given.

Oaths: 5.33-37. The citation is an allusion to several scriptural passages: Lev. 19.12 forbids swearing falsely by the Lord's name; Num. 30.2 forbids breaking an oath or vow to the Lord and requires that the person keep his or her word; Deut. 23.21 emphasizes that someone who takes a vow to the Lord should not be slow in carrying it out, and the next verse asserts: 'if you refrain from vowing, it shall be no sin in you'. Jesus' teaching accepts the view expressed in Deut. 23.22 and forbids all forms of oath, even those not made in the name of the Lord. Straightforward honesty is required, and oaths are said to arise from evil. They are necessary only if a person's integrity cannot be relied upon. At the time of Jesus and of the narrative, oaths of allegiance were sometimes required by the state. Following the teaching would therefore have marked Jesus' followers as potential subversives. The Essenes were not punished by Herod the Great when they refused to take an oath of allegiance, but Josephus makes clear that their case was exceptional (*War* 2.135-39; *Ant.* 15.371). But oaths were also used in other circumstances. For example, a person might take an oath to return something he needed to borrow. The sermon seems to take such a circumstance into account, however, by making borrowing unnecessary (see next section).

Generosity: 5.38-48.[1] 'An eye for an eye' and 'a tooth for a tooth' was a general principle applied to particular cases in order that restitution or punishment should be appropriate, neither too light nor too heavy (Exod. 21.23-24; Lev. 24.20; Deut. 19.21). The sermon seems to understand the principle as a safeguard against excessive retaliation, and carries the concern further: 'Do not resist evil'. 'Evil' is exemplified through concrete examples: 'whoever slaps you on the right cheek, turn to him the other; to him who wishes to sue you for your tunic, let him have your cloak [these two garments would represent the whole of a poorer person's wardrobe]; and whoever would force you to go one mile [as soldiers might do], go with him two'. These evils are not to be met with violence but with generosity. Later, Jesus would be depicted meeting the evils of torture and crucifixion without resistance. In other words, the cycle of violence which characterized society and which God abhorred should be brought to an end by the refusal of people to meet violence with violence. Hence those who suffered persecution without retaliating had been called the salt of the earth and the light of the world (5.13-16). The teaching continues with other examples: give to anyone who asks you and do not refuse anyone who would borrow from you. Any community in which people behaved in this way would not need to safeguard property rights by oaths.

The same generosity is advocated in the next section, in which it is grounded theologically. 'Love your neighbour' is a summary of the law in Lev. 19.18, but 'hate your enemy' is found nowhere in Scripture. Indeed the reverse is advocated in the same chapter of Leviticus: not only neighbours but strangers are to be loved (Lev. 19.34). Elsewhere in Scripture generosity to enemies is commanded (Prov. 25.21). But no doubt for most people, then as now, hatred of enemies seemed natural. In the sermon, what Jesus commands is both love of enemy, in line with Scripture, and also prayer for persecutors. So far no exact parallel to this second injunction has been found in Jewish literature, which generally warns persecutors about God's judgment against them (e.g. 2 Maccabees 7 and see later in the Gospel, 22.7 and 23.29-36). Since the teaching of the sermon understands the prophetic calling to lead to persecution, however, even followers' behaviour towards persecutors has to be integrated into the teaching about generosity.

And all this teaching is related to God's activity. Human beings are to become sons of their heavenly Father, whose generosity is demonstrated by his making his sun rise on the evil as well as the good, and by his sending rain both on the just and the unjust. Rhetorical questions reinforce the teaching: 'If you love those who love you, what reward have you? Don't even tax collectors [some of the most extortionate members of society] do the same? If you greet your brothers only,

1   See Lk. 6.27-36.

what more [see 5.20] are you doing than others? Do not even Gentiles [those outside the covenant community, idolaters] do the same?' Rather followers of Jesus are to be perfect as their heavenly Father is perfect, perfectly generous to those whose behaviour is evil and unjust. In other words, God is gracious and generous and human beings should imitate his generosity. Religion is the determinant of ethical behaviour (see 18.23-35).

Through all these examples in ch. 5, the sermon illustrates what fulfilment of the law and justice entail. Nothing in the teaching abrogates the law. Everyone following the teaching would keep the law. Moreover, merciful and extraordinarily generous behaviour is seen as the appropriate human response to God's mercy and generosity. The examples, about alienated relations between people, between men and women, between people and God, and between people and their enemies, concretize the teaching. True piety and the ethics which express it are the subjects. The teaching is not concerned with prudential considerations in human society. It does not suggest that acting generously would turn enemies and persecutors into friends. On the contrary, it realistically depicts the consequences of following the teaching in an unjust society: reproach, reviling, persecution. The only reward to which followers could look forward is a reward from God in heaven (5.11-12). Later in the Gospel, some sense of a minority community of mutual care will be provided (ch. 18), but it is left undeveloped. There is, however, no encouragement to Christians to cut themselves off from God's world and pursue their own minority interests. What comes into focus is the relationship of Jesus and his followers, especially missionaries, with the rest of human society, and Jesus' life will be described in the narrative as the exemplary expression of a commitment to his teaching which results in martyrdom. Missionary leaders will be invited to make disciples of all nations (28.19) in the short period that remains before God's final judgment, but in doing so, they are to expect persecution from the powerful in society (10.16-25), and even betrayal from within their own community (24.10). Their hopes rest on God's vindication in a post-mortem existence in a new world (e.g. 19.28; 5.3-16).

The Gospel's belief in the imminence of the eschaton excludes from consideration any possible long-term developments in relations between the Christian community and its wider society. Modern Christians, looking back over nearly two thousand years of history, naturally have a different perspective. The teaching of the Sermon on the Mount has inspired both Christians and non-Christians to live lives which express God's generosity and mercy, and the lives of saints and martyrs have exemplified the Gospel's understanding of fidelity to God in different circumstances and at different times. Moreover, their lives have inspired others to work for the expression of God's justice in the larger societies to which they belonged. Hard-won democratic institutions have created societies which are far more just than was the Roman imperial system of the first century, or than modern totalitarian regimes. This is not to suggest, however, that democratic societies express the generosity that the sermon advocates. Far from it. Most women and men, ethnic minorities and the physically and mentally disabled within those societies still have to work for justice, let alone mercy. And Western societies' relations with the rest of the world are usually exploitative or paternalistic. People involved in struggles against injustice are still reproached, reviled and martyred in the present world, even in the world's greatest democracy, the United States of America. But when Christians join with others in working for justice, they have long-term aims which are not countenanced in the Gospel, and they express hopes for God's present and continuing world as well as for God's final vindication. This involves them in compromises. They find themselves aiming for lesser attainable goods as necessary steps towards a more just society, and these compromises raise the question whether the pursuit of lesser goods betrays their Christian calling. For example, in what ways and how far should people defend themselves and others against the violence of the state or the violence of an alien state? Should Christians serve in the defence forces of democratic societies? Should Christians try to assassinate a dictator? The Gospel according to Matthew provides the answer 'no' to all these questions, and some modern Christians have insisted that Christians should never meet violence with violence. On the other hand, Christians can also cite examples in which freedom fighters have achieved their aims of toppling repressive regimes and replacing them with less oppressive systems, and they have tried to define the circumstances in which war might be justified.

Modern Christians cannot avoid another perspective on history which, however, they can share with the Matthaean narrative. This is the realization that members of the Christian church, and the churches as institutions in society, have very often failed to live in accordance with their Christian beliefs and values. In the Gospel, the narrow way of devotion to God and his kingdom is contrasted to the broad way which most people follow, gaining what security they can from money, social status and family solidarity. Even the portrait of the disciples is one of people with little faith, of people who were cowardly in the face of danger, who betrayed their master, denied their allegiance or ran away. And without the examples of the churches' saints and martyrs, the churches' histories would too readily illustrate the same themes.

Dedication to God: 6.1-34
Chapter 6 takes up the theme of justice from ch. 5 and explores it in a new way. First a contrast is made between performing good deeds in

order that they may be seen by other people and performing good deeds which are known only to God (6.1-18). The former alternative is said to bring its own reward, that is, reputation among people; the latter, reward from God at the final judgment. The introductory remarks are in the form of a warning: 'Beware of practising your justice before people in order to be seen by them; for then you will have no reward from your Father who is in heaven'. The teaching is illustrated by examples, charitable giving, prayer and fasting. The sermon then goes on to consider other aspects of devotion to God. Reliance on riches, another way of securing honour in society, is construed as excluding devotion to God, and vice versa (6.19-26). Finally, positive teaching about trust in God as Father is given which obviates the need for lesser forms of security (6.25-34).

Charitable Giving: 6.2-4. The Greek word for 'charitable gift' is from the same root as the noun 'mercy' and the verb 'to show mercy'. It refers to deeds which exhibit mercy towards others in need. Scripture emphasizes that those who serve God should help people in need (e.g. Deut. 15.11; 24.13; Ecclus 7.10). But it is, of course, possible to make a show of charitable giving, in order to gain a good reputation in a society which honours it, as Judaism did and does, and as Christianity came to do. Individuals who make such a show, metaphorically 'sounding a trumpet', are called hypocrites or dissemblers (see Job 36.13) because they serve themselves in the guise of serving others. Those who gave publicly, in the synagogues where people assembled for prayers or meetings, or in the streets, where the Mediterranean climate allowed public transactions to take place, gained a good reputation amongst those who saw their action. Hence they received their reward. Through hyperbole, the sermon advocates another course of action: 'When you give a charitable gift, don't let your left hand know what your right hand is doing, so that your charitable gift may be in secret' (6.4). In other words, charitable giving is not hypocritical if it is effected both unselfconsciously and in circumstances in which no reputation may be gained. The hyperbolic form is important because it excludes another hypocritical possibility, that people give gifts in order to gain favour with God. The teaching goes on to suggest that 'your Father who sees in secret will reward you' but avoids the statement 'give in secret *so that* your Father who sees in secret will reward you'. Rather, 'don't let your left hand know what your right hand is doing...*and* your Father who sees in secret will reward you' (see the similar emphasis in 25.37-40, and the mishnaic saying attributed to the third century BCE scribe, Simon the Just: 'Be not like slaves that minister to the master for the sake of receiving a bounty, but be like slaves that minister to the master not for the sake of receiving a bounty; and let the fear of heaven be upon you' [*Ab.* 1.3]).

Prayer: 6.5-15.[1] Similar teaching is given about prayer. It is possible to dissemble piety by standing to pray (cf. 1 Sam. 1.26; Neh. 9.4; Jer. 18.20) in public, in synagogues or at street corners, so that other people would notice and accord the reward of a reputation for piety. To avoid this, the sermon advocates praying in secret, in a room behind closed doors, '*and* your Father who sees in secret will reward you'. Probably the intention was not to exclude all community prayer but to exclude all prayer directed to others' notice rather than to God.

This teaching is elaborated in a different direction: 'When you pray, don't heap up empty phrases like the Gentiles, for they think they will be heard for their many words' (cf. Ecclus 7.14). As in 5.47, the Gentiles are idolaters whose practice should not be imitated. Rather the audience is reminded that the God they worship is 'your Father' who 'knows what you need before you ask him' (cf. Isa. 65.24). But this is not given as a reason for not praying at all. Instead, a model prayer is presented for use and imitation, which briefly expresses the following convictions and petitions:

1. 'Our Father who is in heaven' acknowledges God's transcendence and fatherhood of all people; that is, it acknowledges that the God who is Creator, from whom all existence comes, cares for human beings as a father, but, like a father, requires devotion and imitation from his children.

2. 'Let your name be sanctified' asks that God may be honoured and praised in acknowledgment of who he is, the holy transcendent Creator, and the Gospel envisages this happening when people perform good deeds (5.16).

3. 'Let your kingdom come' asks for the dawning of God's kingdom from which all forms of evil would be excluded.

4. 'Let your will be done, as in heaven, so also on earth' gives substance to the request for God's kingdom to come. It would bring about a new world in which God's purpose would be accomplished on earth as is imagined to be the case 'in heaven'.

5. 'Give us today bread for this day.' The perspective seems to shift from petitions for an eschatological transformation to a petition which relates to present circumstances. At least, that is the case if 'bread for this day' is an appropriate translation. The adjective is found only in this prayer (see the parallel in Lk. 11.2-4) and nowhere else in the whole of Greek literature. Other possible translations are: 'Give us today bread that belongs to the day' or 'Give us today bread for the coming day'. Moreover, 'bread' could be construed metaphorically to represent anything that is needed. The last of the possible translations could be understood in an eschatological sense: 'Give us today whatever is

1   See Lk. 11.2-4.

needed for the coming eschatological day', in line with the previous petitions.

6. 'Forgive us our debts as we have forgiven our debtors.' 'Debts' are understood metaphorically, as in the parable in 18.21-35, which illustrates forgiveness of sins (and see the alternative metaphor 'transgressions' in 6.14. Cf. Ecclus 28.2-5). The petition asks for forgiveness at the eschatological judgment, but includes a comparison: God is asked to forgive debts *as* we have forgiven our debtors. The petition provides an incentive for people to act mercifully in the present. The same point will be made again at the end of the prayer.

7. 'Lead us not into a test but rescue us from evil.' Jesus had been led by the spirit to be tested by the slanderer (4.1), and later he and the disciples would be put to the test in Gethsemane (26.36-46), where Jesus would pray to remain faithful to God's purpose, but the disciples would fail both to pray and to remain faithful. This seems to be the evil from which the petition asks to be rescued.

This prayer, therefore, expresses the beliefs and concerns of those committed to God, the Father who is about to transform the world into his eschatological kingdom. But the sermon concludes the section with a warning: 'If you forgive people their transgressions, your heavenly Father will also forgive you, but if you don't forgive others, neither will your heavenly Father forgive your transgressions' (6.14-15). The emphasis was so important that the narrative will return to it in 18.21-35.

Fasting: 6.16-18. Fasting, which was a common expression of acknowledged dependence on God (e.g. 2 Sam. 12.15-17) and of contrition for sins (especially on the Day of Atonement; Leviticus 16) was also susceptible to dissembling, since it could be accompanied by sullen looks and disfigurements which made the practice of fasting obvious to others (e.g. sackcloth and ashes, Dan. 9.3; Jon. 3.5). The sermon advocates that there be no outward show (see Isa. 58.5) but rather normal behaviour, anointing the head and washing the face (2 Sam. 14.2), so that others would not know when someone was fasting, '*and* your Father who sees in secret will reward you'.

Here the practice of fasting is taken for granted. Moreover, Jesus had been pictured fasting in the prelude to one of his tests in the wilderness (4.1-11). Later in the Gospel, Jesus' followers will be distinguished from those of the Baptist and from the Pharisees because they, unlike the others, did not fast (9.14-17; see also 11.16-19). In 9.14-17, Jesus is presented replying to John's disciples' question about this with a rhetorical question: 'Can the wedding guests mourn as long as the bridegroom is with them?' But this is followed by the addition: 'The days will come when the bridegroom is taken away from them, and then they will fast'. Jesus' followers, then, would fast after his death. Hence the need for the narrative to guard against hypocritical fasting practice in the sermon, which is addressed to disciples and crowds in the story but to later Christian readers and listeners in the narrative. This is the only instance in the Gospel in which behaviour appropriate to historical associates of Jesus is distinguished from behaviour appropriate to later followers of Jesus.

Treasure on Earth and in Heaven: 6.19-21.[1] The contrast between devotion to God and to a human reputation is now considered in relation to riches. Those who are rich are usually influential in society and are usually accorded the honour which power demands, then as now. Jesus' teaching in the sermon, however, suggests that riches bring no real security. Earthly treasures are subject to decay or they can be stolen by thieves. 'Treasures in heaven', on the other hand, suffer neither fate. 'Treasures in heaven' seem to represent God's rewards in the kingdom of heaven. The sermon therefore encourages people to lay up treasures in heaven. Moreover it points out that 'where your treasure is, there will your heart be also'. It advocates trust in God and purity of heart (5.8), so that devotion to God would obviate devotion to earthly riches.

Light and Darkness: 6.22-23.[2] Yet another metaphor serves to inculcate the practice of single-minded devotion to God. Modern physiology has taught us to recognize the function of the eye as part of a process by which light external to the body allows us to interpret images of the external world. But we, like pre-modern communities, including the Gospel's, also recognize the eye as the most expressive indicator of a person's thoughts, emotions and physical well-being. A bright eye which is gentle can express robust health as well as interest and concern. A bright eye which is hard can express determination, even fanaticism. A dull eye can express distraction, boredom, tiredness or illness. It is in this sense that 'the eye is the light of the body'. So, if the eye is healthy, this shows that the whole body is healthy. Conversely, if the eye is in poor condition, this shows that the whole body is sick. But the use of the expressions 'full of light' and 'full of darkness', together with the general context of the teaching, suggest that its meaning is metaphorical. Healthy means sincere, in poor condition means evil, light means insight and darkness means confusion. That is, 'if therefore you are sincere, your whole existence expresses insight; if you are evil, your whole existence expresses confusion'. Hence the final paradox: 'If the light [insight] which is in you is darkness [confusion], how great is the darkness'. In the context, the metaphor illustrates the impossibility of devotion both to God and to riches.

1   See Lk. 12.33-34.
2   See Lk. 11.34-36.

God and Mammon: 6.24.[1] The same message is repeated through a different metaphor, this time taken from the social institution of service. 'No one is able to serve two masters' is explained as follows: 'for either he will hate the one and love the other, or he will cling to one and scorn the other'. Common experience in the domain of servitude is applied to human relations with God: 'You cannot serve God and mammon'. 'Mammon' is Aramaic for wealth or property, here personified as a subject of devotion. The statement sums up the teaching of 6.19-24. Later in the Gospel 'love of riches' will be presented as a stumbling block to devotion to God (13.22; 19.19-26).

Trust in God: 6.25-34.[2] No matter how compelling these metaphors are for an audience, demanding as they do undivided loyalty to God, any audience would soon start wondering about the prudence of such teaching. It is one thing to be devoted to God in a society characterized by love, in which human needs would be met with generosity—and it is that kind of society which the sermon's teaching seeks to create—but when such a society does not yet exist, are people not supposed to behave responsibly by providing for their dependants and by seeking the security of respect from others? On the contrary, the sermon excludes that kind of prudence, even in the present. The society it advocates could not be created if prudence were to rule behaviour. If people continued to behave in an unjust world in ways which safeguarded them against injustice, such behaviour would only serve to perpetuate the injustice. And from the sermon's perspective, that injustice had no long-term future because God was about to destroy all evil in the final judgment. The narrative recognizes, however, that anyone who put the sermon's teaching into practice in the present unjust world could rely only on God's vindication, as Jesus' story would show.

Hence the sermon meets the difficulty head on in teaching about anxiety. People are urged to be unconcerned about their life and about what supports it at the most basic level, what they are to eat or drink or wear. From the Matthaean perspective, life was given by God, so even the provisions essential for life to continue were not to be people's chief concern. In the exemplary prayer, the petition for bread follows and does not precede the petitions about the sanctification of God's name, the coming of God's kingdom and the enacting of God's purpose (6.9-13) because life is more than food and the body is more than clothing. In support of this view, much rhetorical play is made of the heavenly Father's feeding of birds and clothing of flowers (cf. Job 12.10; 38.41; Psalm 104 and Ps. 147.9; Isa. 40.6-7). It is argued that, since human beings are different from birds (more capable?) and yet cannot through

1   See Lk. 16.13.
2   See Lk. 12.22-32.

their own care add to their span of life, and are different from lilies and yet cannot match their splendour, human anxiety is useless. Moreover, if God even clothed the hay for its short existence before it was thrown into the furnace, how much more would he clothe the human audience, who are urged to greater faith by being characterized as people of little faith. Once more, the negative example of Gentiles serves to enforce the positive message against anxiety. The audience's heavenly Father, in contrast to idols, knows that people have need of all these things (food and clothing). Hence those who seek first the kingdom and his justice would have all these things added.

But is this assurance really as convincing as it is rhetorically satisfying? Birds do die from starvation, plants do wither in drought, and human beings do die because of lack of food and clothing (cf. 10.28-31; 25.35-36, 42-43). The narrative does not deny these realities, but insists that they should not be causes of anxiety. Rather, every contingency is to be understood as encompassed by God's purpose. And if human beings truly dedicated themselves to that merciful purpose, there would be food and clothing in abundance. In any case, anxiety against unknown future contingencies is ruled out: 'Don't be concerned for tomorrow, for tomorrow will be concerned with itself' (6.34). Those of us who wear ourselves out worrying about eventualities which either never happen or which happen in circumstances beyond our imagination can see the sense in the injunction, although our whole social ethos, which encourages and sometimes requires us to insure against disasters in the future, helps to bolster a refusal to let the future take care of itself. And prudential insurance can mitigate some disasters. The point of the sermon's teaching, however, is that prudential insurance cannot sustain people against the disaster of a life wasted by anxiety, nor can it insure people against death. The sermon's teaching argues against prudence, narrowly conceived: 'Sufficient to the day is its evil' (6.34). It offers a realistic option: to live day by day, trusting in the Creator God. Since only God could restore life to the dead, for those faced with persecution and martyrdom, only trust in God could save them from despair.

Warnings and Encouragements: 7.1-27
Interfering Concern: 7.1-6.[1] 'Do not judge that you may not be judged' can be understood in one of two possible senses. It could refer solely to human relations: do not judge others that you may not be judged by them. Alternatively, it could refer to God's judgment: do not judge others now that you may not be judged by God at the eschatological judgment. The second interpretation fits more adequately into the sermon and the whole Gospel (see 6.12, 14-15; 13.36-43, 47-50; 18.21-35). This also makes the best sense of the reason given for the prohibition:

1   See Mk 4.24; Lk. 6.37-38, 41-42.

'For with the judgment with which you judge [now], you will be judged [at the eschatological judgment], and the measure with which you measure [now] will be applied to you [at the eschatological judgment]'. The hyperbolic metaphor which follows illustrates the absurdity of criticizing the small failings of someone else (the speck in your brother's eye) while ignoring your own large failings (the beam in your own eye), and of offering to help your brother when your own sight (insight) is so impaired. Such a person in the audience is addressed as dissembler, since his claim to insight is mere pretence, and he is urged to remove the obstacle which obscures his own vision so that he could be of real service to his brother. Again, the language of 'brothers' suggests an egalitarian mutuality among those who acknowledged the Creator God as Father, but, as usual, fails explicitly to include 'sisters'.

But how are readers to understand 7.6: 'Do not give what is holy to dogs nor throw your pearls before swine, lest they trample them under foot [as pigs would pearls] and turn and rend you [as dissatisfied dogs would]'? How does this teaching connect to 7.1-5? The hyperbolic metaphors prohibit wasting what is precious on the unappreciative. They inculcate the same attitude and the same kind of behaviour as do the teachings of 7.1-5, namely not to be overconcerned about other people. In 7.1-5, intrusive concern is expressed by criticizing other people's petty faults. In 7.6, intrusive concern is expressed by forcing people to notice things that do not concern them. The narrative will return to the same subject in the parable of the wheat and the weeds (13.27-30). Powerful church institutions have often ignored the teaching.

Encouragement: God's Assured Care: 7.7-12.[1] Reassurance is offered to the audience: 'Ask and it shall be given to you, seek and you will find, knock and it will be opened to you, for everyone who asks receives and who seeks finds and it is opened to the one who knocks'. That God is the implied subject who will answer is made clear by the illustration of the first proposition which follows. Two rhetorical questions highlight the lack of cynicism in a human father's care for his son. The theological significance is then brought out in terms both of similarity and difference: 'If, then, you who are evil know that you give good gifts to your children, how much more will your Father who is in heaven give good things to those who ask him'. The harsh valuation of human frailty, 'you who are evil', reinforces the message to trust God. God's generosity is a central theme of the sermon and of the Gospel, yet there is nothing sentimental about its conception. The good gifts that this Father will give to his sons (eternal life in the kingdom of heaven), will be given only after a mortal life which could bring reproach,

1   See Lk. 11.9-13; 6.31.

reviling and martyrdom (5.11-12; 26.36-46).

In the light of the reassurance, a concluding summons returns to the original subject of the sermon, the fulfilment of the law and the prophets in a just life (5.17-20): 'Therefore, whatever you wish people to do to you, do so to them, for this is the law and the prophets' (7.12). This is the ethical behaviour which is to express trust in the Creator God. In Moses' teaching in Scripture, the detailed lists of commands are often summarized. The ten commandments (Exodus 20; Deuteronomy 5) summarize teaching on relations with God and relations between people, and these twin aspects are also summarized more succinctly as love of God (Deut. 6.5; see Mt. 22.37) and love of neighbour and stranger (Lev. 19.18 and 24; see Mt. 5.43; 19.19; 22.39). Earlier in the sermon, love of neighbour had been interpreted to include love of enemies and prayer for persecutors in the context of God's generosity (5.43-48. Cf. Prov. 25.21). The particular form of the summary in 7.12, 'Whatever you wish people to do to you, do so to them', encourages the same kind of imaginative love towards others as in the command to love your neighbour as yourself. It is similar to: 'Judge your neighbour's feelings by your own, and in every matter be thoughtful' (Ecclus 31.15), and expresses in a positive form the negative admonition: 'What you hate do not do to anyone' (Tob. 4.15) or 'What is hateful to you do not do to your neighbour; that is the whole law while the rest is commentary upon it', attributed to Hillel (*b. Šab.* 31a). Mt. 7.12 serves as a summary of all the ethical teaching in the sermon.

The Narrow Gate: 7.13-14.[1] Just as Moses' sermon in Deuteronomy is concluded with exhortations and warnings (e.g. Deuteronomy 28), so is Jesus' in the Gospel. Scripture often makes use of the metaphor of the two ways, one leading to life and the other to destruction, in order to discourage people from failure to love God and neighbour (e.g. Deuteronomy 28; Deut. 30.15-20; Jer. 21.8; Ecclus 21.10). The metaphor is strengthened in the Matthaean version by contrasting the broad way and the wide gate, which leads to destruction and which many enter, with the compressed way through the narrow gate, which leads to life and which only a few seek. (The Semitic idiom in 7.14, '*how* narrow is the gate' has been altered in some manuscripts to the more familiar Greek idiom, '*because* the gate is narrow'.) The eschatological perspective of the narrative means that life and destruction are not confined to this world but encompass rewards at the final judgment (e.g. 25.34, 41). The narrative will describe Jesus' way leading through persecution and death to eternal life. Hence the way is appropriately described as 'the compressed way through the narrow gate'. The Greek verb for 'compressed' also means 'to persecute'. Further warnings follow which

1   See Lk. 13.24.

provide concrete illustrations of the false ways which are not to be taken.

False Prophets: 7.15-20.[1] The audience is warned to beware of false prophets (cf. Deut. 13.1-5 and 20-22; Jer. 14.14; 27.15; and see later, Mt. 24.24-28). False prophets are described as people who present themselves in the garb of sheep while underneath they are rapacious wolves, since their way would lead to destruction. But just as Deuteronomy goes on to suggest how a false prophet could be recognized, so the sermon indicates, through a change of metaphor, that, like plants, people can be known by their fruits (see John's teaching, Mt. 3.8, 10; and see Isa. 5.2; Jer. 8.13). The reader of the narrative would be able to apply the same test to the prophet Jesus. Rhetorical questions challenge readers to supply appropriate answers, which are then confirmed in general principles: 'Every good tree produces fine fruit but the rotten tree produces bad fruit'. The message is so important that it is repeated: 'the good tree is unable to produce bad fruit and the rotten tree fine fruit'. And just as John's sermon had drawn an inference about the fate of the bad tree (3.10), so does Jesus': 'Every tree which does not produce fine fruit is cut down and thrown into fire'. Once again, an image of the eschatological judgment gives force to the teaching. Finally, this method of recognition is summed up: 'Therefore by their fruits you shall know them' (see again 12.33-35).

The sermon has repeatedly warned against hypocrisy or dissembling, against pretending devotion to God, generosity to other people or insight. Here it suggests that such falsity can be recognized, not just by God but also by human beings. People's way of life would give them away. Moreover, people could apply the same test to themselves. The warnings and the test repeat the teachings of the classical prophets in Scripture. Although the prophecies do not use the word 'dissemblers', they describe the practice. Amos, for example, depicts God's abhorrence of worship from people who oppressed the poor (Amos 4.1, 4-5; 5.11-13, 21-24). Hosea criticizes Israel for infidelity to God which showed itself in lying, killing, stealing and committing adultery (Hos. 4.1-3). Isaiah depicts Jerusalem and Judah as God's vineyard which had produced only wild grapes, its people murderers, thieves, lovers of bribes, drunkards, who failed to defend the fatherless and widows, who called evil good and good evil, who were wise only in their own sight (Isa. 1.21-23; 5.1-25). Jeremiah pictures God's finding no grapes on the vine nor figs on the fig tree, since the people had held fast to deceit, had refused to repent, had been greedy for unjust gain, and yet had prided themselves on their wisdom (Jer. 8.4-13). Jeremiah also complains about false prophets who said 'peace, peace' when there was no peace (Jer. 8.11;

1   See Lk. 6.43-44.

see also 2.8, 26-27; 5.13, 30-31; 14.13-18; 18.18; 23.9-40; 27.14-15). The classical prophets had predicted God's punishment in the form of military defeat and exile. The sermon predicts God's destruction at the final judgment. But all of them point to the same reasons for destruction: empty piety which is a mask for injustice, a mask which can be recognized as such by noticing the injustice.

This emphasis in the sermon and in the rest of the Gospel (e.g. 15.6-9, 13-14; 23.1-39; 25.31-46) is explained by the fact that hypocrisy is the antithesis of the Gospel's positive teaching, it is the dangerous corruption to which the positive teaching is prone. Wholehearted devotion to God and his kingdom could and can be dissembled. Hence, the exhortation to beware is addressed as much to the Christian readers of the Gospel as it is to the audience, crowds and disciples, within the narrative.

False Followers: 7.21-23.[1] The same test is applied to those who acknowledged Jesus as their master. Acknowledgment without its expression in appropriate action would lead to rejection at the final judgment: 'Not everyone who says to me lord, lord will enter the kingdom of heaven but he who does the will of my Father who is in heaven'. Since Jesus was God's obedient son, those who followed him should also act as obedient agents of their Father (e.g. 5.45). At the final judgment, this would be the principle for dividing 'sheep' from 'goats' (25.31-46). 'On that day' is the eschatological day of judgment (see e.g. Zechariah 14; Matthew 24). Those who called Jesus lord, who prophesied in his name, who even cast out demons and performed other mighty works in his name, would not be able effectively to appeal to these in their defence. Jesus' reply, 'I never knew you, depart from me' would be addressed to all those who worked lawlessness (see Ps. 6.8; Mt. 5.17-20; 25.12, 41-46). In other words the whole of a person's life, not just spectacular individual works, are taken to be significant of a person's commitments.

Hearing and Doing: 7.24-27.[2] The sermon's final admonition, therefore, encourages the audience not only to hear but also to practise the teaching (cf. Deut. 28.1, 15). Everyone who does so is likened to a wise man who built his house upon a rock (see 16.18). Such a building would not fall when rain and rivers and wind beat against it (an image both of trials within the world and of God's judgment; compare Genesis 6–7; *1 Enoch* 6–11; Ezek. 13.10-16; Mt. 8.23-27). But everyone who hears and does not practise is likened to a foolish man who built his house upon sand. When rain and rivers and wind beat against it, its fall would

1   See Lk. 6.46; 13.25-27.
2   See Lk. 6.47-49.

be great (that is, complete). The admonition and the metaphor encourage trust in and dedication to God. The person who acts differently is characterized as a fool (cf. Ps. 94.8).

Like Moses' sermon in Deuteronomy, Jesus' Sermon on the Mount includes blessings and warnings, and sets before its audience a way of life dedicated to God, in imitation of God's generosity. But the way of life Jesus' sermon encourages would lead inevitably to persecution and death, and through death to eternal life. The rest of the Gospel will depict Jesus' taking that path in order to persuade readers to follow. The readers' response to the sermon is structured by the brief depiction of the crowds' reaction: 'the crowds were amazed at his teaching, for he was teaching them as someone who had authority and not as their scribes' (7.28-29; see Mk 1.55). The Gospel's portrait of Jesus is more like that of the prophet Moses than like scribes whose authority rested, not on their prophetic calling, but on their interpretive skill. The formulaic notice of the ending of Jesus' teaching (7.28) will be repeated at the end of subsequent discourses (11.1; 13.53; 19.1; 26.1; but not at the end of 23.39). It marks the conclusion of a long speech before going on to relate a series of episodes.

Matthew 8.1–11.1: Passive and Active Responses to Jesus

The second aspect of Jesus' ministry, healing and renewal, is highlighted in chs. 8 and 9 by recounting ten of Jesus' miracles. Although each of the miracles has parallels in Mark or Luke, the order in which they are related is unique to the First Gospel. Since earlier chapters had depicted Jesus as a prophet like Moses, the recounting of a series of ten miracles may recall Moses' ten miracles in Egypt (Exodus 7–12). The number ten suggests this connection, rather than the content of each of the miracle stories.

Only one of the miracles described was performed to save Jesus' disciples (8.23-27). All the others were performed to help people who were and remained outsiders, that is, people who did not become followers of Jesus' way of life. They trusted him to the extent that they or their friends believed he was God's prophetic agent who could perform miracles, but, unlike his disciples, they did not then leave everything to follow him. Moreover, in the narrative summaries of Jesus' activities (e.g. 4.23-24), only healing people's diseases and infirmities, like epilepsy or paralysis, and exorcisms of demons are mentioned. The narrative, therefore, seems to distinguish these kinds of miracles from what we would call 'nature miracles' like that performed to save the disciples in 8.23-27.

Nevertheless, calling people to become followers of Jesus is one of the themes of chs. 8 and 9. The sequence of miracle stories is interrupted by conversations between Jesus and people whom he called (8.18-22; 9.9-13). 9.14-17 also serves to make a distinction between, on the one hand, the disciples of the Baptist and the Pharisees, and, on the other hand, the disciples of Jesus. Two different kinds of response to Jesus are thereby countenanced. Those who wished to be healed, or their friends, expressed a passive trust in Jesus. Those whom Jesus called to follow him had to go beyond a passive trust to an active participation in his mission, as ch. 10 will make clear.

It is appropriate that these stories about renewal and about the reorientation of people's lives through Jesus' activity should follow immediately after the preaching. Jesus' summons in the sermon to live in wholehearted dedication to God could have struck readers as so difficult that they might have been inclined to place themselves among those whom God would finally exclude from his eschatological kingdom. Chapters 8 and 9 help to recreate the impression made at the end of the narrative's first chapter, namely, that God was working through his agent Jesus to save people from their sins.

Three Miracles, a General Summary and an Interpretation of Jesus' Healings as a Fulfilment of Prophecy: 8.1-17

Jesus Cleanses a Leper: 8.1-4.[1] In comparison with the accounts of Jesus' cleansing of a leper in Mark and Luke, the Matthaean version is more succinct and has a different setting. Mt. 8.1 places the healing in the presence of great crowds who followed Jesus, and the story ends with Jesus' command to the man, not with a reference to a report of the incident's spreading abroad, nor with the Markan reference to the man's disobedience of Jesus' command to tell no one. The Matthaean story does not depict the cleansed leper as a missionary.

According to Scripture, leprosy (understood as skin disease) made a person unclean, and people who were unclean could not enter the temple (Leviticus 13). Lepers were also to keep apart from other people, presumably to stop the spread of the disease (Num. 5.2). When they were cleansed, the priest was required to make an offering of two birds with cedarwood, scarlet stuff and hyssop, and the person was required to wash himself and his clothes, shave off his hair, remain apart from human society for seven more days, and then bring an offering of three lambs and cereal with oil (unless he was too poor, in which case he could substitute less expensive offerings [Lev. 14.1-32]).

The Matthaean story pictures the leper's treating Jesus with the kind of respect due to eminent people. He knelt before him and called him lord, just as people knelt before David and called him lord (e.g. 1 Sam.

1   See Mk 1.40-45; Lk. 5.12-16.

25.23-24; 2 Sam. 18.28) or before Elijah (e.g. 1 Kgs 18.7). He expressed his trust in Jesus by asserting Jesus' ability to make him clean. Jesus is described cleansing him by touch and command. The narrative emphasizes that the cure was immediate. Jesus' final command warned the man not to tell people about his cleansing, but to fulfil the requirements of the law: 'Go, show yourself to the priest, and offer the gift that Moses commanded', the purpose of which was 'for a testimony to them'. In other words, the priest's acknowledgment of the cleansing and the appropriate sacrifice were to provide a better testimony than the man's claims. The story succinctly depicts the reclamation into the community of a person whose only action was an expression of trust in Jesus. Readers and listeners could feel encouraged by such a story. The story presents Jesus as a prophet like Elisha (2 Kings 5) through whom God cleansed a leper. It also depicts him as a law-abiding Jew, concerned that God's commands through Moses should be obeyed, as in the preceding sermon.

Jesus Heals a Centurion's Son or Servant: 8.5-13.[1] The request made by a centurion for the healing of his paralysed servant or child (cf. Luke: 'a slave near to death') is set at Capernaum, a fishing village on the lake in Galilee. But the centurion is understood to be a Gentile. In the historical context of the time, however, a Roman centurion would not have lived in Galilee, which was ruled by Herod Antipas who had his own army. Roman troops were stationed at Caesarea, and some served in the Antonia fortress in Jerusalem. Presumably, both author and readers in the first century were ignorant of these details.

According to the narrative, Jesus' activity was directed first of all to Jews, although Gentiles are occasionally pictured coming into contact with him, here and elsewhere (e.g. 2.1-12; 4.25; 8.28-34; 15.21-39). These stories about Gentiles hint at the significance of Jesus' mission for all peoples. In comparison with the Lukan version of the miracle, the Matthaean as usual is more succinct (there is no mention of initial requests by the centurion's friends, for example). In general, the First Gospel refrains from narrating distracting details in order to concentrate on what is essential, Jesus' words and deeds.

The narrative relates that Jesus' response to the centurion's request was an offer to go and heal the servant or child (although his response could be construed as a question: 'Should I come and heal him?'), but the centurion is described expressing great respect for Jesus by mentioning his own unworthiness and by drawing a parallel between his own situation and that of Jesus: just as he needed merely to speak his commands and they were obeyed in his absence, so could Jesus. Jesus' reply emphasizes his appreciation of the strength of this Gentile's trust,

---

1   See Lk. 7.1-10; 13.28-29.

which was greater than any he had found in Israel, presumably because the Gentile had asserted the possibility of Jesus' healing from a distance. Only two healings from a distance are recounted in the Gospel, this one and the healing of a Canaanite woman's daughter (15.21-28), both involving Gentiles. It is just possible that the spatial distance symbolizes temporal distance, a recognition that the Gentile mission was undertaken after Jesus' death.

In the Matthaean version, Jesus' response continues with his depiction of the time of the eschatological kingdom when Gentiles, like the centurion, would come from east and west (see Ps. 107.3) to sit at table with the Jewish patriarchs Abraham, Isaac and Jacob (compare *4 Macc.* 13.17), while 'the sons of the kingdom', a Semitic expression for Jewish descendants of the patriarchs who should have inherited God's kingdom, would be thrown into outer darkness, that is, excluded from the kingdom to a place where people would 'weep and gnash their teeth', a favourite Matthaean depiction of despair (see 13.42, 50; 22.13; 24.51; 25.30. Cf. Ps. 112.10. For other Jewish parallels to the imagery, see *1 En.* 103.7 and 108.3. Note that Luke places this section in a different context, 13.28-29.) The extremism of this contrast between the fate of Gentiles and that of Jews, however, cannot be understood to mean that all Jews would be excluded from the kingdom or that all Gentiles would inherit it. Jesus was a Jew and so were his disciples. Some later followers were Gentiles, but the majority of Gentiles, like the majority of Jews, did not become followers of Jesus. The Matthaean text sometimes uses concrete imagery to depict the reality of eschatological bliss or despair, as here. The life of the kingdom is like the enjoyment of a feast (e.g. 22.1-14) and those exluded are those who weep and gnash their teeth in anger. More abstractly, they are in 'outer darkness', separated from God who gives light.

The story ends, however, on a reassuring note: Jesus' command to the centurion to go, and his promise, 'As you believed, let it happen to you', and the narrator's notice that the servant or child was healed at that hour.

Jesus Heals Peter's Mother-in-law: 8.14-15.[1] The third of Jesus' healings in the Matthaean narrative is set in Peter's house, where Jesus cured the latter's mother-in-law's fever. There is no mention of the disciples' presence; the focus is on Jesus and the person healed. This cure is said to take effect merely by touch without either a request for help or a command from Jesus (contrast Mark and Luke). The reality of the cure is conveyed by noting the woman's arising and beginning to serve Jesus.

These three miracles are set apart from those which follow by the

1   See Mk 1.29-31; Lk. 4.38-39.

summary and the prophetic citation in 8.16-17. Moreover, they have something in common. The leper, the Gentile and the woman were all character-types whose lives were peripheral to those of male Jewish members of the covenant community. These accounts of Jesus' cures make it clear that none is peripheral to God's purpose. Since the woman is identified as Peter's mother-in-law, readers can infer that Peter was married, as Paul's letter also indicates (1 Cor. 9.5). They can also infer that following Jesus after leaving everything was not understood to involve complete separation from family. But the Gospel never spells out the effects on family life in detail.

Summary and Citation: 8.16-17.[1] The crowds had been left behind when Jesus entered Peter's house, but they are reintroduced at evening. The summary relates that they brought people possessed by demons and others who were ill, and that Jesus exorcized by word and healed them all (contrast Mark's 'many'. It is typical of the Matthaean presentation that Jesus' activity, whether healing or preaching, is said to include 'all'.) Mental derangement is understood to be caused by demon possession, a belief common to Jews and pagans in the Hellenistic world. In Scripture only the book of Tobit describes demon possession. Modern Westerners recognize both social and physical causes of madness, but our language retains the perception that people who are mad are 'not themselves'.

The Matthaean version (contrast Mark and Luke) concludes this section by depicting Jesus' activity as a fulfilment of Isaiah's prophecy. The quotation of Isa. 53.4, however, differs from the Septuagint wording and conveys a different sense. According to Isaiah, the servant bore sickness and endured pains by suffering himself, whereas, according to Matthew, Jesus removed sickness from others without becoming ill.

Prospective Disciples: 8.18-22[2]

The next section is introduced by Jesus' decision to leave the crowds and depart to the other side of the lake, but before this is reported, a new subject is introduced by noting the approach of people who wanted to follow Jesus. A scribe (in Luke, 'a man') made the claim that he would follow Jesus wherever he went. Nothing further is heard of him, however, when Jesus replied that 'the son of man has nowhere to lay his head'.

In the narrative, this is the first occurrence of the Semitic expression 'the son of the human being' or 'the son of man'. In Scripture, a 'son of man', always without the definite article, means a human being. It is often used in contexts in which human frailty is contrasted with God's

1   See Mk 1.32-34; Lk. 4.40-41.
2   See Lk. 9.57-60.

power (e.g. Ps. 8.4; Ezek. 2.1; 3.1). The use of the definite article in Mt. 8.20 is appropriate to a proverbial expression, but what does 'the son of man has nowhere to lay his head' imply? Like foxes and birds, people usually have homes which provide shelter. Moreover, the narrative provides Jesus with a home in Capernaum (4.13; 9.1, 10, 28; 13.1, 36; 17.25). In spite of this, however, the narrative depicts Jesus' ministry away from home, not only in other towns in Galilee (e.g. 9.35; 11.1), but across the lake (8.23–9.1), in the region of Tyre and Sidon (15.21-28), in Judaea (20.29-34) and in and around Jerusalem (21.1–27.66). Moreover, Jesus is said to withdraw from places to avoid confrontations (12.15; 14.13; 15.21; 16.4). If Jesus is to be identified with 'the son of man', the narrative describes his lifestyle as insecure, and the saying in 8.20 draws attention to this. That Jesus is to be identified with 'the son of man' is clear from the passion predictions (17.22-23; 20.18-19; compare 16.21) and their fulfilment in Jesus' death and resurrection (chs. 26–28). But if the narrative so clearly identifies Jesus with 'the son of man' why are these sayings on the lips of Jesus not expressed in the first person singular? Why does he not say 'I have nowhere to lay my head'? Why is Jesus represented talking about 'the son of man'? The idiom makes sense if readers understand 'the son of man' to refer to Jesus and also to everyone who shares his lifestyle. Jesus is depicted not just talking about himself, but talking about a kind of human being, himself and others who share his way of life. Hence, when Jesus replied to the scribe who had promised to follow wherever he went that 'the son of man has nowhere to lay his head', he was asserting not only that he lived an insecure lifestyle but that those who followed him would also share that insecurity. The first disciples had been described leaving everything to follow him (4.18-22). 'The son of man' in the First Gospel, therefore, means not every human being, however he or she lives, but every human being who, like Jesus, lives in dedication to God's purpose, trusting solely in God and expecting his vindication. The saying in 8.20, therefore, warns both the scribe and the readers that following Jesus would involve abandoning the usual security of a safe home.

The narrative continues with a story about 'another of the disciples' (contrast Luke). Presumably, readers are to infer that Jesus had called him to become a disciple, but the narrative notes only the man's request to be allowed first to go and bury his father. Jesus' reply, 'Follow me and let the dead [metaphorical] bury their own dead [literal]' would have struck first-century people as extremely offensive, whether they were Jews or Gentiles. Honouring parents was commanded in the Decalogue, and honouring fathers was fundamental to first-century patriarchal societies. Even in our more individualistic cultures, failure to attend one's father's funeral would be regarded as scandalous. The narrative could not more forcefully have represented the importance of following Jesus. Elsewhere in the Gospel, too, following Jesus is set above family loyalties (e.g. 10.35-39). Disciples of Jesus, therefore, would have to forego a further source of security in their lives, that which normally comes from family support. The narrative concludes the story with Jesus' command, without noting what the disciple did. The reader is left with the responsibility of recognizing the importance of following Jesus and acting accordingly. (The Lukan version adds a further command, to go and proclaim the kingdom of God, but the Matthaean version will describe Jesus' call to missionary activity in ch. 10.)

Jesus Calms a Storm: 8.23-27[1]

After these conversations with would-be disciples, Jesus is described carrying out his intention to go to the other side of the lake by embarking in a boat, followed by those disciples who had not withdrawn. And the story continues with a description of a great storm which threatened to engulf the boat while Jesus was sleeping. The narrative relates how the disciples woke him and urged him to 'save, lord, we are perishing'. Jesus' immediate response, however, was to ask the disciples why they were afraid (in Mark and Luke this is the second response). He characterized them as people of 'little faith' (Mark's version is more severe, 'no faith'). In spite of their becoming disciples, then, their faith was less than adequate in the face of danger. Nevertheless, Jesus is described rebuking winds and sea and restoring calm, so that the disciples were amazed and wondered what kind of man he was whom winds and sea obeyed. Thus readers are led to wonder and amazement with the disciples.

This is the only miracle recounted in chs. 8 and 9 which involved the disciples, and which is said to have saved them from danger to their lives. How are readers to construe the story? In Scripture, the sea and floods are always viewed as dangerous (e.g. Genesis 6–9; Ps. 104.25-26; Jon. 1.4-6; Amos 9.3; Isa. 5.30; 17.12) and sometimes symbolize chaos (e.g. Gen. 1.2). Should readers therefore understand this story as representative of the dangers, social and political, which Jesus' and the disciples' insecure lifestyle would bring (cf. Psalm 69)? But why is Jesus represented in the story as intervening to save the disciples? He is first depicted asleep, oblivious to the dangers, and the disciples were those who awoke him and urged him to save them. Moreover, Jesus' response suggests that they should not have been afraid and that they were afraid only because of their lack of faith. Are readers to understand that following Jesus may require them to forfeit their lives (see 5.11-12; 10.26-31)? On this occasion, however, Jesus is represented as meeting their request to be saved and provoking the disciples' amazement and their question, 'What kind of man is this that even the winds and sea obey him?' Such questions in the narrative are designed to

1   See Mk 4.35-41; Lk. 8.22-25.

encourage readers to provide appropriate answers, but what answer would be appropriate? The answer that Jesus was the kind of man who acted as God's agent seems most appropriate, since, in Scripture, God is sometimes depicted saving even his faithless covenant people from the dangers of the sea, most notably through Moses in the story of Israel's crossing the Red Sea (Exodus 14–15).

Nevertheless, the rhetoric of the narrative discourages readers from supposing that Jesus would always save them from dangers. On the contrary, it encourages them to understand that faithful followers of Jesus should meet martyrdom with courage. And this is what will be required of them in Jesus' sermon to his missionary disciples in ch. 10.

Jesus Exorcizes Two People Possessed by Demons: 8.28-34[1]

This story of exorcism forms a pair with the previous one in that Jesus is represented as bringing calm out of destructive chaos, and the sea once more functions as a destructive element. The story is set in Gentile territory on the far side of the lake of Galilee, where herds of pigs might be found. The three names of the region in different manuscripts, 'of the Gadarenes', 'of the Gergesenes' or 'of the Gerasenes', seem to reflect the scribes' difficulties in identifying a place near a city or village on that side of the lake from which the herd could rush over a cliff into the sea.

As usual, the Matthaean version is more succinct than that in Mark or Luke, but it also ends with the people's request for Jesus' departure, not with an account of the man's missionary activity in the Decapolis (cf. Mt. 8.22 and Lk. 9.60). Only the twelve are seen as missionaries in the Matthaean narrative (10.1-5; 28.16-20). Another difference between the Matthaean version and those in Mark and Luke is more difficult to explain: the fact that there are two demoniacs in Matthew and only one in Mark and Luke. If Mark's Gospel was used as a source by the author of Matthew's, perhaps this one story represents two exorcisms in Mark. In Matthew there is no other parallel to the exorcism recounted in Mk 1.23-27.

The story emphasizes the fearful affects of the madness which the demons produced in the possessed men. It is particularly appropriate that Gentiles, who were idolaters, should be represented as demon-possessed (see Deut. 32.17; Isa. 65.11). Their speech, however, is not taken to be insignificant: they recognized Jesus as son of God, as God's agent, so confirming the narrator's view, and they asked whether he had come to torment them before the time, that is, before the final judgment when they would be destroyed. The demons seem to have assumed that their destruction would be effected by Jesus, since they tried to negotiate terms, namely that when they were exorcized from the men they be allowed to enter the pigs nearby. Jesus' response is

1   See Mk 5.1-20; Lk. 8.26-39.

simply to tell them to go, but the narrative relates that this resulted in the panic of the herd, which plunged to destruction over the cliff into the sea. In this way, the effectiveness of Jesus' command, as well as an implied refusal to save the demons from destruction, are confirmed, but the story does not end there. It continues with an account of the swineherds' fleeing into the city and reporting what had happened. The reaction of the citizens is also related: they went out to Jesus with a request for his departure. Moreover, nothing is said about the men who were exorcized (contrast Mark and Luke). Earlier readers had been led to expect that Jesus would bring light to the Gentiles (4.16), and the story of Jesus' healing of the centurion's servant or child depicts his doing so. This story, however, ends with Gentile rejection of Jesus. It serves to warn readers that not all Gentiles would show the kind of appreciation which the centurion did (8.5-13; and see later 10.18).

Jesus Heals a Paralysed Man: 9.1-8[1]

Jesus' departure by boat and arrival at the other side of the lake once more sets the scene 'in his own city', which was Capernaum (4.13). Again the Matthaean version of the story is more succinct than the parallel accounts. There is no reference to the house or to the difficulties the paralysed man's friends experienced in reaching Jesus, difficulties which led to their lowering the man through the roof. The Matthaean narrative simply notes Jesus' observing the faith of those who brought the man. Jesus' immediate response pronounces God's forgiveness of the man's sins: 'Your sins are forgiven', a statement which assumes a causal connection between sin and illness (see Deut. 28.5-35; Ps. 103.3). Paralysis aptly dramatizes the stultifying effects of sin. The statement, however, is said to have prompted scribes, whose presence had not been noted earlier (contrast Luke), to say amongst themselves that Jesus blasphemed, presumably in misrepresenting and therefore reviling God. Remarkably, Jesus is depicted criticizing the scribes' evil thoughts without his hearing their expression, just, as earlier, he had known about the bearers' faith. Should readers infer that Jesus was thought to be able to read other people's minds as the narrator could do? Probably not. The story is told in a kind of shorthand which misses out unnecessary details. Jesus' reply is a challenge: whether it was easier to pronounce God's forgiveness or to command the paralysed man to walk. In this context, Jesus' command to the man, to take up his bed and walk, and the man's obedience, are presented as proof that 'the son of man has authority on earth to forgive sins'. At the end of the story the crowds, but not the scribes, are described as perceiving this meaning by honouring God who had given such authority to human beings (note the plural and contrast Mark and Luke). Once more, Jesus'

1   See Mk 2.1-12; Lk. 5.17-26.

activity as 'the son of man' is taken to be representative, the activity of a particular kind of human being, one who can act as God's agent in forgiving sins and healing. Later, the disciples would be commissioned to become the same kind of human beings, acting in the same ways (10.8; 18.18).

Jesus with Tax Collectors and Sinners: 9.9-13[1]

The theme of forgiveness of sin is continued in the following stories, but whereas the paralysed man was restored to live an ordinary life, Matthew the tax collector, an archetypal sinner because tax collectors were extortioners, was called to leave his old life and follow Jesus (Mark and Luke call the tax collector Levi, who is never mentioned again, whereas in the First Gospel Matthew will be listed as one of the twelve [10.3]). Jesus is then depicted at a meal with tax collectors and sinners. As in the story about the paralysed man, his behaviour is said to have engendered criticism, this time voiced by Pharisees to his disciples, but heard by Jesus. His reply, 'Those who are well have no need of a doctor but those who are ill', uses illness as an appropriate metaphor for sin, implying a claim that he saved sinners (see 1.21). His reference to Hos. 6.6 (no synoptic parallels), in which the prophet spoke God's oracle—'I desire mercy and not sacrifice'—provides his justification for his behaviour and for his general assertion that he had come not to call the just but sinners. In each of the statements, Hosea's and Jesus', the exaggerated rhetorical form should not be pressed. The emphasis lies on 'mercy' and 'sinners' without implying either the abrogation of sacrifice (see 5.23-24; 8.4) or that just people could not follow Jesus (5.20). In each case 'not' only has the force 'even more than'. The expression 'I came', often placed on Jesus' lips as here, gives to Jesus' ministry a sense of purpose.

Jesus' Mission Contrasted with those of John and the Pharisees: 9.14-17[2]

The emphasis on Jesus' mercy towards sinners in the last two stories leads to a series of contrasts between Jesus' mission and those of John and the Pharisees. The disciples of John (contrast Mark and Luke) are the people who introduce the topic by asking why Jesus' disciples did not fast (John's imprisonment had been mentioned earlier: 4.12). The question may cause readers surprise since Jesus had fasted and had provided positive teaching about fasting in the sermon (4.2; 6.16-18). The immediate context, however, suggests that the question is an implied criticism of Jesus' eating with tax collectors and sinners instead of encouraging them to fast in repentance. Jesus' first reply distinguishes

1   See Mk 2.13-17; Lk. 5.27-32.
2   See Mk 2.18-22; Lk. 5.33-38.

the time of his present ministry as a time of celebratory feasts like weddings from a future time when fasting would be appropriate because 'the bridegroom' (Jesus) would no longer be with them. The later time seems to refer to the period of his arrest and execution. But a more complete contrast between Jesus' mission and those of the others is made in his second reply: his mission is like new cloth or new wine which could not be associated with the old without destroying it. A similar negative appraisal of the Baptist's mission will be made in 11.11 with a similar contrast in 11.16-19. The Gospel seems to suppose that the missions of John and the Pharisees represented only a repentant attitude whereas Jesus' mission represented an acceptance of God's mercy in the present, in view of the future kingdom. The contrast involves some historical exaggeration since the historical Pharisees emphasized God's present mercy, but perhaps it also reflects Jesus' acceptance of sinners as sinners, without repentance. His eating with tax collectors and sinners seems to make that point, and the Gospel will picture his commissioning cowardly disciples.[1]

Jesus Restores Life to Two Women: 9.18-26[2]

The shorter Matthaean version of the story retains its sandwich form. The unnamed (contrast Jairus in Mark and Luke) ruler's request that Jesus restore his daughter's life is met by Jesus' accompanying him to his house, with his disciples. No crowds are mentioned (contrast Mark and Luke). En route, a woman who had been suffering with a haemorrhage for twelve years is described touching the tassel of Jesus' cloak as an expression of her belief that this would save her. Jesus is said to have turned and seen the woman (contrast Mark and Luke), recognized her faith and informed her that her faith had saved her. The narrative notes that her cure was immediate. The narrative goes on to notice that, on arrival at the ruler's house, mourners had already gathered, a detail which confirms that the daughter was dead. Jesus' command of dismissal because the little girl was not dead but sleeping is said to have raised scornful laughter, so that readers are still aware that the girl was really dead, but now they are led to expect that her death may not be final. Sleep is a common metaphor for death in Scripture (e.g. Dan. 12.2). Hence the story continues by depicting the withdrawal of the mourners and Jesus' taking the girl's hand and raising her back to life (there is no word of command; contrast Mark and Luke). This is the most remarkable of the miracles attributed to Jesus, and the narrative highlights this by noting that a report of the miracle spread through the land (cf. Elijah, 1 Kgs 17.17-24; and Elisha, 2 Kgs 4.18-37).

---

1   See E.P. Sanders, *Jesus and Judaism* (London: SCM Press, 1985), ch. 6.
2   See Mk 5.21-43; Lk. 8.40-56.

Jesus Heals Two Blind Men: 9.27-31[1]

In order that Jesus' miracles in this section should number ten, like Moses', the Gospel duplicates a healing which will be recounted again later, in 20.29-34. The gradual cure of a blind man in Mk 8.22-26 may also offer a parallel, but Matthew is less interested than Mark in details of healing techniques. According to both the Matthaean versions, two blind men were healed (contrast Mark and Luke). In both they are depicted addressing Jesus as son of David, a reminder to readers of Jesus' messianic status, in spite of the fact that the Christ was not expected to perform healing miracles. Their request that Jesus show them mercy and their persistence indicate their faith in Jesus. In this Matthaean version, however, no-one tries to silence them (contrast the later version). The issue of faith is then focused through Jesus' question, the men's reply and Jesus' command: 'According to your faith let it happen to you'. Jesus' touch and command issued in the healing. Finally, Jesus' instruction that they let no-one know of the healing, and their disobedience, is not said to result in their blindness returning (cf. Mk 1.44-45, without exact parallel in Matthew). No explanation of Jesus' prohibition is offered, but it fits into the pattern established, that people who had been healed did not become authorized missionaries.

Jesus Heals a Dumb Man: 9.32-34[2]

If Matthew is dependent on Mark as a source, a healing is brought forward to complete the number ten, but without the Markan interest in technique. In this story, unusually, demon possession is given as the cause of dumbness rather than madness. The healing is therefore presented as an exorcism. This seems to be determined by the ending of the story: while the crowds were amazed at an event which they declared had never happened in Israel (there are no parallels in Scripture), the Pharisees are said to have accused Jesus of casting out demons by the prince of demons. The charge will be taken up later in 12.22-32, where it is again introduced by a similar story about Jesus' exorcism of a blind and dumb demoniac. Now the reference serves to introduce a note of opposition, in contrast to the enthusiastic acceptance of Jesus by the sick and the crowds.

Jesus' Compassion for the Crowds: 9.35-38[3]

The series of miracle stories is brought to an end by a general summary of Jesus' teaching, preaching and healing, recalling 4.23-25. Again the narrative notes that 'all' were cured (contrast Mark's 'many'). The presence of crowds is said to prompt Jesus' compassion, because they were

1   See Mk 8.22-26; 10.46-52; Mt. 20.29-34; Lk. 18.35-43.
2   See Mk 7.32-36.
3   See Mk 6.6, 34; Lk. 8.1; 10.2.

like sheep without a shepherd. In Scripture, the Christ is commonly seen as a shepherd who restores the oppressed flock (e.g. Jer. 50.6; Ezek. 34.23-24; and see Mt. 2.6). But immediately the disciples in the story and the readers of the narrative are made aware of their responsibility by Jesus' command to pray 'to the Lord of the harvest that he send workers for his harvest'. Harvest is an image of the final judgment and the Lord of the harvest is God. The command prepares readers for the subject of the next section which will be concerned with the disciples' mission.

Miracles and Modern Readers. Modern readers of these chapters cannot help feeling alienated from the world which the narrative creates. We do not treat madness or other forms of illness as demon possession, although we do think of them as evils afflicting people. We are also worried by the ethical and theological implications of the stories. If God cures illness through human agents, why does he not cure all illness? The problem cannot be resolved by suggesting that modern people lack faith in such cures, since Jesus is depicted healing when no faith was expressed (8.14-15). Moreover, Jesus' saving of disciples is not even taken by the narrative to imply that they would escape from all dangers, as the following chapters will illustrate. It is tempting for modern readers to see all these stories as symbolic: Jesus brought outsiders into a community, defeated chaos, removed the paralysing effects of sin, restored the spiritually dead, blind and deaf. Certainly the miracles are presented as typical, without distracting details and without any interest shown in the continuing lives of the individuals involved, who are never named, or in the sort of concrete particulars which would allow people to check the stories' historical veracity. But no doubt the original readers believed in the actualization of these spiritual realities in genuine physical cures. They did not think of nature as independent of the Creator God. The miracles are presented as typical instances of God's creative activity through human agents, as evidence of God's merciful benevolence, as indications that, in Jesus' ministry, God 'is with us' not against us. It is of a piece with this perception that Jesus is presented in association with sinners.

We should notice, however, that the narrative insists that human agents must act for God's creative mercy to become a reality. Even the passive trust of those who requested healing is an essential element in the drama. Moreover, Jesus' acceptance of responsibility for sinners, whether they were physically ill or not, and his drawing others into the acceptance of the same responsibility (see 10.8), encourages readers to accept it too (see 25.36, 43). But modern readers who accept it do so in a world in which scientific advances in medicine give them opportunities beyond the wildest dreams of first-century Christians. The policies of the World Health Organization, for example, have succeeded in eradicating smallpox. Life expectancy and its quality among richer people in the Western world are greater than ever before. On the other hand, cynicism towards the poor and callousness towards those who are ill continue to characterize political policies of Western democracies, both in their treatment of their own citizens and in their treatment of people in the Third World. Some Western drug companies have no qualms about exporting their unsafe products to the Third World, and some Western manufacturers of baby milk have killed thousands of babies by offering free samples to their mothers and then selling the milk at prices the mothers could not afford. This worship of mammon by Western industries makes nonsense of the West's pretensions to democracy. Modern Christians who accept the Matthaean call to responsibility for the sick, therefore, will have to fight against the ethos of Western societies' institutionalized greed in order to make God's fatherly care a reality in the present world. And if they gain inspiration for that battle from the First Gospel, it will make them aware that following Jesus will involve them in suffering persecution and reviling.

Jesus' Summons of Twelve Followers to become Participants in his Mission: 10.1-4[1]

The Gospel depicts Jesus' summons to his twelve disciples and his giving them authority to preach about God's imminent eschatological kingdom, to cast out unclean spirits, and to heal every disease and weakness. The twelve were not to be passive recipients but active participants in Jesus' mission. The names of the twelve whom he sent are given: Simon called Peter, Andrew his brother, James the son of Zebedee, John his brother (see 4.18-22), Philip and Bartholomew, Thomas and Matthew the tax collector (see 9.9), James the son of Alphaeus and Thaddaeus (or Lebbaeus in some manuscripts), Simon the Canaanean and Judas Iscariot who betrayed him. The form of the narrative suggests that the number twelve, their names arranged in pairs, as well as the shocking detail that one of them, Judas, was a betrayer, were already familiar to readers and listeners, although it is unlikely that any was known personally to them. The names differ only slightly from those in Mark: Mark supplies a nickname for the sons of Zebedee, 'sons of thunder', does not identify Matthew as the tax collector, whom the Gospel calls Levi, and includes Thaddaeus not Lebbaeus. The Lukan list differs from the other two in calling Simon 'the zealous one' instead of the Canaanean, a Greek translation of the Aramaic term which meant 'enthusiast', and in replacing Thaddaeus or Lebbaeus with Judas the son of James (also included in the Fourth Gospel, 14.22, which however, does not include a complete list of the twelve). No explicit indication of the significance of the number twelve is supplied, but readers

1   See Mk 3.13-19; Lk. 6.12-16.

should probably infer that it represents the twelve tribes of Israel, the remnant and nucleus of a new covenant community (26.28). Most of the names will never be mentioned again in the narrative. Peter, however, is usually depicted as the spokesman, voicing the concerns or beliefs of the others (e.g. 14.28; 16.16, 22; 17.4; 18.21). Together with James and John, he is sometimes seen accompanying Jesus in the absence of the others, at the transfiguration of Jesus (17.1-8) and in Gethsemane (26.36-46). The request for the sons of Zebedee to sit at Jesus' right and left in his kingdom is attributed to their mother (20.20-28; contrast Mark). Peter's denial and Judas' betrayal will be described in chs. 26–27.

Jesus' Instructions: 10.5-15[1]
The second of Jesus' long discourses in the Gospel (10.5-42) gives instructions for the mission of these twelve, but, like the earlier sermon, it creates the illusion that Jesus directly addresses the readers. Their mission is to conform to Jesus'. They are not yet to embark on a mission to Samaritans or Gentiles. Rather they are to go to 'the lost sheep of the house of Israel', that is, they are to become shepherds like Jesus (9.36; cf. 15.24). Instructions to embark on a Gentile mission will be given only after Jesus' resurrection (28.19-20). Their preaching is to have the same content as that of the Baptist and Jesus; 'the kingdom of heaven has drawn near' (see 3.2; 4.17), and they are to heal the sick, raise the dead, cleanse lepers and cast out demons, as Jesus had been shown doing (chs. 8 and 9). The discourse reminds them that their generosity is only a reflection of the generosity they had received (no synoptic parallel). They are also to adopt an insecure lifestyle like Jesus' (8.20), relying on the hospitality of anyone who is worthy. If they are rejected by any city, as Jesus had been (8.34), they are simply to shake the dust from their feet (which collected in the cloak; shaking the cloak was a gesture of abandonment; see Neh. 5.13) and to await the eschatological day of judgment, when it would be more acceptable to the land of Sodom and Gomorrah, the archetypally sinful places which God had destroyed (Gen. 19.24-28) than to that city. The disciples, then, are seen as agents of the God who would vindicate them at the last judgment, but they are warned against taking judgment into their own hands (as in 13.27-30). In comparison with the parallel accounts in Mark and Luke, this Matthaean account is more detailed, bringing out more clearly the conformity of the disciples' mission to Jesus'.

1   See Mk 6.7-13; Lk. 9.1-6; 10.4-12.

Jesus' Warnings about Dangers in the Future: 10.16-25[1]

The Matthaean discourse goes on to warn the disciples and readers about dangers to be encountered, warnings which the Markan and Lukan accounts hold over until later to include in their 'apocalyptic discourses'. The disciples would be like sheep among wolves. They would need to be as shrewd as serpents and as pure as doves (no synoptic parallels), not so that they could avoid persecution but so that they could meet it faithfully. Presumably doves are symbols of purity because they are white (see 3.16 where God's spirit is likened to a dove, and compare the blessing on the pure of heart, 5.8). Serpents are symbols of shrewdness, presumably because of the serpent's part in persuading Eve (Genesis 3; and see Ps. 140.3). The disciples would be endangered by other people who would hand them over to councils (cities had councils of leading citizens) and who would flog them in synagogues. Preachers and healers who attracted crowds could be seen as security risks who should be discouraged. Paul mentions such reactions to his mission among Gentiles (e.g. 2 Cor. 11.23-26). Apparently, synagogue authorities could discourage people through floggings (see Deut. 25.1-3 and 2 Cor. 11.24). The disciples should also expect to be dragged before governors and kings on Jesus' account, but this experience is interpreted as an opportunity for testimony to them and to Gentiles. The use of the plurals, governors and kings, and the reference to Gentiles suggests that the discourse, while restricting the disciples to an immediate mission among Jews, encompasses a timespan beyond that of the story when a mission to Gentiles would also be included (28.19). These warnings in the discourse are followed by reassurance in the form of a promise that what they should say would be given to them through the spirit of their Father (God). But there is no reassurance that God would rescue them from the danger itself (contrast 8.23-27).

Besides opposition from strangers, they should also expect the kind of betrayal from their families that could result in their deaths. Indeed, they would be hated by everyone because of Jesus' name, but they are encouraged to endure their sufferings because 'he who endures to the end will be saved'. Since death is in view, salvation must refer to post-mortem vindication by God.

The next section of the Matthaean discourse (10.23-25) is without parallel in the Markan and Lukan 'apocalyptic discourses'. It tells the disciples not to court persecution but to flee from it (cf. 2.13-15; 4.12). And it assures them that they would not have completed their mission to the cities of Israel before the son of man's arrival. In chs. 8 and 9, Jesus' present mission had been described as the mission of the son of man, in which the disciples were supposed to participate by following

1   See Mk 13.9-13; Lk. 6.40; 12.11-12; 21.12-17.

Jesus. This reference to a future advent, however, is a reference to Jesus' return at the day of judgment, which will be described in the discourse in chs. 24 and 25. It would bring about the final vindication of faithful disciples and followers. This reference to it in ch. 10 suggests that it was already a familiar expectation for readers and listeners. It serves to confirm the impression that the disciples' mission to Jews would continue for some years, not only during Jesus' lifetime but after his death.

The parallel features of reactions to Jesus' and to the disciples' mission are now brought into focus: since a disciple is not above his master, nor a slave above his lord, 'it is enough for the disciple to be like his master and the slave like his lord'. Hence, 'if they call the head of the household Beelzebul, how much more the members of his household?' The saying recalls the note of opposition voiced by the Pharisees, 'by the ruler of demons he casts out demons' (9.34). Now the ruler of demons is called Beelzebul, the name of the god of Ekron whom Elijah opposed (2 Kgs 1.2-8). Later he will be called Satan (12.22-32).

Fear: 10.26-31[1]

This and the rest of the teaching in the discourse has parallels in other settings in Luke or Mark. In spite of the ghastly picture of the disciples' fate which had just been painted, the universal hatred which disciples would encounter, and the persecutions they would suffer, the discourse goes on to discourage them from fear of persecutors. Rather they are to look beyond their immediate sufferings to their eschatological vindication when what was hidden would be revealed, that is, the accusation of allegiance to Beelzebul would be revealed as false. More than that, however, by looking to the eschaton they would realize that those who kill the body are unable to destroy life. The disciple, therefore, should fear only him who is able to destroy body and life in Gehenna, that is, God. (The Gospel refers to the place of eschatological destruction both by the Hebrew name, Gehenna [5.22, 29, 30; 18.9; 22.23], and by the Greek name, Hades [11.23; 16.18].) But this warning to fear God is immediately followed by a depiction of God's care for his creation. Not even the lives of sparrows come to an end without 'your Father'. This Father's concern even encompasses the numbering of the hairs of their heads. The illustrations justify the statement that God values the disciples more highly than many sparrows. The disciples are encouraged to accept martyrdom in the hope of renewed life after death. Suffering persecution and martyrdom, then, is not a mark of God's disfavour but a significant contribution to God's purpose for human beings.

---

1   See Lk. 12.2-7.

Acknowledgment: 10.32-33[1]

Disciples, therefore, should fearlessly acknowledge their allegiance to Jesus (see 10.18). They are encouraged to do so by the promise that everyone who acknowledges him before people would be acknowledged by him before his Father in heaven. Again the final judgment is in view (25.31-46). But the section ends on a negative note by warning about the fate of everyone who denied Jesus. Nevertheless, this harsh picture is modified later in the Gospel in the portrayal of Peter who denied Jesus but whom Jesus commissioned.

Division and Life: 10.34-39[2]

Again the discourse highlights the divisions which acknowledging Jesus would bring to the disciples' families (see 10.21). It states that Jesus did not come to bring peace but a sword. The language, 'coming to do something', gives a sense of purpose to Jesus' whole mission and its consequences. The reference to a sword is metonymic for division. There is no suggestion that Jesus trained his followers as guerilla fighters. On the contrary, his followers are forbidden to retaliate violently (see 5.38-43: 26.51-54). The statements about family divisions allude to Mic. 7.6, where trust in God rather than in fellow human beings is advocated. As in 8.22, the teaching sets following Jesus above family loyalty and requires a greater love for Jesus than for relatives. But the statement in 10.38 takes a surprising form: 'And he who does not take up his cross and follow after me is not worthy of me'. This is the first reference to crucifixion in the Gospel. Jesus' predictions about his own death in Jerusalem will not be related until later (16.21; 17.22-23; 20.17-19) and crucifixion is not mentioned until 20.19. But the fact of Jesus' crucifixion cannot have been unknown to readers and listeners. 10.38 assumes that Jesus was crucified and that his followers should therefore expect a similar fate. The statement is interpreted through a warning and corresponding reassurance: 'He who finds his life will lose it, and he who loses his life for my sake will find it', although he will find it in another world or age (19.28; 12.32; 13.39, 40, 49; 24.3; 25.46).

Receiving: 10.40-42[3]

The discourse ends with further promises and warnings. The only synoptic parallel is to 10.42 in Mark 9.41. 'He who receives you receives me, and he who receives me receives him who sent me' assumes that agents represent those who commission them. The disciples are to be agents of Jesus as Jesus was God's agent. The teaching is developed to include rewards. A prophet's reward is vindication (e.g. Deut. 18.15-22; Elijah in

1   See Lk. 12.8-9.
2   See Lk. 12.51-53; 14.26-27; 17.33.
3   See Mk 9.41.

2 Kgs 2.11). The reward of a just person is entry into the kingdom of heaven (5.20; 6.1). The narrative will associate prophets and just people again in 13.17 and 23.29. Finally, 'whoever only gives a cup of cold water to one of these little ones in the name of a disciple will never lose his reward'. Reference to disciples as 'little ones' draws attention to their political and social powerlessness, a matter which is often stressed in various ways. They are to be meek or humble (5.5) like Jesus (11.29; 21.5), they are to become humble like children (18.3-4), members of Jesus' community are 'little ones' (18.10), and those who want to be great among them are to be servants like Jesus (20.25-28). Offering help to such people could involve the helpers in persecution too.

Conclusion: 11.1

This verse notes in a stylized form the end of Jesus' discourse (see 7.28-29; 13.53; 19.1; 26.1). Here the narrative takes no notice of the disciples' reaction. It gives no account of the disciples' departure and return, as Mark and Luke do (Mk 6.12-13, 30; Lk. 9.6, 10). Rather the impression created by the discourse is that Jesus' teaching relates not to a single journey, but to the longer-term mission of the disciples. It refers not only to the disciples' immediate future but also to their mission after Jesus' death and resurrection, when it would be extended to include Gentiles (10.18; 28.19). The perspective of the discourse includes the whole of the church's mission till the end of the age (10.22-23; 28.20).

How would first-century readers and listeners have understood this discourse addressed to the twelve disciples in the story but addressed to themselves in the narrative? Would they have identified their role with that of the disciples? No doubt some of them would have done so, but not all. Not everyone in the community that read the Gospel would have been a missionary. Although the Gospel stresses the egalitarian nature of the community (20.25-28; 23.8-12), it envisages different groups taking particular responsibilities. 23.34 distinguishes prophets, wise men and scribes from others. One of the parables in ch. 13 distinguishes ordinary followers (wheat) from leaders (servants; 13.24-30, 36-43), and both 18.10-14 and the parables in 21.28–22.14 highlight the special responsibilities of leaders. The judgment scene in 25.31-46, too, distinguishes those in prison from those who visit them. Moreover, the resurrected Jesus will be presented appearing to women but reserving his missionary command for the eleven disciples (28.9-10, 16-20). The Sermon on the Mount had directly addressed every member of the community. This discourse is addressed first of all to wandering missionaries. Those who were not called to become missionaries would be in the position of those who received prophets and just people, mentioned in 10.40-42 (and see 10.11-12). They had become followers of Jesus because of the mission of earlier disciple-missionaries.

Modern readers too have to make such a distinction. But they also have to modify the eschatological expectation which is stressed here and throughout the Gospel. The end of the age, the last judgment and the life of the world to come did not materialize as the Gospel expected it would in the near future. Its failure to arrive caused crises during the continuing history of churches, and, gradually, eschatology was transformed into teleology. Teleology expresses the doctrine of the last things, as in the Creed's 'we look for the resurrection of the dead and the life of the world to come', but that doctrine does not emphasize, as eschatology does, that this would happen in the near future. The eschatological perspective gave to the Gospel's first-century readers a sense of urgency, but it also encouraged them to live their present lives in the light of God's final judgment. Teleology provides modern Christians with the same encouragement. Moreover, the discourse gives to readers' present threatened existence a significance which prevents them from understanding their sufferings as tragic. Their modelling their lives on Jesus', who was crucified by his enemies but whom God raised from the dead, is conceived as the expression of the Creator God's purpose for humanity. Insofar as they refused to meet the violence of persecution with retaliatory violence, they were creating a new kind of community dedicated to the Creator God who cared for them in the present and who would renew their lives after death. It is this theological perspective, shared by modern Christians with first-century Christians, which justifies heroic endurance. But modern Christians who no longer hope for an imminent eschatological judgment also have to work for long-term social and political reforms as God's agents in his continuing world.

Matthew 11.2–13.52: Inadequate Reactions to Jesus' Ministry and Jesus' Responses

Jesus and John the Baptist: 11.2-19[1]

The narrative had noted John's imprisonment before the beginning of Jesus' public ministry (4.12). Hence his question to Jesus arises from reports of Jesus' deeds and is addressed through his disciples (cf. 9.14). 'The deeds of Jesus', the reading of some manuscripts, is probably original, since the alternative reading, 'the deeds of Christ', in the majority of manuscripts, already interprets their significance. 'The deeds of Jesus' leaves open the question of what the deeds may signify. John's question 'Are you he who is to come?' could refer to the expectation concerning either the prophet like Moses (Deut. 18.15, 18) or the Christ (e.g. 2 Sam. 7.16; Isaiah 9 and 11). Since the Christ was not expected to

1 See Lk. 7.18-35; 16.16.

perform healing miracles, but prophetic figures like Moses, Elijah and Elisha were, the expectation of a prophet like Moses makes better sense of Jesus' reply. That reply instructed John's disciples to tell him what they heard about Jesus' miracles and preaching to the poor, phrased as an allusion to Isa. 35.5-6. Isaiah's prophecy, which looks forward to God's future saving of his people, mentions the healings of blind, deaf, lame and dumb people. Jesus' reply mentions the healings of lepers, the blind, lame and deaf, and the raising of the dead, all in the plural. The miracles described in chs. 8 and 9 are therefore understood as exemplary of many healings, as the summaries suggest (e.g. 8.16; 9.35). The miracles described include cleansing a leper, healing two paralysed people, raising the ruler's dead daughter, healing a woman with a haemorrhage, two blind men and a deaf and dumb man. The Isaiah prophecy does not refer to exorcisms because the conception of demon possession was a later development in Judaism, but the Matthaean Jesus' miracles had included exorcisms (e.g. 8.16, 28-34; 9.32-34). The good news preached to the poor is that found in Matthew 5–7 (see Isa. 61.1). The question raised by John, therefore, is used to highlight the significance of Jesus' activities up to this point in the narrative. No direct answer to the question is supplied, but readers could supply the implied answer that Jesus was the prophet like Moses who was to come. Finally, a blessing is pronounced on the one who was not offended by Jesus. The narrative will go on, however, to depict people's taking offence at Jesus.

First, though, Jesus' appreciation of John is provided. The departure of John's disciples forms the introduction to Jesus' question to the crowds about John. The repetition of the question 'What did you go out to see?' (or 'Why did you go out? To see...') is supplied with two absurd answers and then a reasonable answer: a prophet. John had been described as a prophet dressed like Elijah (3.4). Here, however, he is immediately described by Jesus as 'more than a prophet', as the messenger who would prepare Israel's way according to Exod. 23.20 and Mal. 3.1 (see Mk 1.2; Lk. 1.76). The citation in Matthew seems to allude to both passages without exactly quoting either. But what does 'more than a prophet' mean? It implies that he was the prophet who announced the imminence of God's eschatological kingdom, that he was someone greater than any other person 'born of a woman', but that 'the one who is least [the comparative used with superlative force] in the kingdom of heaven is greater than he'. The contrast implies that those who would enter the kingdom of heaven would be born not just of women but also of God, through God's spirit (3.11; 5.3, 48; 28.19). Further reflections on John's significance by Jesus follow, but 11.12 is difficult to interpret because the Greek expressions are ambiguous (the Lukan parallel in 16.16 is different). The verb *biazetai* could be either middle or passive, that is, either 'forces its way' or 'suffers violence'. Moreover, the present of the verb *harpazousin* could mean 'are siezing' or 'are trying to sieze'. The sentence could therefore be translated in the following ways:

1. 'From the days of John the Baptist until now, the kingdom of heaven suffers violence and men of violence are siezing it'. This would view the kingdom of heaven as an existing reality between the time of John's ministry and this point in Jesus' ministry. Such a rendering makes no sense in the context, however, since the disciples had just been told to preach the imminence of the kingdom of heaven, not its past arrival (10.7). Moreover, according to ch. 10, it is not the kingdom of heaven which would suffer violence but the messengers of its imminence.

2. 'From the days of John the Baptist until now, the kingdom of heaven forces its way and men of violence are trying to sieze it'. This translation makes much better sense in the context of the Gospel. It graphically depicts the inevitability of the future arrival of the kingdom of heaven while excluding people's violent attempts to bring it in. Jesus' sermon had already excluded violence as a means of serving God's purpose (5.38-48). John, Jesus and Jesus' followers were all to suffer violence without inflicting it, in their commitment to the future eschatological kingdom of heaven.

The teaching then returns to John's role: 'All the prophets and the law prophesied until John' conceives the whole of Scripture as prophetically looking forward to the present events. The frequent citations and allusions to Scripture had already suggested as much. Hence John is identified with the messenger Elijah who was to come, according to Mal. 4.5. At first the identification is suggested tentatively, 'if you want to receive', but is then reinforced, 'he who has ears let him hear'.

In spite of John's importance, however, the teaching distinguishes John's type of ministry from Jesus' (see 3.11-12; 9.14-17), while ridiculing 'this generation' which criticized both. 'This generation' is likened to children calling to others in market places: 'We piped and you did not dance' represents a celebration; 'we wailed and you did not mourn' represents a funeral. Readers are to infer that the first criticism was addressed to John and the second to Jesus. John is depicted as an ascetic, neither eating nor drinking (in celebration), which people are said to have taken as a sign of demon possession. Jesus, the son of man, is depicted as someone who enjoyed eating and drinking (see 9.10-13), which people are said to have construed as a sign that he was a glutton and a drunkard, a friend of tax collectors and sinners. These popular appraisals, however, are interpreted as trivial by the challenge, 'wisdom is justified by its deeds' (contrast Luke). John had preached repentance and baptized the repentant. Jesus had preached about the imminent eschatological reversal, as John had done, but he had also healed the sick and associated with tax collectors and sinners, demonstrating God's desire to save sinners. The crowds in the story and the readers of the narrative are encouraged to make the distinction and are left to draw inferences for their own way of life. The implied rejection of both Jesus and John by 'this generation' leads into the following series of woes.

Prophetic Woes against Unrepentant Cities: 11.20-24[1]

Jesus' woes against the cities (compare Hos. 7.13; 9.12; Amos 5.18; 6.1; Isa. 1.4; 3.9, 11; 5.11-30; Ezek. 24.6-14; Nah. 3.1) are introduced with the statement that he began to reproach the cities in which most of his mighty works had happened, because they did not repent. But of the cities named, Chorazin, Bethsaida and Capernaum, only the last is ever mentioned elsewhere in the Gospel. Readers have to assume that the others were among the places visited without their being named in the general summaries (e.g. 9.35). The responses of Chorazin and Bethsaida are contrasted negatively with the responses that would have been expected from Tyre and Sidon had Jesus performed such mighty works there. Tyre and Sidon were two fortified cities on the Mediterranean coast, sometimes condemned by prophets (e.g. Isaiah 23; Ezekiel 26–28). Later, Jesus will be described extending his ministry to the regions of Tyre and Sidon, where the crowds responded by praising God (15.21-39). Hence, on the day of judgment, it would be more tolerable for Tyre and Sidon than for Chorazin and Bethsaida. Worse, however, would be Capernaum's fate, in spite of the fact that Jesus' ministry had been pictured as centring there. Capernaum would not be exalted but humiliated (Capernaum is not mentioned in Lk. 10.12-15. See Isa. 14.13-15). It is unfavourably compared even to Sodom which God had destroyed (Gen. 18.16–19.28. Cf. Mt. 10.15), because even Sodom would have remained had it witnessed Jesus' deeds. On the day of judgment, therefore, it would be more tolerable for Sodom than for Capernaum. This negative appraisal of Capernaum draws out more clearly what can only be inferred from earlier descriptions, namely, that most of its inhabitants did not respond positively to Jesus' ministry (8.5-22; perhaps 9.1-31). Earlier, at the end of ch. 9, a more positive impression had been created: 'The harvest is plentiful but the labourers are few'. Between 9.37 and 11.24, however, the narrative had noted the persecutions which Jesus' disciples would suffer and had described the crowd's rejection of Jesus' way of life (10.16-39; 11.16-19).

This teaching, like that of the classical prophets in Scripture, treats communities as wholes, without distinguishing individuals within them. Later judgment will be pronounced against the whole of Jerusalem (23.37-38). Elsewhere, however, the teaching does envisage a judgment of individuals (e.g. 7.21-27). But these dramatic warnings against whole communities emphasize the interdependence of individuals and prevent

1   See Lk. 10.12-15.

readers from supposing that they could live a separate existence in a world of their own.

Jesus' Prayer and Invitation: 11.25-30[1]

In the context of these stories which indicate inadequate responses to Jesus' ministry, it is appropriate that readers should be reminded of his significance. In Jesus' prayer, God is addressed as Father, Lord of heaven and earth, acknowledging both his fatherly care and his final control of everything that exists, and God is praised for hiding these things (the significance of Jesus' activities) from the wise and understanding, but revealing them to babies. Earlier, the disciples had been likened to 'little ones' because they were socially vulnerable (10.42). Later they will be told to become like children, that is to be humble (18.3-4). The 'wise and understanding' in this context, then, must refer to the powerful in society, reckoned to be wise and understanding in worldly affairs. By contrast, the disciples' understanding (13.51-52) would be an understanding of what God was bringing about. They will be called 'wise men and scribes' (23.34) whom the powerful would persecute. The prayer understands God's revelation to these 'babies' as an expression of what pleases God rather than human beings.

The teaching then reflects on Jesus' relationship with God, drawing on the metaphor of a son's relationship to his father. All things were given to Jesus by this father, no one recognized the son except the father, and no one recognized the father except the son and anyone to whom the son decided to reveal him. Both the son's dependence on the father and the son's importance as the father's agent are stressed, while readers are encouraged to understand themselves as among those to whom the son decided to reveal the father. The stark disclaimer that 'no-one recognized the son except the father' prepares readers for the disciples' abandonment of Jesus at his arrest (26.56).

In the light of this father–son relationship, an invitation is issued to all who labour and are heavy laden. They should come to Jesus since he would give them rest (cf. Exod. 33.12-14). They should take his yoke and learn from him, because he was humble and lowly in heart, and they would find rest for their lives. Jesus' yoke is said to be easy and his burden light (no parallel in Luke). Later, scribes and Pharisees will be criticized for binding heaven burdens, hard to bear, on people's shoulders (23.4). What is described as easy and light, however, is a life lived in complete dedication to God, a dedication which would free people from self-concern (6.24-34) and for generosity (5.38-42), but which would inevitably bring persecution from fellow human beings (5.11-12; 10.16-25). Nevertheless, this way is understood to give rest, not from persecution and hardship, nor through temporary worldly honour, but

1   See Lk. 10.21-22.

through reliance on the God who is Father and Lord of heaven and earth. It would be easy and light because it would be free from trivial concerns. The prayer and invitation summarize earlier teaching, prepare readers to understand the episodes which follow, and invite readers to dedicate their lives to God as Jesus did.

Jesus Defends the Behaviour of his Disciples from Criticism: 12.1-8[1]

The incident that gave rise to criticism is briefly described: on the Sabbath Jesus went through the grain fields, and his disciples were hungry and began to pluck grain and eat. Scriptural commands allowed the poor to take gleanings (Lev. 19.9; 23.22; Deut. 23.25). Mark and Luke do not contain the explanatory detail that the disciples were hungry. The Matthaean detail helps to forge a link between the disciples' plight and that of David (12.3-4). Perhaps it also illustrates their obedience to Jesus' command to take no provisions on journeys (10.9-10) and implies that the towns and villages through which they had passed had proved unworthy (10.11-15 and see 11.20-24). It is the Pharisees who are named as those who criticized the disciples' behaviour as unlawful on the Sabbath. The command in the Decalogue states that on the Sabbath 'you shall do no work, you or your son or your daughter, your manservant or your maidservant, or your cattle, or the sojourner who is within your gates' (Exod. 20.10; Deut. 5.14). The command clearly forbids ordinary work on the Sabbath day, but it does not define exactly what work is. Pharisees and other Jews, who were concerned to obey the command, agreed that people should rest from their everyday work and that they should make the necessary provisions for a Sabbath meal in advance of the Sabbath (see Exod. 16.5). But they disagreed over details. For example, what exactly were people to do in preparing the meal on the Sabbath? Since the Sabbath celebrated God's generosity to his people, relaxing and enjoying a meal was essential to the celebration (see Exod. 16.29).

Nevertheless, Jews had come to realize that, in particular circumstances, other concerns might take precedence over the Sabbath rest. For example, during the Maccabean revolt in the second century BCE, Jews needed to decide whether they should fight on the Sabbath or not. Those who did nothing to defend themselves were killed by their enemies (1 Macc. 2.29-38). Eventually, they decided to defend themselves when attacked on the Sabbath, but not to initiate an attack on the Sabbath (1 Macc. 2.39-41; Josephus, *War* 1.145-46). They seem to have recognized that saving life, even by working, should take precedence over the Sabbath rest. Work which did not save life, however, would have been less acceptable on the Sabbath. In the context of

1   See Mk 2.23-38; Lk. 6.1-5.

first-century Judaism, therefore, some people might have objected to the disciples' plucking grain on the Sabbath, but the issue was far from clear-cut. If readers infer that the disciples' itinerant lifestyle and their rejection by local communities made normal provision for a Sabbath meal impossible, their behaviour could not be construed as wanton Sabbath-breaking.

The reference to Pharisaic criticism is somewhat artificial. They are said to have seen the disciples' plucking grain as they walked through the fields. So readers have to imagine Pharisees out in the grain fields at a time when they would have been eating their Sabbath meal. Moreover, the Gospel sets the incident in Galilee, and it is historically unlikely that Pharisees lived there in the early part of the first century. Repeatedly, however, the narrative picks out the Pharisees as those who criticized Jesus and his disciples (e.g. 9.34; 12.24, 38; 15.1). They are caricatured as dissemblers whose unjust opposition to Jesus stemmed not from true piety towards God but from a concern to gain honour from other people (e.g. 23.5-7). Christians who know nothing about Pharisees apart from their depiction in the Gospels have too readily accepted a polemical caricature as if it depicted historical realities. One-dimensional caricatures can never do justice to the religious ethos of any group. Modern Judaism draws insight and succour from the profound teachings of the historical Pharisees. And the Matthaean caricature fails to appreciate how much the Matthaean Jesus had in common with Pharisees and other Jews in their emphasis on God's bounteous mercy (e.g. Josephus, *Apion* 2.190-97). In a short work like the Gospel, however, a caricature usefully served as a warning to readers against dissembling. It becomes dangerous only when people overlook its literary function and take it to be a true depiction of historical reality. This story in Matthew discourages readers from behaving like these 'Pharisees'.

Jesus is represented as justifying his disciples' behaviour by reference to scriptural precedents. When David and his followers were hungry, they ate bread which had been offered to God and which only priests were allowed to eat (1 Sam. 21.1-6; see Lev. 24.5-9). Moreover, it is possible to infer from Scripture that the David incident took place on the Sabbath, since that was when the shewbread was set out (Lev. 24.5-9). Matthew's account (contrast Mark and Luke) then cites a second precedent which makes explicit a connection with the Sabbath. To perform their duties on the Sabbath, priests were required by the law to do things which would normally be construed as work (Num. 28.9-10), but temple sacrifices were allowed to take precedence over the Sabbath rest because they were ordained by God.

These precedents are then applied to the case of the disciples' plucking corn on the Sabbath. The argument runs like this: satisfaction of hunger takes precedence over the restriction of offerings on the

Sabbath to priests; temple offerings take precedence over the Sabbath rest; 'something greater than the temple is here', something that takes precedence over temple sacrifice. What is this 'something greater'? The answer is supplied by God's oracle in Hos. 6.6: 'I desire mercy and not sacrifice'. It is mercy, then, which takes precedence over temple sacrifice. The rhetoric of the oracle does not imply an abrogation of sacrifice but the greater importance of mercy. Had the 'Pharisees' acted mercifully, they would not have condemned the disciples' satisfaction of hunger, which is pronounced 'guiltless'. The general statement at the end, 'for the son of man is lord of the Sabbath', must be understood in this context. It does not justify any type of behaviour on the Sabbath, only merciful behaviour. Other references to the Sabbath in the narrative imply that the Sabbath rest was generally kept (24.20; 28.1). 'The son of man' is the human being who lives in dedication to God, who fulfils God's purpose for humanity. In the story, the son of man's lordship had been exemplified by the disciples. In the following story it will be exemplified by Jesus. (The First Gospel does not contain the opaque Markan statement: 'The Sabbath was made for man and not man for the Sabbath').

Jesus Heals a Man with a Withered Hand: 12.9-14[1]
This second Sabbath story is set in a synagogue, a meeting place where Jews would have been free to assemble on the Sabbath. The presence of a man with a withered hand is said to have prompted a question from bystanders, 'Is it lawful to heal on the Sabbath?', but the narrator construes the question as a trick that could have led Jesus to reply in a manner which would have justified accusations against him. His reply, however, begins from what is presumed to have been a generally accepted practice on the Sabbath, namely the rescue of a sheep which had fallen into a pit (see Lk. 14.5). We do not know for certain whether it was a generally accepted practice, but since the Covenanters at Qumran did not allow it (CD 11.13-14), we may assume that less strict Jews did. Further, another generally accepted proposition, that a human being is more important than a sheep, is used to justify the conclusion that it is lawful to do good on the Sabbath. On the basis of the general conclusion, Jesus' healing of the man with the withered hand is presented as a lawful action on the Sabbath. Remarkably, however, the 'Pharisees' are depicted taking council to destroy Jesus (Mark includes Herodians, Luke scribes).

In the historical context of the time, however, nothing Jesus is described saying or doing could be construed as breaking the Sabbath. Speech was not forbidden on the Sabbath, and Jesus did no work to facilitate the healing. Even the most strict of the Pharisees could have

1   See Mk 3.1-6; Lk. 6.6-11; 14.1-6.

found no fault with Jesus' behaviour. Moreover, the Pharisees at the time had no legal power to destroy Jesus literally. They could have attempted to destroy his popularity by suggesting that he worked miracles as an agent of Satan, not of God, as they will be depicted doing in 12.22-24, so readers should probably understand 'destroy' in that sense. It is significant that Pharisees are not included at the Jewish council which condemned Jesus according to Mt. 26.57-68 and that breaking the Sabbath is not an accusation brought against Jesus. But in the earlier part of the narrative, 'Pharisees' are caricatured as impious opponents of Jesus who ignored all evidence that his activity made God's mercy known. Readers are discouraged from following their example.

Jesus the Servant of God: 12.15-21[1]

In response to 'Pharisaic' plans, Jesus is pictured withdrawing, and this allows the narrator to reflect on the significance of Jesus' ministry in a way which makes it clear to readers that 'Pharisaic' offence at Jesus was opposition to God's purpose. The summary of Jesus' healing activity and his prohibition of making it known are said to fulfil Isaiah's prophecy about God's servant Israel. Jesus' withdrawal and prohibition are seen to exemplify the servant's silence and confirm that he had been chosen and was beloved by God who had given him his spirit. This reminds readers of what they had already heard from the heavenly voice at Jesus' baptism (3.17). Jesus' healing is interpreted both as the servant's refusal to destroy the weak and feeble and as his establishment of justice which brought hope to Gentiles: 'a bruised reed he will not break, and a smoking wick he will not quench, until he brings justice to victory, and in his name will the Gentiles hope'. (The wording of the quotation does not correspond exactly either to the Hebrew or to the Septuagint versions as we have them, Isa. 42.1-4). The Isaianic expectations about Israel's role are understood to be fulfilled by the obedient Jew, Jesus. Readers are reminded of the universal significance of Jesus' life in the context of accounts about opposition from some of his Jewish contemporaries. The narrator's reflections predispose readers to understand 'Pharisaic' criticism in the next episode as obtuse.

The Beelzebul Controversy: 12.22-32[2]

The story opens with Jesus' exorcism of a blind and dumb demon-possessed man (cf. 9.27-34). The amazement of the crowd is said to lead to their question, 'could this be the son of David?', to which readers had been encouraged to answer yes, but to which 'Pharisees' answered: 'It is only by Beelzebul, the prince of demons, that this man casts out

1   See Mk 3.7-12; Lk. 6.17-19.
2   See Mk 3.22-30; Lk. 11.14-23; 12.10.

demons' (the Markan introduction is different). This interpretation of Jesus' exorcisms picks up their statement in 9.34 and represents their attempt to destroy Jesus (12.14) by influencing the crowds to understand him as a sorcerer rather than as God's agent. Readers, however, had already been prepared to understand the accusation as false, not only by the preceding quotation from Isaiah, but also by the story of Jesus' tests in the wilderness (4.1-11). Jesus' reply confirms the readers' perception. Jesus is presented as 'knowing their [the Pharisees'] thoughts', that is, perceiving the purpose of their accusation. His reply begins with general statements about every divided kingdom, city and house suffering ruin, and then applies them to Satan's household. Beelzebul, the idol of Ekron (2 Kgs 1.2), is taken to be a synonym for Satan, God's spiritual adversary (1 Chron. 21.1). The argument runs: if Satan were to cast out demons, he would be acting against his own household, which would be divided and would therefore suffer ruin. A second argument appeals to the practice of Jewish exorcists through a rhetorical question: 'If I cast out demons by Beelzebul, by whom do your sons cast them out? Therefore they shall be your judges'. The narrative acknowledges that Jesus' exorcisms, or his disciples' exorcisms, were not unique. Jews who were not followers also acted as God's agents in performing exorcisms. All these exorcisms are interpreted as evidence of the activity of God's spirit (compare Luke's 'the finger of God') and of the establishment of God's kingdom rather than Satan's. As elsewhere in the narrative, 'the kingdom of God' refers to God's eternal reign as Creator of the world, and should be distinguished from the 'kingdom of heaven' which refers to the kingdom God would finally establish in the future at the eschatological judgment, when all forms of evil would be eradicated. Jesus' argument then reverts to the image of the household, asserting that it is impossible to plunder a strong man's household without first binding him (Luke develops the image differently). The strong man represents Satan. Jesus' exorcisms, therefore, are not to be understood as evidence of Jesus' allegiance to Satan, but, on the contrary, as evidence of Jesus' opposition to Satan through the inspiration of God's spirit.

These arguments against the accusation that Jesus cast out demons by Beelzebul are presented in such a compelling manner that the opposition which voiced them is seen to be foolish. This is the subject of Jesus' concluding remarks. No middle ground is allowed to exist between Jesus and his opponents: 'he who is not with me is against me, and he who does not gather with me scatters' (see Mk 9.40). The opponents had been misrepresenting not only God's agent but God himself in attributing his activity to Satan. The teaching therefore concludes with a warning: 'Every sin and slander shall be forgiven people, but the slander of the spirit shall not be forgiven'. In other words, people who attributed God's activity to Satan were beyond even God's power to save. The message is reinforced: 'Whoever makes a statement against the son of man will be forgiven, but whoever speaks against the Holy Spirit will be forgiven neither in this age nor in the age to come' (the Markan version is different). The saying suggests that the behaviour of the son of man, Jesus and his followers, may be inadvertently misinterpreted, whereas denying incontrovertible evidence of the Holy Spirit's activity precludes the re-creative activity through forgiveness that God's spirit brings (cf. Num. 15.30-31; Isa. 5.20). 'This age' is present historical existence, 'the age to come' is the age which would follow God's eschatological judgment (Markan phraseology is different. See Mt. 13.39, 40, 49; 24.3; 28.20, and compare Jewish apocalyptic literature: 2 Esd. 7.47, 50; 2 Bar. 15.7-8; 44.15).

The rhetoric of the passage suggests that everyone ought to be able to discern the creative activity of God's spirit. Modern readers are more likely to discern such activity in the fact of the world's continuing existence, in birth, in nature's re-creative process and in instances of individual and social renewal than in exorcisms which are foreign to our world view. Moreover, we are impressed and encouraged when we know people who suffer from incurable illnesses but who behave with courage and generosity.

Jesus' Condemnation of People's False Statements: 12.33-37[1]

Condemnation of the audience as a 'brood of vipers', that is, as poisonous destroyers, is introduced by a command to make or recognize the connection between a good tree and good fruit and between a rotten tree and rotten fruit, which allows the inference that a tree may be known by its fruit. The metaphor, applied to human behaviour, had been explored earlier as part of a warning (7.17-20). Now it is given more force by placing it after the Beelzebul controversy. The metaphor prepares for the question, 'How are you who are evil able to say good things, for out of the abundance of the heart the mouth speaks'. The heart is pictured as a treasury out of which good or bad things are brought forth. Hence the warning, 'Truly I say to you, every idle word which people utter will be brought to account on the day of judgment'. In effect, then, people would condemn themselves. The pronouncement ends, 'By your [singular] statements you will be justified, and by your statements you will be condemned', applying the teaching to individuals in the audience. The Gospel sees everything that people do or say in the light of the eschatological judgment.

---

1   See Mt. 7.16-20; Mk 3.30; Lk. 6.43-45.

Opponents Replied with a Request for a Sign: 12.38-42[1]

According to the narrative, Jesus' arguments and warnings did not silence the 'Pharisees'. On the contrary, they and the scribes are pictured replying with a request for a sign, presumably a sign which would signify Jesus' status as a teacher from God (see Exod. 4.7-10). Clearly they had rejected exorcisms as such signs. Their request, however, provides an occasion for further condemnations from Jesus. Jesus' reply states that an evil and adulterous (that is, in the sense of infidelity to God) generation seeks a sign. The proposition seems to interpret their request as an attempt to test God (see 4.5-7). Nevertheless, the reply continues with a kind of promise, that no sign would be given (implied by God) except the sign of Jonah (contrast Mark). This sign is then explained: the son of man would be three days and three nights in the heart of the earth as Jonah had been three days and three nights in the belly of the sea monster (Jon. 1.17). The reference is cryptic in the story but readers familiar with the later account of Jesus' crucifixion and resurrection would recognize the reference to those future events. Nevertheless, the narrative will relate that even Jesus' resurrection failed to impress his opponents (28.11-14). Hence the reply goes on to represent the Ninevites (those to whom Jonah was sent) condemning 'this generation' at the eschatological judgment because they repented at the preaching of Jonah, and now 'something greater than Jonah is here'. The 'something greater' refers to Jesus' resurrection from the dead which was an even greater sign of God's mercy than Jonah's survival. A second example repeats the message. The queen of the south who came from the ends of the earth to hear Solomon's wisdom (1 Kgs 10.1-10; 2 Chron. 9.1-12) would rise up in judgment against 'this generation' because something even more remarkable than Solomon's wisdom, that is Jesus' resurrection, 'is here'. These references to Gentiles, the Ninevites and the queen of the south, point forward to the Gentile mission which the disciples would undertake after Jesus' resurrection (28.19-20).

Jesus' Warning of Worse Evil: 12.43-45[2]

Jesus' discourse continues with a story about an unclean spirit, exorcized from a person, seeking rest, finding none, and returning to its original dwelling-place, which had been swept and put in order, bringing seven other spirits more evil than itself to dwell there. The person's final state is pronounced worse than his first. The story is then applied to 'this evil generation' (contrast Luke). The teaching seems to be warning both the audience in the story and the readers of the narrative against complacency. Rescue from the influence of evil may be but the prelude to worse enslavement. The warning is appropriate at the end of

1   See Mt. 16.1-2, 4; Mk 8.11-12; Lk. 11.16, 24-26, 29-32.
2   See Lk. 11.24-26.

a series of accounts in which readers might too easily identify with Jesus against his opponents.

An Instance of Complacency: 12.46-50[1]

Jesus' warning is then illustrated by an example of complacency in which Jesus' mother and brothers presumed on their family relationship to gain access to Jesus. The story seems to presuppose that Jesus had gone into his house (see 13.1), outside of which his mother and brothers stood. Jesus, however, did not go out to greet them. This rejection of family would have been even more shocking to first-century readers than to modern Western readers, but it is one of the Gospel's themes (e.g. 10.34-39). Instead Jesus is presented identifying his disciples as his mother and brothers, that is, as those who were close to him. But his next statement broadens the reference to include the readers: not only the disciples but 'whoever does the will of my Father in heaven is my brother and sister and mother'. It encourages readers to play those roles. In spite of the usual male myopia of the Gospel, this saying specifically includes women as well as men and warrants the addition 'and sisters' to all the statements about brothers in the narrative's teaching.

Jesus' Public Discourse in Parables: 13.1-35

Matthew 4–12 had depicted the development of a complex situation in which Jesus' activities of preaching and healing had met with different responses. Often the crowds had been impressed, but their leaders, scribes and Pharisees, had decided that Jesus was working as an agent of Satan and should be opposed. Only twelve disciples, and those people who lacked courage and whose faith was inadequate, had followed Jesus and shared his task. This is the context of Jesus' third discourse, addressed first to crowds and disciples and then to disciples alone (13.36-52). The discourse consists of seven short stories, two of them interpreted (cf. the seven woes of ch. 23). Each short story is called a parable, that is, a comparison, but what is being compared to what? In the previous chapter, Jesus' teaching had made use of metaphors from nature, but in most of the stories in ch. 13 the focus of the stories will be on human activity, the activity of stock figures: farmers, servants, a baker, a merchant, fishermen. The stories are indicative, not imperative. What do they indicate? In Scripture, short stories are sometimes found as illustrations in teaching, but many of them are fables (e.g. Judg. 9.7-21; 2 Kgs 14.8-14; Ezek. 17.1-24). Only Nathan's parable to David (2 Sam. 12.1-15) is like Jesus' parables in Matthew 13.

The context of Jesus' parables discourse in the First Gospel leads readers to expect it to contain some comment upon and interpretation of the various responses which his ministry had been seen to engender.

1   See Mk 3.31-45; Lk. 8.19-21.

Setting and Parable of the Sower: 13.1-9.[1] Jesus is pictured leaving the house and sitting by the sea, but, because many crowds gathered, he had to sit in a boat while the crowds stood on the shore. His first parable describes a common activity and its consequences. The sower cast seeds; some seeds fell by the way and were eaten by the birds; other seeds fell on stony ground where they grew but, since there was no depth of soil, the plants (understood) were burned by the sun and withered because they had developed no roots; others fell among thorns which choked them; and others fell on good ground and began to bear fruit, a hundredfold, sixtyfold and thirtyfold (contrast Mark and Luke). At the end of the story, people are encouraged to understand its significance: 'he who has ears to hear, let him hear', that is, let him really hear and understand. But what is he to understand? Surely not a commonplace story about a sower and the fate of the seeds. But if the story throws light on something else, to what does it refer, and to what to the various details, sower, seed, soil and plant (understood) refer?

The Purpose of Parables: 13.10-17.[2] Before answers to these questions are supplied, as they will be in the interpretation of the parable (13.18-23), the disciples' question and Jesus' answer provide readers with hints about how to read the parables. The narrative distinguishes disciples from crowds (perhaps readers are supposed to imagine them in the boat with Jesus). They are the ones who asked, 'Why are you speaking to them in parables?' Jesus' reply points out that the disciples had been given (by God) the ability to know (that is, recognize) the mysteries of the kingdom of heaven. They were the people who had accepted and repeated Jesus' message about the imminence of the kingdom of heaven (4.17; 10.7) and who had followed him. Their response is interpreted as a gift from God. The crowds, on the other hand, had not been given this insight. An inference is then drawn: the disciples could receive even more insight, but the crowds were in danger of losing even the little understanding they had attained. Hence when Jesus taught the crowds in parables, they were in danger of seeing and hearing only the commonplace story without understanding its significance. Isaiah's prophecy would then be fulfilled (the quotation conforms to the Septuagint except for the omission of 'their' with 'ears'; 6.9-10). The quotation challenges crowds and readers to 'turn around' and God would heal them; that is, they should turn to God and recognize that he was saving them through Jesus. This distinction between crowds and disciples does not imply that Jesus would abandon a mission to the crowds, but rather that crowds should become disciples.

1   See Mk 4.1-9; Lk. 8.4-8.
2   See Mk 4.10-12; Lk. 8.9-10.

In the rest of the Gospel, much teaching will be directed to crowds in parables and other ways. Nevertheless, disciples are described as already more privileged than prophets and wise people who had wanted to see and hear what they did, but had not. The rhetoric urges disciples in the story and readers of the narrative to appreciate what they had received and would receive, and to recognize that the gift was from God. The rest of the chapter will illustrate Jesus' appeals in parables both to the crowds and to the disciples.

Explanation of the Parable of the Sower: 13.18-23.[1] The explanation is addressed to the disciples ('you') in the foreground with the crowds in the background. Readers are allowed to share this further instruction which will teach them how to understand not only the parable of the sower but also the following parable which uses similar imagery. The explanation shows that sowing seed is an image for preaching about the imminence of the kingdom. This is the point of comparison. Jesus, then, had been playing the role of the sower. Casting seed by the way is therefore preaching to someone who hears but does not understand, and the evil one plays the role of the birds in snatching what had been sown in that person's heart. This illustrates the way in which the crowds were in danger of losing even the little they had (13.12). Casting seed on stony ground is preaching to someone who hears and immediately receives the message with joy, but who is like a plant without roots and, in the face of affliction and persecution, is offended at the preaching. The disciples had been depicted playing that role (4.18-22 and 8.23-27). Casting seed among brambles is preaching to someone who hears the message, but the concerns of this age and the desire for money choke the message so that it becomes fruitless. This repeats the teaching from 6.24. Casting seed upon good soil is preaching to someone who hears and understands the message and whose own response engenders that of others, a hundredfold, sixtyfold and thirty-fold. This is the role disciples in the story and readers of the narrative are encouraged to play.

The parable and its explanation, then, helps to throw light on the variety of responses which had been depicted in chs. 4–12. It helps to mitigate a sense of failure, since failure is seen as no more surprising than failures in sowing, and the failures are set alongside extraordinary success.

Parable of the Weeds among the Wheat: 13.24-30. This parable is introduced with, 'Another parable he set before them' (see 13.31 and cf. 13.33). It is addressed to crowds as well as disciples (13.34). The parable, like those which follow, begins, 'The kingdom of heaven may

1   See Mk 4.13-20; Lk. 8.11-15.

be likened to [or is like]... ' Following this introduction in each case is a noun in the dative: a man who sowed, a grain of mustard seed, leaven, treasure hidden in a field, a merchant seeking beautiful pearls, a net thrown into the sea. Are readers to suppose that the kingdom which God is about to establish is like whatever noun follows in the dative, or should they rather see a comparison between that kingdom and the whole of the short story which follows? Since it is impossible to make sense of the teaching, presented as a short story, if the first option is adopted, readers should adopt the second option.

This second parable develops imagery from the parable of the sower. This time a man sowed good seed in his field but, while he slept, an enemy sowed weeds. When the crops grew, the weeds appeared. The servants of the landlord brought this to his attention by asking whether he did sow good seed and whence came the weeds. When the lord explained the weeds as the work of an enemy, the servants asked whether they should gather the weeds, but were told to let both crops grow together until the harvest, lest the wheat be damaged. The lord promised that, at the time of the harvest, he would tell harvesters to gather the weeds to be burnt but to gather the wheat into his granary.

After the interpretation of the parable of the sower, disciples and readers would have an initial understanding of the significance of this parable, since sowing can again be interpreted as preaching. The preaching of Jesus about the imminence of the kingdom of heaven was fruitful in producing followers (wheat). But not everyone became a follower. When the landlord slept, an enemy, probably the evil one of the previous parable, also gained followers (weeds). The parable sees these as worthless and doomed to destruction. The servants of the landlord, presumably the disciples and the leaders of the community to which the narrative was addressed, are instructed not to separate the followers from others, since that would be the task of harvesters, perhaps angels, at the time of the harvest (the establishment of the kingdom of heaven at the eschatological judgment).

The parable offers further encouragement to disciples, crowds and readers. In spite of the activity of an enemy, the mission would be fruitful, but they are warned not to separate followers from other people, not to form a separate clique and harm those followers. Rather they should leave that separation to other agents at the time when the kingdom was established.

Parable of the Mustard Seed: 13.31-32.[1] Again the same imagery is employed. Now, a man sowed a grain of mustard seed in his field. This seed is said to be the smallest of all the seeds, but, when grown, is the greatest of the herbs, even becoming a tree, so that the birds of the air

1   See Mk 4.30-32; Lk. 13.18-19.

come and nest in its branches. Clearly some exaggeration is involved in this story. If the seed again represents the preaching, the story assures disciples, crowds and readers of its extraordinary effectiveness, as in the parable of the sower, but this time the emphasis is on the strong growth, like a tree whose branches can be used by nesting birds. It provides a more positive vision of the eschatological community, after the destruction of evil at the last judgment (13.30), and the reference to 'birds' could represent those Gentiles who would enter the kingdom of heaven (see Ezek. 31.6).

Parable of the Leaven: 13.33.[1] Next, imagery from farming is replaced by imagery from baking. This time it is a woman who is described taking leaven and hiding it in a large quantity of flour until the whole was leavened. In the context, this could represent a positive way of viewing the community which the preaching about the imminent kingdom had brought into being. In spite of its smallness, it would have an effect on the whole of God's world. At least that is one possible meaning of this opaque parable. Alternatively, read in the light of 13.44 about treasure hidden in a field, perhaps the detail in this parable about the woman *hiding* the leaven should be given more weight. If so, the hidden leaven would refer to the future hidden eschatological kingdom, which, although in the future, exerts a powerful influence on people's present lives.

Fulfilment of Scripture: 13.34-35.[2] Jesus' speaking to the crowds only in parables is interpreted as fulfilment of a prophetic oracle, Ps. 78.2 taken as prophetic in force (contrast Mark). Asaph, the author of the psalm, is called a prophet in 1 Chron. 25.2 and 2 Chron. 29.30. (The quotation conforms exactly neither to the Hebrew nor to the Septuagint as we have them.) The things hidden from the foundation (of the world) seem to refer to the assurances given by Jesus in the parables about the effectiveness of his mission in making people aware of, and in preparing them for, God's eschatological judgment.

Jesus' Private Teaching to the Disciples: 13.36-52
Explanation of the Parable of the Weeds among the Wheat: 13.36-43. Jesus' withdrawal from the crowds into the house (see 13.1) provides the setting for further teaching to the disciples alone. It is introduced by their request for an explanation of the parable of the weeds in the field. The explanation identifies the sower as the son of man (that is, Jesus and those who would follow him), the field as the world, the good seed as the sons of the kingdom (that is, those who

1   See Lk. 13.20-21.
2   See Mk 4.33-34.

would inherit God's eschatological kingdom), the weeds as the sons of the evil one (that is, agents of the evil one), the enemy as the slanderer, the harvest as the end of the age, and the harvesters as angels. As the weeds were gathered and burned, so would it be at the end of the age, that is, agents of the evil one would be destroyed. In this list, one of the items is anomalous. The 'good seed' should surely read 'the wheat' to correspond to 'the weeds'. 'Wheat' is what the good seed, the preaching, brought into being. The explanation serves to confirm or correct the readers' understanding of the original parable, but it also highlights aspects of the eschatological events which had received no attention in the original parable: the son of man would send his angels and gather from his kingdom all offensive things and those who did lawlessness, and they would throw them into the furnace of fire. This image is intensified by a favourite Matthean depiction of despair: 'There shall be weeping and gnashing of teeth' (cf. 8.12; 13.50; 22.13; 24.51; 25.30). But the interpretation ends with a more attractive image: the just would shine like the sun in the kingdom of their Father (cf. Dan. 12.3).

What are readers to make of this depiction? It is open to the interpretation that there would be two kingdoms, one belonging to the son of man which would include offensive things and those who did lawlessness, and one belonging to God from which they would be excluded. But nowhere else in the narrative is such a distinction drawn. According to ch. 24, the son of man would return to establish God's eschatological kingdom (see also the reference to Jesus' future kingdom in 20.21). It is more likely therefore that the explanation refers throughout to the establishment of the one eschatological kingdom through the son of man's command to the angels that they remove offensive things and those who did lawlessness. The image of the just's shining like the sun, like Daniel's image, creates an impression of everlasting bodily splendour in the age to come. Again, disciples in the story and readers of the narrative are encouraged to understand the teaching: 'he who has ears let him hear'.

Treasure Hidden in a Field: 13.44. The parable tells of a man who found treasure hidden in a field, who buried it again, and who, in his joy, went and sold all that he had and bought that field. Following on from the explanation of the weeds in the field, the hidden treasure seems to represent the future, hidden, eschatological kingdom, belief in whose imminence brought joy in the present (cf. 5.12) and a willingness to give up everything else to gain it (see 4.18-22; 9.9; 19.27-30). The parable illustrates the exhortations about laying up treasure in heaven (6.19-21).

A Precious Pearl: 13.45-46. This parable tells of a merchant who sought beautiful pearls. When he found an exceedingly valuable pearl, he went and sold everything that he had, and bought that pearl. It repeats the same message as the previous parable: the man sold everything (gave up everything else) to buy the precious pearl (to inherit the kingdom of heaven). Similar teaching will be repeated later in the story of the rich young man (19.16-30).

Sorting Fish Caught in a Net: 13.47-50. The final parable recounts a story in which a net, cast into the sea, caught fish of every kind. When it was full, people drew it to the shore and sat and sorted the good fish into vessels and threw the bad away (see the earlier metaphor of the disciples as fishers of people, 4.19). An interpretation of the parable is immediately supplied. The story represents what would happen at the end of the age: angels would come and separate evil people from just people and would throw them into the furnace of fire (cf. 13.42). The interpretation does not explain whether 'fish of every kind' refers to both Jews and Gentiles, as it could do, but focuses on the eschatological separation of bad from good. Here the phrase 'there shall be weeping and gnashing of teeth' intensifies the warning. The whole series of parables, then, ends with this vision of final destructive judgment against human evil. Disciples and readers are warned to avoid all forms of evil in the present for the sake of gaining the future kingdom of heaven.

Conclusion: The Disciples' Understanding: 13.51-52. The conclusion confirms the importance of understanding the teaching. Jesus' question, 'Do you understand all these things?' received the reply 'Yes'. According to Matthew's Gospel, unlike Mark's, the disciples did understand Jesus' teaching, and readers are allowed to share their understanding. Jesus is then presented comparing each of them to 'a scribe, learned in the kingdom of heaven', who in turn is likened to 'a householder who brought out from his treasure new things and old things'. What does this mean? Were the order 'old things and new things', it would be reasonable to interpret the saying to refer to what the disciples already knew before hearing Jesus' parables and what they knew at the end of the discourse (see. 13.10-17). But the order 'new things and old things' seems rather to represent 'everything'. In the Sermon on the Mount, people had been recommended to lay up treasure in heaven 'because where your treasure is, there will your heart be also' (6.21 and see 13.44). So here the disciples are depicted as those who understood Jesus' teaching, whose treasure was in heaven, and whose dedication to God would provide them with all things necessary. 'And when Jesus had finished these parables, he went away from there' (13.53) formally marks the end of Jesus' third discourse (cf. 7.28; 11.1; 19.1; 26.1).

Modern readers of these parables are again made aware of the narrative's expectation about God's final judgment in the near future. Present existence is understood as a prelude to that judgment. The audience is encouraged to behave in the present in ways which would avoid future destruction: to live like fruitful plants or like good fish. Like the man who found treasure hidden in a field or the merchant who came across an exceedingly valuable pearl, they were to give up everything else in the present in order to devote themselves to God and his kingdom. The visions of God's future judgment provide a spur to generous and merciful activity in the present and a warning against becoming agents of evil. And belief in the imminence of the eschaton lends urgency to the message. If modern readers wish to apply the message to their own situation, they have to transform eschatology into teleology. For them, a sense of urgency comes not from belief in the imminence of God's judgment but from revulsion at the evils still perpetrated in the world.

Matthew 13.53–14.36: Jesus the Prophet

The Rejection of Jesus and John the Baptist: 13.53–14.12[1]
The narrative notes Jesus' departure from the house by the sea and his coming to his own country where he taught in the synagogue. Since the house was probably understood to be in Capernaum (4.13), 'his own country' must refer to Nazareth (see 2.23; 26.71; compare Luke). No details of his teaching are supplied. Instead the narrative emphasizes the audience's astonishment at his wisdom (in teaching) and his powers (in healing). The audience's question, 'Where did this man get this wisdom and these powers?' encourages readers to supply the answer 'from God'. Nevertheless, the very impressiveness of his activity is said to have caused offence because he was familiar as the son of the carpenter or builder (contrast Mark's 'the carpenter [or builder], the son of Mary'), whose mother, Mary, whose brothers, James, Joseph, Simon and Judas, and whose sisters were well known. Jesus' reply interprets his role and their offence: 'A prophet is not without honour except in his homeland and in his household' (see Jesus' earlier rejection of his family; 12.46-50). It confirms the role the narrative had assigned to Jesus, the role of the prophet like Moses who preached and performed miracles, and illustrates the rejection that prophets habitually encountered (see 5.12). Moreover, the narrative explains the effect of rejection: 'there he did not perform many mighty works because of their unbelief'. In chs. 8 and 9, miracles had usually but not always been performed in response to people's faith.

1   See Mk 6.1-6, 14-29; Lk. 3.19-20; 4.16-30; 9.7-9.

Listing the names of Jesus' mother and brothers (see also 1.18, 27.56) suggests that they were not unimportant to later Christian communities. The four Gospels create the impression that Jesus' significance went unrecognized by his family during his ministry, but Acts implies that his mother and brothers became followers after his resurrection (Acts 1.14), and that his brother James became the leader of the Christian community in Jerusalem (15.13; 21.18). Paul's letter to the Galatians confirms James' role (1.19; 2.9, 12), and 1 Cor. 15.7 includes James in a list of those to whom the resurrected Jesus appeared. Josephus, too, provides an account of James' martyrdom (*Ant*. 20.200).

In spite of the account of Jesus' rejection, the introduction to the next story mentions that a report about Jesus had reached even Herod the tetrarch, Rome's client ruler of Galilee. Herod's interpretation of the report—'This is John the Baptist; he is raised from the dead and this is why powers are at work in him'—confirms the narrator's reference to Jesus' powers, associates Jesus with John, and introduces belief in resurrection, albeit in a manner which the narrative will later correct. The statement leads into a long explanation of Herod's role in John's execution. Previously the narrative had noted John's imprisonment (4.12; 11.12). Herod is said to have imprisoned John because John had criticized his marriage to his living brother's wife as illegal. (The name of the brother, Philip, is found only in some manuscripts, and has probably been added from the parallel account in Mark. According to Josephus, the half-brother involved was not Philip but another Herod [*Ant*. 18.110-11, 148]). Herod the Great and his sons who ruled Jewish territory normally adhered to the Jewish law, but this is an exception: the marriage was illegal according to Jewish law (Lev. 18.16; 20.21). Herod Antipas' imprisonment, rather than execution, of John, is explained by his fear of the crowd which held John to be a prophet. In the narrative, therefore, both Jesus and John are understood to be prophets. Herod's birthday party, however, is said to have provided an occasion for Herod's hand to be forced: Herodias's daughter, presumably by her previous marriage, danced and pleased Herod to such an extent that he promised to give her whatever she asked. Prompted by her mother, she asked for John's head on a platter. In spite of Herod's qualms, John was beheaded in prison. Josephus' account explains John's execution by Herod Antipas differently: it was because of John's popularity that Herod viewed him as a threat to law and order and had him executed (*Ant*. 18.116-19). This explanation makes better historical sense than that in the Gospels, since princesses did not entertain guests by dancing. The Gospel accounts, however, provide a more dramatic story which has appealed to people's imaginations over the centuries.

But why does the First Gospel devote so much space to an account of John's martyrdom? The account is introduced and concluded by references to Jesus. Herod's superstition that Jesus was John raised from the dead confirms Jesus' status as a great prophet. The reference to John's disciples' burying the corpse and reporting to Jesus (14.12) suggests that John's execution might herald Jesus'. This is confirmed by the note that Jesus withdrew into a deserted place alone (14.13). Although the narrative distinguishes the ministry of Jesus from that of John, recognition of their prophetic status by crowds is something they are seen to share. As the narrative proceeds, it will also become clear that they were to share the fate of martyrdom at the hands of powerful rulers. Recounting John's martyrdom at this stage, therefore, prepares readers for what would happen to Jesus. Nevertheless, Jesus is not depicted courting martyrdom. His reaction to the news of John's execution, like his reaction to the news of John's imprisonment, was to withdraw (4.12; 14.13), and he had given similar advice to disciples (10.23). Later, when Jesus decided to go to Jerusalem in the knowledge that he would be killed there (20.17-19), his action is presented not as a tragic gesture but as the fulfilment of God's purpose in a messianic figure who would not behave like rulers, but who would serve, giving his life as a ransom for many (20.20-28).

Jesus' prophetic status is confirmed by the following stories, his feeding five thousand, his walking on the sea and his healings at Gennesaret.

His Feeding Five Thousand: 14.13-21[1]
The narrative relates that Jesus' withdrawal by boat to a deserted place did not secure seclusion, since crowds from cities followed him on foot. Jesus' compassion rather than people's faith is said to have led to further healings (contrast Mark's reference to teaching and Luke's reference to both teaching and healing. The Markan saying about shepherd-less sheep occurs earlier, in Mt. 9.36). The account relates that, when the disciples suggested Jesus send the crowds away so that they could go into the villages to buy food at evening, his surprising response was to tell the disciples to give them something to eat. The disciples' reply, that they had only five loaves and two fish, led Jesus to ask for the food and to command the crowds to sit (contrast the greater detail of the Markan and Lukan accounts). Then he took the bread and fish, blessed and broke them, as was customary at Jewish meals, and gave them to the disciples who gave them to the crowds. Thus the disciples were included in ministering to the crowds' needs. The narrative notes that all the people ate and were satisfied, and that what was left over filled twelve baskets. The number of the crowds is finally mentioned, about five thousand men, without counting women and children (Mark and Luke mention only men). Nothing is said, however, about the people's recognition of a great miracle, just as nothing had been said about their

1   See Mk 6.30-44; Lk. 9.10-17; Jn 6.1-14.

requesting food. Nor are feeding miracles mentioned in the summaries of Jesus' activities.

The miraculous supply of food, however, is a feature of prophetic activity in Scripture. Like Moses in the desert (Exodus 16; Numbers 11), Jesus supplied food in a deserted place, but unlike the ancient Israelites, the crowds are not depicted testing God by demanding food. Moreover, in the Matthaean miracle there is a superabundance of food, since all were satisfied but fragments were left over. Like Elisha, Jesus multiplied loaves to feed his followers and fragments were left (2 Kgs 4.42-44), although Elisha's multiplication of twenty loaves to feed a hundred was exceeded by Jesus' multiplication of five loaves and two fish to feed more than five thousand (the parallel with the Elisha story is brought out more clearly by the Johannine account). Later, Jesus would recall to the disciples, and the narrative would recall to readers, the five loaves, the five thousand and how many baskets of fragments were left over (16.9), in a context in which Jesus warned disciples to beware of 'the leaven' of the Pharisees and Sadducees; that is, to beware of their teaching (16.5-12). This suggests that these numbers were significant (the two fish are ignored). The gathering of twelve baskets of fragments may therefore symbolize the gathering of the twelve tribes of Israel (e.g. Ezek. 47.13), and the two references to five may recall the five books of Moses, the Torah, which recount the early period of Israel's history, when God provided food in the desert through his prophet Moses. The narrative, then, depicts Jesus' fulfilment of expectations about a prophet like Moses who would restore the covenant community (Deut. 18.15, 18). And the bread would symbolize everything that people need, Jesus' teaching (see 16.12) and his exemplary life. The reference to Jesus' taking, breaking and blessing the food would remind readers already familiar with the whole narrative of his similar actions at the last supper with his disciples, and perhaps of their own practice in the Eucharist. Hence the depiction of bread and fish in early Christian representations of the Eucharist.

How then are readers to understand the nature of this story? What kind of story is it? That the narrative is recounting a typical prophetic act and that it presents feeding the hungry as an act of compassion are clear. But is the story to be taken as a depiction of a single incident which happened once, when Jesus literally multiplied bread and fish to feed more than five thousand people? Or is the story symbolic, a dramatic depiction of God's bounty when people act as God's agents to express compassion for the hungry? And does hunger symbolize their hunger for justice (see 5.6) which Jesus' teaching and exemplary life satisfy? The absence of references to feeding miracles in the summaries, the absence of any reference to the crowds' reaction at the end of the account of the miracle, the numbers five and twelve, the reference back to the incident in 16.5-12, and the echoes of the Eucharist narrative, all suggest the story's symbolic force. The story of Jesus' and his disciples' action in compassion for the hungry, therefore, encourages readers to take every opportunity to act as God's agents in supplying the needs of those who hunger for justice. Such actions would help to restore the covenant community (see 26.28).

His Walking on the Sea: 14.22-33[1]

The narrative immediately goes on to depict another miracle. When the disciples had been sent ahead in the boat (Mark, but not Matthew, notes their destination, Bethsaida), and Jesus had dismissed the crowds, he went up into the mountain alone to pray. This is one of the rare references in the narrative to Jesus' praying (see 11.25-26; 19.13; 26.36-46). The narrative assumes that his praying was a normal and unexceptional activity, an expression of his conscious dedication to God's purpose. Here the reference helps to mark the progression of time between the disciples' departure in the boat and Jesus' meeting with them. Hence 'when it was evening, he was alone' and 'the boat was already many stadia distant from the land, buffeted by the waves, for the wind was against it'. The narrative reads like a typical introduction to a story about dangers at sea, and is reminiscent of the earlier story in which Jesus had calmed the storm (8.23-27). But the development of the story is exceptional: 'In the fourth watch of the night [that is the fourth quarter between 6pm and 6am; cf. 24.43; Ps. 90.4; Lam. 2.19], Jesus went to them walking on the sea'. (Neither Matthew nor John record Mark's statement that Jesus meant to pass by the disciples.)

Nothing in the narrative about Jesus' prophetic and messianic ministry, the ministry of a vulnerable human being whose life was in danger from opponents, had prepared readers for this extraordinary story about Jesus' walking on the sea. Do readers have to revise their view and recognize that the narrative denies Jesus' humanity? The disciples' responses, terror at what they took to be an apparition and cries of fear, confirm the readers' reaction to something unprecedented. It is Jesus who has to identify himself: 'Be courageous, it is I; stop being afraid'.

How should this strange story be understood? Again it is not mentioned in the summaries of Jesus' miracles. It depicts Jesus' moving across the water at night. It is therefore reminiscent of the story of creation in Genesis 1, according to which 'the spirit of God was moving over the face of the waters' as the prelude to the creation of light (Gen. 1.2-3). According to the Matthaean narrative, Jesus was endowed with God's spirit (3.17) and would endow his followers with God's spirit (3.11). In other words, he was a prophet and his followers would become prophets. Moreover, the form of the story is one of recognition (14.28-29, 33). It emphasizes the disciples' acceptance of Jesus as God's

1   See Mk 6.45-52; Jn 6.16-21.

son, in spite of their fears and doubts. And the description of Peter's walking on the water and his suffering doubts and beginning to sink (found only in Matthew) corresponds to his behaviour after Jesus' arrest (26.58, 69-75). In both stories, Peter's original response was more courageous than that of his fellow disciples in that he followed Jesus, but only to fail in the face of difficulties. Furthermore, this story both recalls the earlier symbolic story about disciples in a boat (8.23-27) and offers some contrasts. This time, Jesus is not described as asleep in the boat, but as moving alone over dangerous waters. Then Peter's following him and his failure reinforce for readers the importance and the difficulty of his original following. Jesus' rescue of Peter in this story corresponds to his commissioning his doubting disciples at his resurrection (28.16-20). Both stories highlight the dangers that following Jesus would entail, but both offer an encouragement to readers whose courage and faith may have been as inadequate as the disciples'. Once again, then, the story, like the stories of other so-called nature miracles, is symbolic. There is no reason to suppose that it denies either Jesus' or Peter's humanity.

The Healings at Gennesaret: 14.34-36[1]
The summary of Jesus' healings provides a contrast with the earlier account of his rejection at Nazareth (13.53-58). The people of Gennesaret, unlike the people of his homeland, responded to his presence by bringing all who were ill in the whole region, so that they might beseech only to touch the tassel of his garment (for tassel, see Deut. 22.12, and cf. Mt. 9.20-22). The narrative concludes by confirming that as many as touched were healed. Jesus, then, was recognized as a great prophet away from his homeland.

Matthew 15.1-20: Jesus' Counter-Attack on his Opponents[2]

In ch. 12, the narrative had described attacks on Jesus by Pharisees and scribes and Jesus' replies. 15.1-20 represents Jesus' counter-attack on Pharisaic and scribal tradition, but without their replies. The story opens with a question about the disciples' behaviour, addressed to Jesus by Pharisees and scribes who had come from Jerusalem: 'Why do your disciples transgress the tradition of the elders, for they do not wash their hands when they eat bread?' The Matthaean version of the dispute concerns only the tradition of the elders, not the written law

1   See Mk 6.53-56.
2   See Mk 7.1-23.

(contrast the Markan version, which also concerns commands in the law about food). The Matthaean version also explains the custom of washing more succinctly, as part of the elders' tradition, and does not imply, as the Markan version does, that all Jews practised it. The story represents one of the earliest historical references to some Jews' washing hands before they ate. Such washing was not concerned with hygiene but with the removal of ritual uncleanness, contracted by touching unclean or dead animals and insects. There is no such requirement in the written law. Moreover, Pharisees at the time seem to have washed their hands only when eating Sabbath or festival meals (*m. Ber.* 8.2-3; *t. Ber.* 5.25).

In the Matthaean story the scribes' and Pharisees' question was not answered by Jesus, who, instead, criticized the tradition of the elders on quite different grounds: 'Why do you transgress the commandment of God for the sake of your tradition? For God said, honour father and mother, and he who speaks ill of father and mother, let him surely die [see Exod. 20.12; 21.17-18; Lev. 20.9; Deut. 27.16], but you say, whoever says to father and mother, what you would have gained from me is a gift [to God], need not honour his father. And you annul the discourse of God on account of your tradition'. The epithet 'dissemblers', and the quotation from Isa. 29.13 (which is an abridgment of the Septuagint), intensify the criticism. The criticism suggests that Pharisaic and scribal tradition allowed children to dedicate property to God at the temple, and that in that way they prevented their parents from making use of it, a matter which is interpreted as dishonouring parents. Historically, there is no evidence to support the view that scribes and Pharisees would have regarded such a vow of dedication as binding, and some evidence which suggests the reverse, where members of the family were concerned (*m. Ned.* 3.2). In Egypt, however, Philo may have regarded such a vow as binding.[1] Furthermore, the criticism that Pharisaic and scribal tradition led to the dishonouring of parents might more appropriately be applied to the Jesus tradition in the First Gospel (see 8.22; 10.35-37; 12.46-50). The contradiction is easy to overlook, however, and the author must have been oblivious to it, but it does ruin the force of the argument. The narrative actually accepts that dedication to God's service by following Jesus takes priority over responsibilities to parents, except when such dedication is advocated by outsiders.

The story does provide, however, more positive teaching. It continues with Jesus' address to the crowd: 'Not what goes into the mouth defiles a person, but what comes out from the mouth, this defiles a person'. The Markan version takes the saying literally and infers that Jesus declared all foods clean. But the Matthaean version understands

1   *Hypothetica* 7.3; and see the discussion by E.P. Sanders, *Jewish Law from Jesus to the Mishnah* (London: SCM Press, 1990), pp. 56-57.

the saying differently, without reference to clean or unclean food. This means that we do not know whether the author or the community to which he belonged ate kosher food, whereas we can be virtually certain that the Markan community did not. I have already drawn attention to the rhetorical force of statements in the form 'Not this...but that' (cf. 9.13; 12.7), which imply that the second command is even more important than the first command, without implying the negation of the first command. The narrative, however, does not picture Jesus' expounding the saying to the crowd. Instead, the scene shifts to a private conversation between Jesus and his disciples. The disciples pointed out the offence taken by the Pharisees at Jesus' criticism, but Jesus' reply was even more offensive than his original attack: 'Every plant which the heavenly Father did not plant will be uprooted. Leave them alone. They are blind guides. If a blind person leads a blind person, both will fall into a pit'. Clearly, the narrative assumes a complete separation between Jesus' community and Pharisaic and scribal communities.

Peter's request for clarification of Jesus' parable (about what enters and comes out of the mouth) leads first to Jesus' rebuke, 'Are you still without understanding?' The implication is that both they and the readers should have understood, as they had understood the parables in ch. 13. Disciples and readers, however, are provided with an explanation: 'Don't you know that everything which enters into the mouth passes into the stomach and is cast out into the drain? But the things which come out of the mouth proceed from the heart and those defile a person. For out of the heart comes evil thoughts, murders, adulteries, fornications, thefts, false witnessings, slanders. These are the things which defile a person, but to eat with unwashed hands does not defile a person' (Matthew's list includes seven offences, Mark's 13). The explanation denies the necessity of handwashing, but does not abrogate the commands in the law about eating only clean food. 'What comes out of the mouth' is understood metaphorically, to refer to unethical behaviour prompted by an 'impure' heart (see 5.8). After such a trenchant attack on some of the leaders of Judaism and their tradition, the narrative depicts Jesus' turning to Gentiles.

Modern readers feel uncomfortable when they read these attacks on the scribes and Pharisees in the narrative. It treats the whole of their tradition in a polemical fashion, as something alien, and as a disservice to God. It ignores the similarities between Jesus' teaching and that of contemporary scribes and Pharisees, and it even misrepresents scribal and Pharisaic teaching. Those few Christians who have taken the trouble to study scribal and Pharisaic traditions recognize their twin concerns, to love God and to love fellow human beings, and also their remarkable egalitarian and merciful ethos. In a short narrative like the First Gospel, a caricature of opposition helps both to highlight the positive depiction of

Jesus' way of life, and to warn against its most obvious inherent danger, hypocrisy. The caricature of scribes and Pharisees dramatizes the role of hypocrites. This literary technique, however, has had far-reaching consequences for Christian relations with Jews. The Gospels' caricatures have often been understood by Christians as accurate representations of Judaism. The Gospel according to Matthew represents one aspect of Christianity's early attempts at self-definition. It sees Jesus' followers as the covenant community which inherited the promises of Jewish Scriptures, and it applies all those Scriptures' criticisms of Israelites to Jews who did not become followers of Jesus. Most Jews did not recognize Jesus as messiah. Christians like the author of the First Gospel recognized Jesus as messiah, but as a messiah unlike David and much more like a second Moses. In spite of nearly two thousand years of separate development, however, Judaism and Christianity still share perceptions based on Jewish Scriptures, which Christianity adopted. But they also share a history in which Christians have used their political power violently to persecute Jews, in which Christians have shown themselves to be hypocrites in betraying Jesus' way of life. We who call ourselves Christians cannot escape from our history. We can, however, beg forgiveness from God and our Jewish contemporaries, and do everything possible to counter anti-Semitism and its poisonous effects in the world.

Matthew 15.21-39: Jesus' Activities Among Gentiles

This time, Jesus' withdrawal is understood to take him outside Jewish territory and into the regions of Tyre and Sidon, Gentile ports on the Mediterranean coast. Such cities dominated the regions in which they were located and on which they relied for food supplies. This journey of Jesus into Gentile territory where he performed miracles serves to justify his followers' mission to non-Jews after his resurrection. Historically, Jesus could have come across Gentiles within Palestine, but it is unlikely that his mission actually took him outside the Jewish milieu. Had it done so, his followers would not have disputed whether or on what terms a Gentile mission should be undertaken, as we know they did (e.g. Galatians 2; Acts 10–15). It is noticeable that in this section of the narrative we find only the healing of a Canaanite woman's daughter from a distance, a summary of healings, and a repetition of Jesus' feeding miracle.

His Healing a Canaanite Woman's Daughter: 15.21-28[1]

The Matthaean version of the story calls the woman a Canaanite, whereas the Markan calls her a Syrophoenician. The Markan term reflects usage in the first-century Graeco-Roman world, whereas the Matthaean term is scriptural. The Matthaean scene is set in the street (contrast Mark's in the house). The woman's reiterated plea, 'Have mercy on me, lord, son of David', is hardly appropriate on the lips of a Gentile, but is similar to that in other accounts of miracles (e.g. 8.6; 9.27; 20.30-31). Perhaps it is meant to represent the woman's acceptance that Jesus' mission was to Israel. The development in the Matthaean version, in which Jesus ignored the woman's request for her demon-possessed daughter to be healed, his disciples urged him to send her away because she cried after them, and Jesus responded by saying that he was not sent except to the lost sheep of the house of Israel, is not found in Mark. It emphasizes the exceptional character of Jesus' response to a Gentile, as the earlier story about his healing the centurion's son or servant had done (8.5-13), and it echoes Jesus' instructions to his disciples for their mission (10.5-6). The woman's persistence and skill in argument, however, are presented as the means by which she persuaded Jesus to recognize her great faith and grant her request. She is the only character in the narrative who bettered Jesus in argument. The story shares some features with the earlier story of a Gentile healing (8.5-13): both Gentiles demonstrated their faith in their declarations, both interceded on behalf of someone else, in each case the healing was effected from a distance through Jesus' command, 'Let it happen to you', and each is concluded by noting that the person was healed at the time of Jesus' pronouncement (contrast Mark). There are, however, some differences. Jesus accepted the centurion's request with alacrity and was only dissuaded from accompanying him by his pointing out that it was unnecessary and in that way demonstrating his faith. On the other hand, the woman's pleas were ignored by Jesus, rejected by his disciples, then rebuffed by Jesus' reference to Gentiles as 'dogs', and she had to persuade him with an argument which was far from complimentary to Gentiles: 'For even the dogs eat from the crumbs which fall from the table of their masters'. Nevertheless, Jesus' healing justified the mission to the Gentiles which the narrative finally gives to the disciples (28.19-20).

Would the original Gentile Christian readers of the narrative have been offended by Jesus' reference to Gentiles as 'dogs'? In the end the offence is mitigated by the healing, and those readers who identified with the woman could at least identify with her faith. Moreover, Gentiles who became Christians would necessarily have rejected aspects of their former lives, especially any idolatrous and unethical

1   See Mk 7.24-30.

practices. Paul did not scruple in writing to Gentile converts about pointing out the sinful failings of their former lifestyles (e.g. 1 Cor. 6.9-11; Rom. 1.18-22). The First Gospel also exhibits a negative attitude to Gentiles as Gentiles (e.g. 5.47; 6.7). But the original Gentile Christian readers of the Gospel were probably second generation Christians, rather than converts, and would have shared the narrative's attitude to paganism. Once again, the narrative's caricature of what is alien, in this case paganism rather than Judaism, fails to recognize or draw on its insights. In subsequent centuries, however, Christians inherited and made creative use of traditions of Greek philosophy and Roman law.

His Healings of Other Gentiles: 15.29-31[1]
The setting of these healings is near the lake of Galilee but apparently still in Gentile territory, since Jesus later had to cross the lake by boat to reach the region of Magadan, presumably in Galilee, although its exact location is uncertain (15.39. The location of Mark's Dalmanath is also uncertain. Cf. Mark's more elaborate itinerary [7.31]). The narrative relates that Jesus' presence attracted crowds who brought with them lame, blind, maimed, deaf and many others, whom they set at Jesus' feet, and he healed them (cf. the similar prelude to the first feeding miracle [14.13-14], and the list of those healed in 11.5). General note is taken of the responses of the crowds when they saw the healings, which are listed again: they were amazed and praised the God of Israel. In other words, they are represented as converts.

His Feeding Four Thousand: 15.32-39[2]
Jesus' opening remarks set the scene for this second feeding miracle: he had compassion on the crowd and was reluctant to send them away because they had been with him for three days and might faint on the way. Both the crowd's fidelity and Jesus' compassion are emphasized. The disciples' question about where in a deserted place to procure the amount of food needed to satisfy such a large crowd highlights the magnitude of the coming miracle (contrast Mark). As in the previous feeding account, Jesus inquired how many loaves they had but received a slightly different reply: seven and a few small fish (Mark mentions fish separately). The miracle story follows the pattern of the previous one, with Jesus' command to the crowd to sit on the ground, his taking, breaking and blessing the food, his giving it to the disciples and the disciples to the crowd. Again, the crowd ate and was satisfied, a fact confirmed by the amount of fragments taken up, this time filling seven baskets. Finally the number of the crowd is noted, four thousand men without counting women and children (Mark mentions only men).

1   See Mk 7.31-37.
2   See Mk 8.1-10.

Again, there is no mention of the crowd's response to the miracle. The setting and the numbers, recalled at 16.10, suggest that this is a symbolic story about Jesus' and his disciples' supplying the needs of Gentiles, and bringing them into the covenant community: four represents the four corners of the world and seven represents completion. The story encourages readers to follow the examples of Jesus and his disciples. The account of Jesus' sortie into Gentile territory is brought to an end with the note that he sent away the crowds and got into a boat and came to the regions of Magadan (15.39).

Matthew 16.1–18.35: Jesus' Formation of his own Group of Leaders, Separate from the Jewish Leadership

Request for a Sign: 16.1-4[1]
The Pharisees and Sadducees (Mark mentions only Pharisees), that is, lay and priestly leaders within the Jewish community, are pictured testing Jesus by asking him to show them a sign from heaven, that is, some indication that he was acting as God's agent. The reference to testing reminds readers of Jesus' testing in the wilderness (see especially 4.5-7). At this stage in the narrative, after the depiction of Jesus' teaching and miracles, the request must strike readers as obtuse. The manuscripts supply either a longer or a shorter form of Jesus' reply. The longer form includes vv. 2 and 3 (not in the Markan parallel), with their reference to interpreting the significance of a red sky, the ancient equivalent of our maxim 'red sky at night, shepherd's delight, red sky in the morning, shepherd's warning' (contrast Luke's version). This leads to Jesus' accusation, 'You know how to interpret the appearance of the sky, but you are unable [to interpret] the signs of the times', that is, the signs that God is about to bring this age to an end (see 3.2; 4.17; 10.7; 12.32; 13.39-40, 49). All the manuscripts include v. 4 with its assertion that an evil and adulterous generation, a generation unfaithful to God, seeks a sign, but to whom no sign would be given except the sign of Jonah (Mark does not mention the sign of Jonah). This is exactly the same response as that attributed to Jesus earlier, when some scribes and Pharisees had requested a sign (12.38-39) except that there the sign of Jonah was explained and judgment on 'this generation' was pronounced. This second, briefer, account merely recalls the earlier one as a reminder of the blindness of the Jewish leaders, in preparation for the following stories.

1   See Mk 8.11-13; Lk. 12.54-56.

The Leaven of the Pharisees and Sadducees: 16.5-12[1]

The scene shifts to a conversation between Jesus and his disciples who had subsequently followed him from the other side of the lake (16.5; see 15.39). It is introduced by noting that the disciples had forgotten to buy bread. The fact led to their misunderstanding Jesus' metaphorical warning against the leaven of the Pharisees and Sadducees (Mark has Pharisees and Herod), that is, against the influence of their teaching. Jesus' response to their concern about having no bread is a reminder both of their little faith and of the two feeding miracles, with the question about how many fragments they took up. Readers are left to supply the appropriate numbers (the Markan version is harsher and longer, and the disciples supplied the answer, twelve and seven). Then he explained that his warning about Pharisees and Sadducees had not referred to bread but, metaphorically, to teaching (Mark does not contain this explanation. Luke interprets Jesus' saying about Pharisees as a reference to leaven in 12.1). The conversation highlights the adequacy of Jesus' provisions and distinguishes his and his disciples' leadership from Jewish leadership. The distinction serves to justify the separate identity of Jesus' followers realized by the churches whose members have read the narrative, and the episode prepares the way for the formation of Jesus' disciples into a group of leaders who were to follow his way of life.

Peter's Confession that Jesus is the Christ: 16.13-20[2]

This section is marked off from the previous one by a change of location, to Caesarea-Philippi, about 25 miles north of Galilee, in Philip the tetrarch's territory. The setting, away from Galilee and Judaea, perhaps suggests the separation of Jesus' disciples from Judaism. The dialogue is introduced by Jesus' question to the disciples, 'Whom do people say that the son of man is?' (contrast Mark and Luke). If readers understand 'the son of man' as a reference to a particular kind of human being, dedicated to fulfilling God's purpose, this makes sense of the disciples' reply, 'Some say John the Baptist, others Elijah, others Jeremiah or one of the prophets'. In other words, a persecuted prophet was a person dedicated to fulfilling God's purpose. The narrative assumes that prophets were persecuted (e.g. 5.12); it had already described John's execution (14.8-12), and Scripture depicts the persecution of Elijah, Jeremiah and other prophets (e.g. Moses).

But before applying this insight to himself and his disciples (16.21-28), the narrative depicts Jesus' asking another question: 'Whom do you [the disciples] say that I am?' It is Simon Peter, the usual spokesman of the disciples (15.15; 18.21; 19.27), who provides an answer: 'You are the

1   See Mk 8.14-21.
2   See Mk 8.27-30; Lk. 9.18-21.

Christ, the son of the living God' (contrast Mark and Luke). The two
expressions 'Christ' and 'son of God' are used in apposition. 'Son of
God' in Scripture and in the narrative refers to a person who does the
will of his heavenly Father (e.g. 4.1-11; 5.45). In the Matthaean narrative,
Jesus' confirmation of Peter's confession takes the form of a blessing on
him, because what he said had not been revealed by human beings
('flesh and blood') but by God ('my Father in heaven'). (Note that this
and the following verses have no parallel in Mark and Luke). At this
point, what had been known to readers from the beginning of the
narrative is confirmed by Peter and Jesus, and is interpreted as a revelation from God (see 1.1).

Why, however, is Jesus' blessing in the form, 'Blessed are you, Simon
bar Jonah'? *Bar* is the Aramaic word for 'son'. Are readers to infer that
Jonah was the name of Peter's father? This would be the most obvious
meaning of the term, but compare Jn 1.42, in which Simon Peter is called
'son of John' not 'son of Jonah'. A less obvious but possible
interpretation of 'son of Jonah' involves understanding Jonah as the
prophet mentioned earlier in the chapter (16.4 and see 12.39-40). In
Scripture and in the First Gospel, 'son' is often used metaphorically to
indicate shared characteristics, as in the case of 'son of God'. If this is the
correct interpretation, Peter was blessed because he had spoken as a
prophet like Jonah, revealing God's purpose, and this would make sense
in view of Jesus' remarks about God's revelation.

Next, Jesus goes on to interpret the significance of Simon Peter's
nickname, Peter, which should have indicated his stone-like quality of
firmness but, given the stories about him (e.g. 14.30-31; 26.69-75), perhaps functioned ironically. We often nickname very large people 'Tiny'.
The Greek word *petros* means a boulder or rock and is generally
restricted to poetic diction. The form *petra*, meaning 'rock', was in
common use and this is the word found in 'upon this rock'. (Paul and
the Fourth Gospel refer to Simon by the Aramaic form of the nickname,
Kephas; e.g. Gal. 1.18; 2.9; Jn 1.42.) Clearly there is a play on words: 'You
are *Petros*, and upon this *petra* I shall build my church and the gates of
hell will not prevail against it'. The statement seems to mean that Jesus
would build his church on the rock which was God's revelation to
Peter that Jesus was the Christ. Belief in Jesus as the Christ is what the
narrative advocates. The Greek word for church, *ekklesia*, which
comes from the verb 'to call out', is used in Scripture to refer to the
congregation of Israelites (e.g. Deut. 31.30; 1 Sam. 17.47), and this desig-
nation was taken over to refer to Christian communities (e.g. Acts 5.11; 1
Cor. 4.17). Scripture also refers to the congregation of Israelites as a
'gathering', *sunagōgē* (e.g. Num. 16.3; Josh. 22.16; Ps. 74.2), but only in Jas
2.2 in the New Testament is this term used of a Christian congregation.
In the Gospels, it always refers to the place where Jews assembled.
Jesus is depicted referring to 'his church' or 'the church' only in Mt.

16.18 and 18.17. The other Gospels never refer to Jesus' church,
although they frequently refer to his followers. The Gospel according to
Matthew is attributing to Jesus the plan of forming his followers into a
congregation separate from Judaism, and is offering the reassurance that
'the gates of hell' would not prevail against it. The image of gates
prevailing is peculiar and can be understood only when it is recognized
that 'gates of hell' is an idiom for death (see Isa. 38.10; Ps. 107.18; Job
38.17). Not even death, then, would destroy Jesus' church, but at this
point it is not clear whose death is in view. Later (16.21-28) both Jesus'
death and the death of his followers will be mentioned.

Jesus' address to Peter concludes with a promise to give him the keys
to the kingdom of heaven, which is interpreted to imply, 'Whatever you
bind on earth will have been bound in heaven, and whatever you
loose on earth will have been loosed in heaven'. By receiving the
(metaphorical) keys to the kingdom of heaven, Peter would accept the
responsibility of opening the way to the kingdom of heaven for others
(contrast 23.13). This is the responsibility that the resurrected Jesus
would give to him and the other disciples at the end of the narrative
(28.19). The seriousness of this responsibility is accentuated by the
saying about binding and loosing, the form of which suggests that Peter
would be acting in obedience to God (what will have been bound or
loosed in heaven). The same saying will be addressed to all the disciples
in 18.18, where it will refer to the disciples' responsibility towards
recalcitrant sinners in the church. There, the responsibility is safeguarded from abuse both by emphasizing that the disciples would be
gathered 'in Jesus' name' (18.20) and by urging the forgiveness of sins
(18.21-35).

Finally, a warning against making Jesus known as the Christ is
addressed by him to the disciples. The reason for this will soon become
clear, when the nature of Jesus' messiahship will be described in terms
unlike those used of David's kingship.

Jesus Predicts the Way he is to Take, which his Disciples should Follow: 16.21-28[1]

The development of the Matthaean narrative shows that Jesus took
Peter's confession as a starting point for preparing the disciples' understanding of the unexpected nature of his messiahship, namely that 'he
must [implying that this was God's purpose] go to Jerusalem, suffer
many things from the elders and chief priests and scribes, and be killed,
and on the third day be raised'. Matthew's 'on the third day' is a scriptural idiom for a day on which something new would happen (e.g. Hos.
6.2), whereas Mark's 'after three days' makes it clear that Jesus was truly
dead before his resurrection. Jesus had often been called 'son of David',

1   See Mk 8.31–9.1; Lk. 9.22-27.

but this prediction of what would happen to him bears no resemblance to what happened to David. David was a successful military leader who defeated his enemies and was not killed by them. Although the prediction of what would happen to Jesus includes a reference to resurrection after death, it is the necessity of execution which is taken up and emphasized. Jesus was to suffer persecution like the prophets mentioned earlier in the narrative (16.14), and his persecutors are called elders, chief priests and scribes. There is no reference to the part Romans were to play in his execution, probably because it would have been unwise of Christians living in the Roman Empire to draw too much attention to the part played by the Roman governor in Jesus' execution: other Roman governors might follow Pilate's example and persecute Jesus' followers. The narrative, therefore, blames Jewish leaders for Jesus' execution. There is also no mention of Pharisees, who will not appear in the Passion Narrative (chs. 26–27). Historically, scribes and Pharisees had no power to effect Jesus' execution. Whether chief priests had such power will be discussed later, in connection with the accounts in chs. 26 and 27.

Peter's immediate response to Jesus' prediction is formulated as a rebuke: '[God be] merciful to you, lord; this shall never happen to you' (Mark attributes no saying to Peter), but Jesus' reply interprets Peter's statement as the work of Satan, recalling the earlier narrative of Jesus' tests (4.1-11), and as the expression of a human rather than a divine plan. Self-preservation is taken to be a normal human tendency, but one which sometimes conflicts with God's purpose. In spite of Jesus' earlier praise of Peter, which had led to promises about his future responsibilities, then, Peter could still be presented as God's opponent and as an offence to Jesus (Luke does not include this section about Peter).

Jesus' discourse goes on to draw a parallel between his own way of life and that of his followers: 'If someone would come after me, let him deny himself and take up his cross and follow me' (see 10.38). 'Someone' also includes the readers. Jesus' prediction had mentioned execution but had not specified crucifixion. The reference to someone's taking up his cross, in 10.28 and here, assumes the readers' knowledge that Jesus would die by crucifixion. Followers of Jesus, then, were to suffer martyrdom as he would do (Luke tones down the horror of the saying by transforming it into a metaphor: 'take up his cross daily'). The message is then elaborated with general propositions about life and death (in Mark, this saying is addressed to a crowd as well as the disciples): 'For whoever wants to save his life will lose it; and whoever loses his life for my sake will find it. For what will it profit a person if he gains the whole world but forfeits his life? Or what will a person give in exchange for his life?' The rhetoric plays on two meanings of the word 'life'. The person who wants to preserve his life (that is, wants not to die) will lose his life (that is, his true, purposeful life, in dedication to the

Creator God); and the person who loses his life (that is, dies) for Jesus'
sake (that is, who dies in following Jesus' way, never meeting violence
with violence), will find it (that is, will find his true purpose in obedience
to God and gain eternal life in the kingdom of heaven). 'Forfeits his life'
means forfeits his purposeful life in dedication to God. 'In exchange for
his life' has the same meaning. This is confirmed by the vision of
eschatological judgment which follows: 'The son of man is about to
come in the glory of his Father with his angels and then he will repay
each one according to his deed'. The saying repeats imagery from
earlier sayings (10.23; 13.40-43, 49-50), which will be explored in more
detail in Jesus' final discourse (chs. 24–25). It is this son of man, this
human being who shows the way to live a human life dedicated to the
Creator God, who will be responsible for the final eschatological judgment in that he will be both the standard by which others will be
judged and he will be God's agent in judgment. This vision of the eschatological judgment helps to encourage followers to face martyrdom. And
that the judgment is imminent is confirmed by Jesus' final statement:
'Truly I say to you, there are some standing here who will not taste
death [a common metaphor; see for example *4 Ezra* 6.26] until they see
the son of man coming in his kingdom'. In spite of the passage of time
(perhaps fifty years) between Jesus' ministry and the writing of the narrative, the eschatological judgment is still thought to be imminent (see
24.34; compare the different wording in Mark and Luke). Moreover, the
saying suggests that not every follower would actually be killed before
the final judgment.

   This section, which treats Jesus' persecution, execution and resurrection as exemplary for his followers, indicates the way in which his
life would express his teaching in the Sermon on the Mount (chs. 5–7).
Those who wished to follow him were to abandon all forms of self-
concern, even concern for the preservation of their mortal lives. They
were not to retaliate violently but to suffer violence. The fact that Jesus'
and the narrative's expectation of an imminent eschatological transformation proved to be wrong does not rob this way of life of its value. It
raises the question whether the long-term aims of modern Christians to
obviate injustice in God's world should ever be attempted through
violent means, and it requires of Jesus' followers that they be prepared
to meet persecution from day to day. Even Christians fortunate enough
to live in Western democracies face day-to-day difficulties in finding and
keeping a job which does not involve them in unjust behaviour. At the
very least they may find themselves denigrated or ignored because of
their commitment to a lifestyle at odds with the general ethos of con-
sumerism. Moreover, if they become well-known opponents of injustice,
they run the risk of assassination, as did Martin Luther King. Even more
perilous are the lives of Christians and others who pursue social justice
in totalitarian regimes.

God's Acceptance of Jesus'Teaching and Way of Life: 17.1-13[1]

In the account of Jesus' baptism (3.13-17), God's acceptance of Jesus' ministry had been indicated by the voice from heaven and by endowment with God's spirit. Then the story of Jesus' tests had shown that essential to Jesus' sonship was his obedience to God. Now, after Jesus' prediction of his future suffering and martyrdom, it is necessary that another account should make clear that God accepted and confirmed the way of life which the prediction encompassed. The narrative of Jesus' transfiguration is reminiscent of the narrative of Moses' transfiguration, although there are differences in vocabulary (see Exod. 34.29-35, and notice the similarity between Matthew's 'his face shone like the sun' and Exodus's 'the skin of his face shone', and contrast Mark and Luke). Both in Exodus and in Matthew, the transfiguration of the prophet on the mountain signified to followers that the prophet truly made God's purpose known. In Matthew, Moses and Elijah are appropriately associated with Jesus because both suffered rejection by their own people, but were vindicated by God.

Only Peter, James and John, not the rest of the disciples, are said to have shared this experience (cf. Joshua's presence with Moses; e.g. Exod. 24.13; 33.11; and see Mt. 26.37). Peter, as usual, is presented as spokesman, responding with a suggestion that he make three tabernacles, one for each of the prophets, Moses, Elijah and Jesus. According to Exodus, Moses used to enter the tabernacle to learn God's purpose: 'The Lord used to speak to Moses face to face' (Exod. 33.11). Peter's suggestion implies a recognition of Jesus as a prophet as great as Moses and Elijah. But 'while he was still speaking, behold a bright cloud overshadowed them', an image of God's presence. In the Exodus narrative, a pillar of cloud descended when Moses entered the tabernacle 'and the Lord would speak with Moses' (e.g. Exod. 33.9). But in Exodus, the cloud also covered the mountain for six days 'and on the seventh day the Lord called to Moses out of the midst of the cloud' (Exod. 24.15-16). So, in the Matthaean narrative, Jesus took the three disciples onto the mountain 'after six days' (17.1), and on the (implied) seventh day 'a voice from the cloud said, "This is my beloved son with whom I am well pleased"', repeating the message of the voice at Jesus' baptism (3.17; compare Mark and Luke). But this time, the voice commanded the disciples, 'Hear him' (see Deut. 18.15). Hence, the voice endorsed Jesus' description of his destiny and his call to his disciples to follow him. The description of the disciples' response confirms the awesome nature of the experience and encourages readers to share it. Then the narrative depicts Jesus' touching them and saying, 'Rise, don't be afraid', and the disciples' lifting up their eyes to see no one but Jesus. His command to

1   See Mk 9.2-13; Lk. 9.28-36.

tell no one about the vision until the son of man was raised from the dead warns readers that the full significance of Jesus' life would be understood only when the whole of his story had been told.

The narrative calls the incident a vision (17.9), but the manner in which it is related affirms that the vision was from God. It is not to be understood as the hallucination of gullible people, but as an experience of God-inspired insight, which encouraged the disciples to hear Jesus and to take up their cross in following him. Later in the narrative, these same three disciples will be described accompanying Jesus in Gethsemane (26.36-46) where their failure to watch and pray explains their cowardly behaviour at Jesus' arrest. The Gospel encourages readers to share the disciples' insight but not to follow their example when put to the test.

In spite of the disciples' visionary experience, they are immediately depicted raising the question, 'Why therefore do the scribes say that Elijah must come first?' (Mal. 4.5. There is no Lukan parallel to this section. Notice the differences in the Markan version). Elijah, together with Moses, had been associated with Jesus in the vision. Jesus' reply confirms the expectation by affirming its fulfilment: 'Elijah indeed comes and is to restore all things, and I say to you that Elijah has already come, and they did not recognize him but did to him whatever they wanted'. Moreover, what had happened to Elijah is taken to confirm what Jesus had predicted about the son of man's fate: 'Thus also the son of man is about to suffer at their hands'. In case the reader had failed to make the connection earlier, the narrative confirms: 'Then the disciples understood that he spoke to them about John the Baptist'. References to John, both before (16.14) and after (17.12-13) Jesus' prediction of his execution explain why the narrative had devoted space to an account of John's execution (14.3-12). Like the prophets before them, both John and Jesus were to suffer persecution, and their followers should expect a similar fate (e.g. 5.11-12; 16.24).

An Example of the Disciples' Inadequacy: 17.14-20[1]

Once more, Jesus is depicted in the presence of crowds, presumably in Galilee (17.22). The location of the mountain had not been specified (17.1). As in the Exodus narrative, the mountain is a place where the purpose of God is made known to people (see also 5.1; 28.16). The description of the boy's illness suggests epilepsy. The terminology shows that epilepsy was thought to be related to the phases of the moon. The Matthaean version of the story is, as usual, more succinct than the Markan. This healing is distinguished from others in the Gospel by the father's complaint that he had brought his son to Jesus' disciples but

1   See Mk 9.14-29; Lk. 9.37-43.

that they had been unable to heal him. The missionary discourse (10.8) had required the disciples to heal as well as preach. Jesus' response expressed frustration at a faithless and perverse generation (cf. Deut. 32.5), in which the disciples were particularly included. 'How long shall I be with you? How long shall I bear with you?' emphasizes the importance of the disciples' accepting their responsibility in view of Jesus' predicted death. Nevertheless, Jesus healed the boy and the healing is described as an exorcism which was immediately effective ('from that hour'; cf. 8.13; 9.21; 15.28). The following private conversation between Jesus and his disciples about their inability to exorcize again focuses on their little faith (contrast Mark's reference to prayer), but provides the hyperbolic reassurance: 'If you have faith as a grain of mustard, you will say to this mountain, move from here to there, and it will move; and nothing will be impossible to you' (see Lk. 17.6 and cf. 1 Cor. 13.2; Hab. 3.6; Zech. 14.4. Mt. 17.21 is considered to be a secondary addition from Mk 9.29, since it is absent from some manuscripts).

No doubt first-century readers could have heard this assurance as if it were addressed directly to themselves, providing them with encouragement to continue Jesus' healing ministry. Modern Christians can accept responsibility for those who are ill, but no longer understand epilepsy as lunacy or demon-possession.

Jesus' Second Prediction of his Execution and Resurrection: 17.22-23[1]

The mention of Galilee provides, retrospectively, the setting for all the stories in ch. 17. Their gathering together (rather than the alternative reading in some manuscripts, 'their dwelling') in Galilee was the prelude for their departure from Galilee to Judaea (19.1). Jesus' summary of his previous prediction, 'The son of man is to be delivered into the hands of men, and they will kill him, and he will be raised on the third day' (see 16.21 and 17.12) reinforces the message about Jesus' exemplary way. The disciples would soon have to continue Jesus' mission themselves. Their great grief at their imminent loss is appropriate both to the subject of the prediction and to their failure to heal the epileptic boy (contrast Mark's and Luke's reference to their lack of understanding).

Confirmation that a New Community was being Formed: 17.24-27

The earlier lessons about Jesus' followers forming a new community, separate from Judaism, are recalled in this discussion about payment of the temple tax. The amount of money involved shows that the temple tax was in view (Exod. 30.13; 38.26; Hebrew 'the half-shekel', Septuagint

1   See Mk 9.30-32; Lk. 9.43-45.

'the didrachma', as in Mt. 17.24). The temple tax was paid by all Jews to support the functioning of the temple in Jerusalem. When the temple was destroyed by the Romans in 70CE, the emperor Vespasian converted the temple tax into the *fiscus Judaicus* and used it for the support of the temple to Jupiter Capitolinus in Rome (Josephus, *War* 7.218). By paying it, Jews gained exemption from some Roman customs to which they objected, but at the cost of acknowledging Roman power.

The Matthaean account is set at Capernaum once more (cf. 4.13; 8.5; 11.23) and is introduced by a question from those who collected the tax to Peter: 'Does not your teacher pay the didrachma?' to which Peter replied with the expected 'yes'. In the house, however, Jesus challenged Peter with a further question: 'From whom do the kings of the earth take toll or tribute? From their sons or from others?' When Peter replied, 'From others', Jesus drew the inference, 'Then the sons are free'. This suggests that he and his followers, sons of their heavenly Father, need not pay the temple tax. In other words, they were no longer to regard themselves as members of the Jewish community. Nevertheless, Jesus went on to tell Peter to go to the sea, cast a hook, take the first fish which came up, and open its mouth to find a *stratera* (double the amount of the didrachma). This he should give to them for Jesus and himself. The reason for this instruction is 'that we may not give them offence'. 'Them' in the context refers to the Jewish collectors of the temple tax. The miracle suggests God's endorsement of the decision.

During the period of Jesus' life in Palestine, he and his disciples must have paid the temple tax as all Jews did. The Matthaean story depicts their doing so, as obedient law-abiding Jews. Nevertheless, 'the sons are free' seems to give readers a freedom not to pay. The Gospel was probably written after 70 CE, when the temple was destroyed, but when the Romans imposed a substitute tax. The rhetoric of the story leaves open the possibility that Jewish Christians might pay this tax to the Romans, if there were any Jewish Christians in the community to which the narrative was addressed. But it seems more likely that there were none, since the Gospel contains mistakes about Judaism as well as vitriolic attacks on its leaders. Nevertheless, in taking over and regarding as authoritative the Jewish Scriptures, which contain the injunction to pay the temple tax, teaching which explained why it need not be paid was necessary. The new covenant community (26.26-29) could express their freedom as sons of their heavenly Father.

The formation of a Christian community separate from the Jewish community had far-reaching consequences for Christian relations with the Roman imperial power. In the first century BCE, Jews had won for themselves exemptions from Roman customs like sacrificing to Roman gods, and they had the right of assembly in their synagogues. Christians would have abhorred those customs as much as Jews did, and they also wanted to meet together, for example to celebrate the Eucharist, but once they had separated from Jews, they would no longer have shared Jewish privileges. Their neglect of Roman sacrificial customs would have brought them under suspicion of disloyalty to Rome. We know that the emperor Nero was able to distinguish Christians from Jews at Rome in 64 CE, and that he ordered the execution of Christians whom he blamed for the fire in Rome. At the beginning of the second century, the Roman governor of Bithynia, Pliny, was also able to distinguish Christians from Jews, and he ordered the execution of those Christians who refused to offer Roman sacrifices. The Gospel according to Matthew does not describe its community's social situation in detail, but leads readers to expect persecution from Roman authorities (10.18; 24.9).

Jesus' Instructions to his Disciples as Leaders of this New Community: 18.1-35
Who is the Greatest in the Kingdom of Heaven? 18.1-5.[1] This, the fourth of Jesus' discourses in the narrative, given only to his disciples, provides a pause for reflection on the nature of this new community and the leadership appropriate to it, before their departure to Judaea. It is introduced by the disciples' question, 'Who, then, is greatest in the kingdom of heaven?', which allows Jesus' reply to focus on humility: 'Truly I say to you, unless you turn and become like children, you will never enter the kingdom of heaven. And whoever receives one such child in my name, receives me' (notice the differences in the synoptic parallels). Earlier teaching about humility is recalled (5.5; 10.16, 24-25, 40-42; 11.25-30). Making children exemplary for disciples does not imply that they should become childish, but that they should assume the social powerlessness of children. Children had no economic independence and were dependent on their parents for their survival. The disciples' leadership was not to mimic the powerful but the powerless. In fact, they were to conform to Jesus' position, to act in his name, so that whoever received them in effect received him. This last statement encourages acceptance of these humble leaders and missionaries by other members of the community or by outsiders (cf. 10.40-42).

The teaching is antithetical to the ethos of most social structures, in which the rich and powerful dominate others. This was particularly true of Roman society in the first century, but it is still true, even in Western democratic societies. And the Romans imposed their ethos on client states like those in Palestine. Herod Antipas who ruled Galilee and Peraea as a client tetrarch was rich and powerful. But Judaism had long expressed suspicion of such power. In its Scripture, prophets who

1   See Mk 9.33-37; Lk. 9.46-48.

were not rich stood against kings who were, and the ideal king described in Deut. 17.14-17 was to be a humble brother who did not multiply horses or wives or silver and gold. It is true that the priestly families with whom Rome was prepared to negotiate were wealthy, but their influence on Jews depended on their conscientious adherence to the Jewish law, not on their wealth. Moreover, all Jews were members of the covenant community, and lay Jews who were learned in the law gained respect in spite of their poor economic status. The first-century scribe Hillel, one of the most influential of Jewish teachers, was a day labourer. Jesus' teaching in Matthew 18 endorses Judaism's egalitarian ethos.

Warnings against Offending Little Ones: 18.6-9.[1] Since the leaders of the community were to be as powerless as children, it is appropriate that teaching should follow which warns against taking advantage of their vulnerability. Jesus' speech is like that of a prophet: death by drowning would be better than committing an offence against one of these little ones who believed in him. His woe to the world pronounced God's judgment against those who offended his followers, while, at the same time, encouraging his own to remain faithful. 'For it is necessary that offences come' means that even this was encompassed by God's purpose, but this theological perspective did not exempt those who caused offence from ethical responsibility: 'Nevertheless, woe to that person through whom the offence comes'. The saying about cutting off or casting away hand, foot or eye and entering into life maimed rather than being thrown into eternal fire is re-used in this context. Earlier (5.29-30), a similar statement had discouraged followers from lustful behaviour. In this new context, it encouraged leaders to form a community separate from that in which the rich dominated (the context and the force of similar teaching in the synoptic parallels is different).

Care of Those who Go Astray: 18.10-14.[2] The disciples' responsibility towards each other, and probably towards other followers, is expressed through the parable of the lost sheep. Not even the disciples' understanding should lead them to despise those who went astray. The narrative had already given examples of disciples' failures to live up to their calling, because of their little faith. Now they were reminded that each of the little ones had a guardian angel who looked upon God's face ('the face of my Father who is in heaven'). This belief is adopted from contemporary Judaism (e.g. *Jub.* 35.17; cf. Ps. 91.11). It encourages disciples to exercise the same care as guardian angels. Hence they were

1   See Mk 9.42-48; Lk. 17.1-2.
2   See Lk. 15.3-7.

to behave like the shepherd who sought the lost sheep and rejoiced when it was found. They should be 'shepherds' as Jesus was (2.6; 9.36). In this way, they would be doing God's will: 'So it is not the will of my Father who is in heaven that one of these little ones should be lost'. Once again the disciples were to imitate Jesus' example (e.g. 9.10-13. The setting and interpretation of similar teaching in Luke is different). At the end of the narrative, Peter would be commissioned in spite of his denial, ten others would be commissioned in spite of their cowardly escape, but Judas, the betrayer, would hang himself in spite of his repentance (27.3-5; 28.16-20).

Forgiving the Brother who Sins Against You: 18.15-35.[1] This general teaching is next exemplified by a particular example. There are no synoptic parallels to most of this section. Only Lk. 17.3-4 offers a parallel to Mt. 18.15, 21-22. The need to forgive others had been emphasized in the Sermon on the Mount (6.12, 14-15) and Jesus had been depicted putting his teaching into practice (9.1-13). Now the teaching is applied to relations within the community (brothers, but, unfortunately, not sisters), some of whom were clearly expected to behave badly.

Practical advice is given about the treatment of a brother who had sinned against a brother. First, the injured brother should convict the offender privately (see Lev. 19.17). If he succeeded, he would have gained his brother. If he were unsuccessful, he should take with him one or two others, an allusion to Deut. 19.15. Should that be equally ineffective, he should tell the whole church. Here 'church' seems to refer to the particular Christian community to which the Gospel was addressed. The narrative even goes on to suggest what should be done if he refuse to listen even to the church: 'Let him be to you like a Gentile and a tax collector'. This suggests that he should no longer be viewed as a member of the community but as an outsider to whom the community directed its mission, as Jesus did (e.g. 8.5-13; 9.9-13; 15.21-28; 28.19-20).

The seriousness of the disciples' responsibility is stressed by repeating the saying addressed to Peter in 16.19: 'Whatever you bind on earth will have been bound in heaven, and whatever you loose on earth will have been loosed in heaven'. The disciples are to be agents of God's purpose. Reassurance is therefore given that if two agreed about anything they asked, it would be done for them by their Father in heaven. This bold promise, however, could lead to misunderstanding, which is excluded by the following qualification: 'For where two or three are gathered in my name, there am I in the midst of them'. Only if the disciples were living as Jesus lived (in his name) does the promise hold.

1   See Lk. 17.3-4.

The promise looks beyond the time of Jesus' historical ministry to the time when his followers would have to act in his name, but with his continuing support (see 28.20). Jesus would no longer be present with them as he was in his historical ministry, but, after his resurrection, he would be present in all those who continued his work (25.31-46).

The rest of the chapter returns to stress the humble and forgiving behaviour expected of those whom God had forgiven. Peter is again presented as spokesman of the twelve in asking how many times he should forgive a brother who has sinned against him. His suggestion, 'seven times', seems to be generous but it is met with Jesus' response, not seven times but seventy-seven times (early manuscript translations of this Greek expression into Latin took it to mean 'seventy times seven'), that is, in effect, every time it happened. The allegorical parable about the kingdom of heaven which follows tells the story of a king settling accounts (there are some similarities between this parable and the story in Lk. 7.41-43). The king, who represents God, was persuaded to forgive a servant who was indebted to him for an extraordinarily large amount. The servant, however, failed to imitate the king's generosity in his treatment of someone who was indebted to him for a petty amount. When this was brought to the king's attention by his servants, he summoned the servant concerned to ask, 'Should not you have had mercy on your fellow servant as I had mercy on you?' The servant was then punished even more severely than he had punished his fellow (not only imprisonment but torture). The message is applied to the disciples: 'So also my heavenly Father will do to you [plural], if each of you does not forgive his brother from his heart', that is, sincerely (cf. 6.12, 14-15).

Matthew 19.1-2: Jesus Begins his Ministry in Judaea

Jesus' Departure for Judaea: 19.1-2[1]

The usual formula marks the end of Jesus' discourse (cf. 7.28; 11.1; 13.53; 26.1), but this time it is followed by a statement that Jesus left Galilee and came into the regions of Judaea across the Jordan. The first two Gospels structure their stories by depicting Jesus' teaching and healing ministry first in Galilee and its environs, and then in Judaea and Jerusalem. The Third Gospel sets much of Jesus' teaching in the context of his long journey from Galilee to Jerusalem (Lk. 9.51–19.45). The Fourth Gospel juxtaposes accounts of incidents in Galilee and Samaria with those in Jerusalem. Each of the structures serves the purpose of

1   See Mk 10.1.

dramatic effect rather than historical development. Incidents are related to create an overall understanding of Jesus' significance. They reflect history to the extent that we can be sure Jesus pursued his ministry both in Galilee and in Judaea, and that he was crucified outside Jerusalem. But his ministry probably lasted for many more months than would have been needed to achieve what is related in the Gospels. The Fourth Gospel assumes a ministry of at least two years, since three annual Passovers are mentioned (Jn 2.13; 6.4; 12.1).

The 'regions of Judaea across the Jordan' (contrast Mark) suggests that the setting was on the periphery of Judaea until Jesus went to Jerusalem via Jericho and Bethphage (20.17, 29; 21.1). Strictly speaking, the region across the Jordan, Peraea, was not part of Judaea and was ruled by Herod Antipas. Many crowds are said to have followed Jesus, including some Pharisees (19.3), children (19.13) and a rich young man (19.20, 22). The brief introduction notes that Jesus healed people (19.2; contrast Mark's 'taught'), before examples of his teaching are given in detail. The twin aspects of his ministry, then, healing and teaching, are understood to have continued, in spite of the fact that only one story of a particular healing, of two blind men (20.29-34), occurs in these chapters, together with a second summary of healings (21.14).

Matthew 19.3–20.34: Complete Dedication to God

Divorce and Celibacy: 19.3-12[1]

Jesus' teaching about divorce (contrast the less orderly and in some respects different teaching in Mark) is presented as a response to a test question from the Pharisees: 'Is it lawful for a person to divorce his wife for any cause?' Characterizing the Pharisees' behaviour as testing predisposes readers against them. Jesus' reply, 'Have you not read?', and the quotations from Scripture challenge the presumption of the question. 'He made them male and female' (Gen. 1.27, conforming to the Septuagint) sets the teaching in the context of God's purpose for human beings. The word for 'Creator' is not found in the Septuagint, although the verb 'to create' is used of God's activity, as well as the noun 'creation' for what he created. Calling God 'Creator' was a natural extension of this usage (e.g. Josephus, *War* 3.354; Rom. 1.25). The next quotation serves to define God's purpose: 'On account of this, a person shall leave father and mother and shall cleave to his wife, and the two shall become one flesh' (Gen. 2.24, slightly different from the Septuagint). An inference is drawn: 'So they are no longer two but one flesh.

1   See Mk 10.2-12.

Therefore, what God yoked together let not a human being divide'. The warning implies that there could be no justification for divorce.

Unusually, the Pharisees of the story were not silenced by this reply, but asked a further pertinent question: 'Then why did Moses command one to give a bill of divorce and to put her away?', an allusion to Deut. 24.1, which states, 'If a man takes a wife and marries her, if then she finds no favour in his eyes because he has found some indecency in her, and he writes her a bill of divorce and puts it into her hand and sends her out of his house, and she departs out of his house, and if she goes and becomes another man's wife...' The Deuteronomic passage assumes a formal procedure for divorce, including a written document, but is vague about its cause: 'some indecency' could refer to sexual infidelity, before or after marriage, or to something less offensive, and its possible meanings were discussed in Jewish circles. The Matthaean teaching interprets the passage as a concession rather than a command: 'for your hardness of heart', something less than the fulfilment of God's purpose. Nevertheless, the ruling in Mt. 19.9 expresses a possible interpretation of 'some indecency'. It does not state that divorce is impossible in all circumstances, but 'whoever divorces his wife, except for *porneia*, and marries another commits adultery' (cf. 5.32: 'Everyone who divorces his wife, except for the reason of *porneia*, makes her commit adultery, and whoever marries a divorced woman commits adultery'). *porneia* could refer to sexual infidelity before or after marriage. The exception clause in both Matthaean passages (contrast Mark, Lk. 16.18; 1 Cor. 7.10-11; Rom. 7.2-3) allows for divorce, and presumably remarriage, for a man whose wife had been sexually unfaithful, but excludes marriage to a divorced woman. (Only the Markan version countenances women's initiation of divorce, a possibility in Roman society, but not in Jewish or Greek society.)

In modern Western societies, women have more economic and legal freedom to decide whether to marry or whether to continue a marriage. Nevertheless, their choices are by no means easy. The individualistic ethos of our societies makes it difficult for us to appreciate and practise the reciprocal virtues which marriage and a commitment to bringing up children require, while at the same time isolation and loneliness engender desires for close companionship. The rapid pace of social change and the frequent need to move to new homes both cut people off from their roots and devalue long-term commitments. Yet the expression of the ideal, 'the two shall become one flesh', still haunts us, and encourages people to criticize and change societies which militate against it, without returning to a conservatism which would hold women, men and children in a destructive bond.

The Matthaean narrative depicts the reaction of the disciples to Jesus' teaching, in spite of its exception clause, as one of dismay: 'If this is the case of a person with his wife, it is not profitable to marry'. This is an extraordinarily negative expression of a male attitude to marriage, but no rebuke is found in the narrative. Moreover, the Gospel supplies no information about the marital status of most of the disciples. Readers can infer that Peter was married from the story of Jesus' healing his mother-in-law (8.14-15), and the story also suggests that Peter's contact with his wife's family persisted after he left off fishing to follow Jesus. Apart from general statements about the importance of following Jesus, which should come before family obligations (e.g. 10.37-38), nothing is said about the repercussions on wife and children which a married man's commitment to following Jesus would entail. Rather, the disciples' judgment allows the text to introduce a call to celibacy (no synoptic parallel). The call, however, is recognised to be exceptional rather than general: 'Not all make room for this saying, but those to whom it has been given [by God]'. The ability to remain celibate is construed as a gift from God. This perspective is necessary, because otherwise Jesus' call would have directly contradicted God's command in Genesis to be fruitful and multiply and fill the earth (Gen. 1.28; 9.7). The form of the call, with references to eunuchs, is couched in harsh terms. Eunuchs were excluded from the congregation of Israel (Deut. 23.1), although eunuchs are often mentioned at courts (e.g. Gen. 39.1; 40.2, 7; 1 Sam. 8.15; 1 Kgs 22.9; 2 Kgs 8.6). Jesus' call, 'For there are eunuchs who are born so from their mother's womb, and there are eunuchs who are made eunuchs by people, and there are eunuchs who make themselves eunuchs on account of the kingdom of heaven. He who is able to make room, let him make room', uses 'eunuch' literally in the first two state-ments, but metaphorically, to refer to celibacy, in the third. The refer-ence to the kingdom of heaven, which the narrative teaches would arrive in the near future, suggests that celibacy was encouraged in view of the imminence of the kingdom, which would make marriage and begetting children less important. Paul adopts a similar perspective in 1 Corinthians 7. On the basis of God's command in Genesis, Jews regarded marriage and begetting children as a sacred duty. Only the covenanters at Qumran adopted at least a partially celibate way of life, and they shared with Paul and the Jesus of the First Gospel a belief in the imminence of God's eschatological kingdom.

When Christians came to modify belief in the imminence of the eschatological judgment, celibacy for some was advocated on many different grounds. But monastic communities were still seen to represent people's complete dedication to God and freedom from worldly con-cerns, in a community which intimated something of the future life in God's kingdom. Moreover, a celibate priesthood among Roman Catholics has allowed priests to fight injustice in totalitarian regimes without involving families in the persecutions they have suffered.

Jesus' Acceptance of Children: 19.13-15[1]

This short account (contrast the versions in Mark and Luke), in which
people brought children to Jesus so that he might lay his hands on them
and pray, the disciples rebuked them (for which no explanation is
offered, but perhaps their behaviour represents a misunderstanding of
the previous teaching, which could have implied a denigration of children), but Jesus accepted them with the words, 'Let the children come
to me and do not forbid them, for to such belongs the kingdom of
heaven', and his action of laying on his hands, serves to offset any
disparagement of children which the previous advocacy of celibacy
could have implied. Elsewhere, laying on hands is associated with healing (e.g. 8.3; 20.34), but here with blessing. Jesus is represented accepting
and blessing the children, while reminding the disciples of his previous
teaching about their similarly powerless status (18.3), a message which
will be reinforced by the following stories.

In first-century Jewish society, children were regarded as blessings
from God. By contrast, in Roman society babies, especially girls, were
exposed to dangers from starvation, climate and animals, or to the possibility of other people's bringing them up as slaves, when their fathers
did not accept them into the family. Members of modern societies do
not always regard childbirth as a blessing. Some argue that the earth is
already too full of human beings. But the possibilities of effective contra-
ception and abortion have complicated the ethical decisions involved.

The Negative Example of the Rich Young Man: 19.16-22[2]

The narrative relates that, after Jesus' departure from the crowds
(19.15), someone approached him (Matthew's use of 'one' for someone'
is a Semitic idiom), who is only later described as a young man (19.20;
contrast Mark and Luke) who was rich (19.22). He began well, with the
question, 'Teacher, what good shall I do that I may have eternal life?'
(cf. Lev. 18.5, and contrast the versions in Mark and Luke). Jesus'
counter-question, 'Why do you ask me concerning the good? One
there is who is good' receives no reply in the narrative, but leaves
readers to supply the answer: because Jesus was God's agent and God
is good. Obedience to this good God is what is required to enjoy eternal
life in the kingdom of heaven. Hence Jesus' reply, 'If you want to enter
life, keep the commandments'. But the man persisted with a further
question: 'Of what sort?', to which Jesus replied by quoting some of the
ten commandments, though in a different order from that in Scripture
(Exod. 20.12-16; Deut. 5.16-20), together with the summary from Lev.
19.18, 'You shall love your neighbour as yourself'. Again, however, this
failed to satisfy the man, because he claimed to have kept them all.

1   See Mk 10.13-16; Lk. 18.15-17.
2   See Mk 10.17-22; Lk. 18.18-23.

Finally, Jesus asserted: 'If you would be perfect [cf. 5.48], go and sell your belongings and give to the poor, and you will have treasure in heaven [cf. 6.19-21], and come, follow me'. This is the justice already advocated in the Sermon on the Mount. The withdrawal of the grieving young man is explained by the fact that he had many possessions (cf. 13.22). The form of the story echoes earlier teaching and reminds disciples and readers of Jesus' call to a life of generosity and powerlessness.

Jesus Contrasts the Lives of Disciples with those of the Rich: 19.23-30[1]

According to Matthew, Jesus drew out the implications of the incident just related for the disciples alone (contrast Luke). First, there is a general reflection: 'With difficulty will a rich man enter the kingdom of heaven'. 'The kingdom of heaven' is the eschatological kingdom which the narrative proposes as imminent (see 3.2; 4.17; 10.7; chs. 24–25; contrast Mark and Luke). But not only would a rich man find it difficult to enter this future kingdom, he could not really serve God in the present world: 'It is easier for a camel to go through the eye of a needle than for a rich man to enter the kingdom of God'. 'The kingdom of God' refers to the present world as the Creator's kingdom. The statement, with its hyperbolic comparison, captures the difficulty which the rich encounter in acknowledging God's sovereignty, the difficulty illustrated in the account of the rich man's departure. The disciples' astonishment—'Who then can be saved?'—highlights the radical nature of the teaching. It might have been supposed that freedom from day-to-day anxieties would make the rich peculiarly well suited to devote their leisure and their possessions to God's service, and rich Christians have sometimes sought to justify their wealth on such grounds. But that is clearly not the view of the First Gospel. On the contrary, riches are seen to give people the illusion of self-sufficiency, whereas those in need are understood to recognize their dependence on the Creator's God's generosity (5.3-12). Nevertheless, Jesus' reply to the disciples does not entirely rule out the possibility of God's saving even the rich: 'With people this [that is, salvation] is impossible, but with God all things are possible' (contrast 6.24). The claim helps to offset the negative impression of the story of the rich young man.

Again, Peter is represented as speaking for the disciples: 'Behold, we left everything and followed you. What then will there be for us?' Jesus' reply looks beyond the sacrifices which the disciples had made to follow him, and focuses on the reversal of values in the new world: 'In the *paliggenesia*, when the son of man sits upon the throne of his glory, you who followed me will also sit on twelve thrones judging the twelve tribes of Israel'. *paliggenesia*, rebirth, is a technical Stoic term for the

1   See Mk 10.23-31; Lk. 18.24-30.

rebirth of the cosmos after its conflagration, which was thought to happen periodically, not once. The term is used in the First Gospel, however, to refer to the new world which would come into being at the eschatological judgment. The other Gospels do not use the word. Scripture refers to the new heavens and the new earth (Isa. 65.17; see *1 En.* 45.4-5), and the first-century CE apocalyptic work, *2 Baruch*, refers to a new world (44.12; 57.2). In this new world, followers of Jesus would no longer suffer persecution but, together with the son of man (Jesus as the representative of humanity dedicated to God's service), they were to become both judges and the standard by which others were to be judged at the eschatological judgment (see 25.31-46). This vision of the twelve disciples' judging the twelve tribes of Israel suggests that they represent the new Israel, the new covenant people (cf. Lk. 22.30). The number functions in this way in the Gospel despite the betrayal and suicide of Judas, one of the twelve. The saying has no exact parallels in Jewish apocalyptic literature. In *Jub.* 32.19, Israel is given the role of judging the nations, and the covenanters at Qumran, the elect, assigned the same role to their community (1 QpHab. 5.4). In the *Testament of Abraham*, three tribunals are envisaged. At the first, Abel would preside. Since all humanity was thought to descend from Adam, it was considered appropriate that they be judged by Adam's son. At the second tribunal, they would be judged by Israel, and at the third by God (13.6). In the vision in Daniel 7, the one like a son of man is given everlasting dominion, and the saints of the Most High are associated with him. The saying in Mt. 19.28 about the disciples' judging Israel fits into the period of Jesus' ministry depicted, when it was directed to Israel (15.26; 10.5-6), before the command to extend the mission to Gentiles, after Jesus' resurrection (28.19-20).

The teaching goes on to make concrete this vision of the reversal of values: 'Everyone [including the readers] who left houses or brothers or sisters or father or mother or children or fields for my name's sake will receive a hundredfold [or, many times over] and will inherit eternal life. Many that are first will be last and the last first' (contrast Mark and Luke). In other words, those whose status is first in this world (the rich) will be last in the new world, while those who are powerless in this world will be first in the new world. The teaching emphasizes the near impossibility of the rich's serving God in the present or entering the kingdom of heaven in the future, without placing it beyond the power of God's generosity (19.26). On the other hand, those like Jesus' disciples, who had left not only possessions but family for Jesus' sake, would be compensated and rewarded with eternal life.

The form of this teaching has sometimes led Christians to suppose that they could strike a bargain with God, giving up things in this world in order to gain compensation in this world and the next. It has even been used to avoid relieving people's poverty in this word, since God would compensate the poor in the next world. No doubt the teaching was intended to offer assurance of God's mercy and justice to those who were suffering deprivations and persecutions, but earlier teaching had excluded any possibility of calculating or bargaining with God. Dependence upon God's generosity (5.3-12), imitation of God's generosity (5.38-48) and unselfconscious giving (6.2-4) demonstrated the gulf between dedication to God and dedication to mammon (6.24). Dedication to this God is said to characterize Jesus' life and that of his followers, both in this world and in the world to come. The unselfconscious nature of this dedication will be captured again in the vision of the last judgment (25.31-46). Moreover, the vision of the reversal of values in the new world encourages a reversal of values in the present world.

Parable of the Workers in the Vineyard: 20.1-16

Jesus' last statement, 'Many who are first will be last and the last first' (19.30), is illustrated by this parable (see 20.16), introduced by the same formula as that used in ch. 13, 'For the kingdom of heaven is like...' This does not imply that the kingdom of heaven is like the householder, but that something can be learned about the kingdom of heaven from the whole parable. The image of the vineyard and its owner is taken over from Scripture (e.g. Isa. 5.1-7; Jer. 12.10). The vineyard represents Israel and its owner God. Jesus' parable takes this for granted and focuses on the fate of workers in the vineyard, that is, the fate of leaders in Israel. The story relates that the owner went out many times in a day to hire workers for the vineyard, but agreed a wage of a denarius a day only with the first group. The parable reflects a social situation which existed in first-century Palestine in which landless peasants gathered in the market place in the hope of finding casual work. The wage of a denarius a day indicates what was thought to be an average wage (see Tacitus, *Annals* 1.17; Tob. 5.14), and helps readers to understand the values of amounts mentioned in other parables. For example, the servant of the parable in 18.21-35 was indebted for a hundred denarii (18.28), but the servant to whom he was indebted had been forgiven a loan of about 60 million denarii (that is, ten thousand talents, when a talent was worth about six thousand denarii [18.24]).

The five groups of workers, according to the parable, were hired at different times: early in the morning (about 6am, 20.1), about the third hour (9am, 20.3), about the sixth hour (12 noon, 20.5), about the ninth hour (3pm, 20.5), and about the eleventh hour (5pm, 20.6). At the end of the day, the vineyard owner instructed his steward to call the workers and pay them, beginning with the last and ending with the first. Those who had worked from the eleventh hour were paid a denarius each. No reference is made to any of the groups which began at the third, sixth and ninth hours, but the story moves immediately to the payment of those who had worked from early morning, called 'the first'. Readers are told that they supposed they would receive more than a denarius, although that was the wage they had agreed, and it was the wage they received. Their response was to grumble about the house-holder, pointing out that the last had received the same as themselves, while the last had worked only one hour whereas they had borne the burden of the day and the heat. The householder's reply to one of them interprets his decision: 'Friend, I do you no wrong. Did you not agree with me for a denarius? Take what is yours and go. I wanted, however, to give to this man, the last, as I also gave to you. Am I not allowed to do what I like with my own? Or is your eye evil because I am good?' The parable then ends with a repetition of the statement it illustrates: 'Thus the last will be first and the first last'.

The parable dramatically represents the expectations of the first (the rich) at the final payment (the last judgment). They expected their present status to ensure a greater reward at the judgment and were offended by God's (the householder's) generosity to the poor (the last). Their complaint about bearing the burden of the day and the heat represents their excuse that earning and retaining riches and power had involved hard work. The parable reinforces the teaching of the beatitudes (5.3-12) and of ch. 19.

Jesus' Third Prediction of his Suffering, Execution and Resurrection: 20.17-19[1]

At this point, both the disciples in the story and the readers of the narrative should be in a better position to appreciate the significance of the fate awaiting Jesus. This, the most detailed of Jesus' predictions, is occasioned by his going up to Jerusalem. En route, he took his disciples aside to tell them what awaited the son of man there. He would be betrayed to the chief priests and scribes, and condemned to death. They would hand him over to the Gentiles to be mocked and flogged and crucified, and on the third day he would be raised (contrast the details in Mark and Luke). This is the first time that the involvement of Gentiles and the manner of his execution, by crucifixion, had been mentioned. The prediction, however, does not specify that the Gentiles concerned were Romans, although only Romans had the power to crucify in first-century Palestine. What the prediction makes clear is that the son of man, Jesus and those who adopted his powerless lifestyle, would meet persecution and martyrdom. Nevertheless, their dedication to the Creator God would ensure their resurrection.

Jesus' resurrection 'on the third day', which will be recounted at the end of the narrative, represents God's endorsement of his way of life and encourages both disciples and readers to follow his example.

1   See Mk 10.32-34; Lk. 18.31-34.

Moreover, resurrection was an expectation which was associated with that of final eschatological judgment. Jesus' resurrection, therefore, assured first-century Christians about the imminence of the kingdom of heaven. Nearly two thousand years later, Christians who try to follow Jesus' example express their hope in a future resurrection without expecting an imminent transformation of the world. They know that the early disciples of Jesus and their successors were not raised 'on the third day'. Their lives, however, are still inspired by the God who raised Jesus from the dead, and by hope for a new world in which poverty would not entail betrayal, persecution and martyrdom.

The rhetoric of the Gospel, which includes predictions of what would happen later in the story, affords the opportunity to prepare readers for an understanding of Jesus' crucifixion, not as a tragic accident, but as the fulfilment of God's purpose. It does not mitigate the horror of Jesus' suffering and death, nor does it diminish human responsibility for the evils which made it possible, but it presents his death as an integral part of his way of life. Not even the violence of the Roman imperial system would deflect Jesus from his resolve never to retaliate violently.

Requests for Special Honours: 20.20-28[1]

This account of the request by the mother of James and John (contrast Mark) that her sons might sit at Jesus' right and left (that is, in positions of special honour) in his kingdom (contrast Mark) comes as rather a shock at this juncture. Even the ten's indignant response to the request (20.24) hardly suggests their own humility. But the account serves the useful purpose of excluding misunderstandings of the previous teaching in 19.27-30. Jesus' reply is addressed to the brothers rather than to their mother. Their mother will appear later in the narrative, watching Jesus' crucifixion (27.56). 'You do not know what you ask' emphasizes the brothers' misunderstanding, and 'are you able to drink the cup which I am to drink?' reminds them that their lives should conform to Jesus'. 'The cup' which Jesus was about to drink is a metaphor for the suffering and death awaiting him in Jerusalem (see Ezek. 23.33). The assertion of James and John, 'we are able', would be contradicted by their actions in Gethsemane (26.36-46, 56). Nevertheless, Jesus' prediction, 'You will drink my cup; but to sit at my right hand and left hand is not mine to give, but is for those for whom it has been prepared by my Father' reinforces the exemplary nature of Jesus' way of life and reminds people not to presume on God's mercy. The Acts of the Apostles mentions that James was later killed by Herod (Agrippa) (Acts 12.2), and some later patristic references suggest that John was also martyred, although alternative patristic stories about his living into old

1   See Mk 10.35-45; cf. Lk. 22.27.

age at Ephesus contradict them (Eusebius, *Ecclesiastical History* 3.13, 31; 4.14; 5.8).

The narrative's note of the ten's indignation introduces Jesus' remarks to all the disciples, which repeat in a new form his earlier teachings: 'You know that the rulers of the Gentiles lord it over them and great men exercise authority over them. It shall not be so among you. But whoever [including the readers] wants to become great among you will be your servant, and whoever wants to be first among you will be your slave'. The message is reinforced by a reference to the representative life of the son of man: 'Just as [contrast Mark] the son of man came not to be served but to serve and to give his life as a ransom for many' (see Isa. 53.10-12). The reference to 'ransom' assumes a situation in which enslaved prisoners of war could be ransomed from slavery by their relatives. Jesus, the son of man, was to give his life as a ransom for many, that is, was to die voluntarily for the freedom of many others. Later, the account of the Eucharist will make clear that this freedom is freedom from sins (26.28 and 1.21). The statement does not imply that Jesus' martyrdom would make the disciples' martyrdoms unnecessary. On the contrary, they would have to take up their cross and follow him (10.38; 16.24); they would have to drink the cup that he was to drink (20.23). But Jesus' death set a seal on his life of obedience to God. By suffering an unjust and horrible execution, he provided an example for his followers which broke the pattern of sinful, retaliatory violence.

Jesus' Healing of Two Blind Men: 20.29-34[1]

The reference to their departure from Jericho, north-east of Jerusalem, reminds readers that Jesus was on his way to Jerusalem. Now the presence of a great crowd is noted once more (only implied in Mark and Luke). The account relates that, when two blind men seated by the way heard that Jesus was passing by, they cried out, 'Have mercy on us, son of David'. When the crowd required their silence, they cried out the more, 'Have mercy on us, lord, son of David'. The details indicate the men's persistence, and their form of address reminds readers of Jesus' messianic mission, in preparation for the next section of the narrative. Jesus' reaction, standing still, calling them and asking what they wanted him to do, elicits their request, 'Lord, that our eyes may be opened'. The narrative notes Jesus' compassion for them and describes his action, touching their eyes. The immediate cure is confirmed by their following him (contrast Mark's more vivid and detailed account).

Many of the details of the story are reminiscent of the earlier account of Jesus' healing two blind men in 9.27-31. In this second version, however, references to the men's persistence make unnecessary any

1   See Mk 10.46-52; Lk. 18.35-43.

question about their faith (cf. Mark and Luke). Moreover, the presence of a crowd makes a command to keep silent inappropriate (cf. 9.31). In both Matthaean versions, two blind men were cured (contrast one in Mark and Luke). This doubling makes the healing even more impressive. Undoubtedly the implied author and readers believed that Jesus cured physical blindness, but the placing of the incident after a story which depicted the startling lack of insight of Jesus' disciples suggests that the miracle was related to offer hope that Jesus could also help the disciples to 'see' the significance of his life and teaching.

Matthew 21.1-22: Jesus Begins his Mission in Jerusalem

Jerusalem was the religious centre of Judaism and its temple, magnificently and beautifully rebuilt at Herod the Great's instigation, commanded the heights of the city. Not only did Jews from the Middle East and the Mediterranean world make pilgrimages there for the three pilgrim festivals—Passover in the Spring, Weeks seven weeks later, and Tabernacles in the autumn—but Gentiles visited it as one of the wonders of the world. Herod's temple had a court for Gentiles outside the court for Jewish women, the court for Jewish men and the court for priests. Inside the court for priests was the Holy of Holies, which was entered only once a year by the high priest on the Day of Atonement. The high priest and the chief priests, together with thousands of ordinary priests, performed the sacrifices required by Scripture, and Levites helped with the temple services. Jews supported the temple and Jerusalem through their payment of the temple tax, and through the offerings of tithes by Palestinian Jews. Jews from the diaspora also sent gifts of money. Temple guards helped to keep order, especially during the pilgrim festivals. Jews who entered the holy temple had first to go through cleansing rituals to remove uncleanness, and outside the temple were large pools for the purpose. Contact with the dead, the most serious cause of impurity, required a ritual for its removal which lasted seven days (Numbers 19).

The Roman prefect did not normally live in Jerusalem, but in Caesarea on the coast. There were, however, Roman soldiers in the Antonia fortress which overlooked the temple. During the pilgrim festivals the prefect and additional Roman troops moved to Jerusalem in order to deal with any unrest among the huge crowds.

The Humble King Comes to Jerusalem: 21.1-11[1]

The narrative begins by noting that Jesus and his followers drew near
to Jerusalem and came to Bethphage, to the Mount of Olives, just outside the city. Bethphage is not mentioned in Scripture, but the fifth-
century *Babylonian Talmud* refers to it (Mark and Luke also mention
Bethany). The story relates that from there Jesus sent two of his disciples to the village opposite in order to bring a donkey and her foal,
which they would find there. No details are given about prior arrangements, which seem to be presupposed, but Jesus is pictured telling the
disciples what to say should they be questioned: 'The lord has need [of
them]' (cf. the Markan and Lukan longer and more impressive stories.
Only the Matthaean version mentions the foal as well as the donkey; cf.
the quotation from Zechariah).

Jesus' instructions are explained as a fulfilment of Scripture (contrast
Mark and Luke and cf. John), with a quotation of parts of Zech. 9.9 and
Isa. 62.11: 'Say to the daughter of Zion [Isa. 62.11], Behold your king is
coming to you [Septuagint of Zech. 9.9], humble and mounted upon a
donkey [abbreviation of Septuagint of Zech. 9.9], and upon a foal, the
son of a beast of burden' (slightly different from the Septuagint of Zech.
9.9). This story is often called 'the triumphal entry', but the Matthaean
story contains not a hint of triumph. On the contrary, the Zechariah
passage describes the king as 'humble', a term favoured by the Gospel
(5.5; 11.29) and entirely appropriate after the teaching in chs. 18–20. The
quotation helps readers to understand Jesus' action as a demonstration
of the kind of humility he had been advocating for the disciples.

The narrative notes the disciples' successful completion of their task,
and then it relates that they placed cloaks on the donkey and her foal,
and that Jesus sat on the garments. Readers have to assume that Jesus
then rode into Jerusalem (21.10), but the narrator's view shifts to a
description of the behaviour of the very great crowds. They spread
their own cloaks in the way, while some cut branches from trees and
spread those in the way (cf. 2 Kgs 9.13; and especially the account of
Simon's entry into Jerusalem in 1 Macc. 13.50-52). Some of the crowds
went before and others followed Jesus, crying, 'Hosanna to the son of
David; blessed is he who comes in the name of the Lord; hosanna in the
highest'. The Hebrew *hosanna*, which means 'save us', is used as a cry
of jubilation. The crowds' words echo Ps. 118.25-26 and 2 Sam. 14.4, in
recognition that Jesus was the Christ, the son of David, 'he who comes
in the name of the Lord' as God's agent. In this way, Jesus' humility is
interpreted as obedience to God, as a true fulfilment of messianic expectations (see Deut. 17.14-17). The narrative ends by recounting a question from people who were disturbed in Jerusalem, 'Who is this?', and
the reply of the crowds who accompanied Jesus: 'This is the prophet

1   See Mk 11.1-11; Lk. 19.28-38; Jn 12.12-19.

Jesus who is from Nazareth in Galilee' (no Gospel parallels). The reply
suggests that Jesus was to be understood as a prophetic figure. The
reference to Nazareth in Galilee reminds readers that he was brought
up there (2.22-23).

The form of the story serves an essential purpose in creating readers'
understanding. Jesus' entry into Jerusalem is presented as the action of
a humble Christ, an action which exemplified the teaching which
preceded it and which prepared for what would follow. The crowds
are used to voice the significance of his messianic mission for readers.
And their calling him a prophet reminds readers of a prophet's fate,
persecution (e.g. 5.11-12). But the form of the story causes historians
difficulties. If vast crowds were involved and the city of Jerusalem was
disturbed, it is impossible to explain how the chief priests and the
Roman soldiers remained ignorant of the incident. Moreover, had they
looked into the matter and discovered that Jesus had been hailed by
great crowds as the messiah, Roman soldiers would have acted quickly
to destroy this threat to Roman power. Only if the huge crowds were
removed from the account would Jesus' continuing freedom to teach in
Jerusalem be historically comprehensible.

Jesus' Action in the Temple: 21.12-17[1]

According to the Matthaean account, the incident in the temple immediately followed Jesus' entry into Jerusalem (contrast the other Gospels).
Nothing is said about Jesus' going through the necessary purity rites
before entering the temple. The narrative relates that, in the temple,
Jesus threw out those who sold and bought, turned over the tables of
money-changers and the seats of those who sold pigeons, and said: 'It
is written, my house shall be called a house of prayer, but you have
made it a cave of robbers'. The first part of the scriptural quotation is
from Isa. 56.7. 'Cave of robbers' is an allusion to Jer. 7.11. In that passage, Jeremiah complained that people supposed they could steal, kill,
commit adultery, burn incense to Baal, go after other gods, and then go
to the temple, called by God's name, and declare, 'We are saved'. The
oracle asks: 'Has this house which is called by my name become a cave
of robbers in your eyes?' In other words, Jeremiah's oracle criticized
people for supposing that they could behave unethically and idola-
trously and still expect God to save them. This was to treat the temple
of God as if it were a cave of robbers. There is no implication that the
temple officials were acting as robbers in extorting money from pilgrims.

Jesus' actions and words make sense in the Matthaean narrative if his
quotation is taken to express a similar criticism. The depiction of his
actions seems to intimate God's destructive judgment against his immoral
and unfaithful people, and his words serve to interpret his actions: the

1   See Mk 11.15-19; Lk. 19.45-48; Jn 2.13-22.

temple should be called a house of prayer, but when people behaved badly and went there to worship, they treated it as if it were a cave of robbers. The narrative will draw out this meaning more clearly in Jesus' later teaching (23.37–24.2).

The story is surprising, coming as it does after the story of the crowds' recognition of Jesus as their prophetic Christ. In the preceding sections of the Gospel, it was Jewish leaders rather than Jewish crowds who had been criticized for their hypocrisy, blindness and opposition to Jesus. Only in 11.20-24 had Jesus been depicted uttering woes against whole Galilean cities. But Jesus' action in the temple seems to symbolize the destruction of the whole people without distinction. This kind of action, however, was typical of the scriptural prophets. The books of the classical eighth- and seventh-century prophets criticized the rich and powerful but predicted destruction for the whole people in their accounts both of preaching and symbolic acts, and their oracles were understood to be fulfilled by the victories of the Assyrians and the Babylonians over Israel and Judah. These scriptural condemnations of Israel help to explain the similar condemnations of Jews in the Matthaean narrative. Nevertheless, some Jews survived the conquests, and subsequent generations were able to return to Judaea and live lives dedicated to the God who had brought punishment but also renewal. The Gospel according to Matthew predicts the destruction of the Jewish people as God's punishment, but also looks forward to renewal. Jesus and his twelve disciples, all of them Jews, represent the remnant from which renewal would begin. By the time the Gospel was written, probably in the eighties of the first century, it would have become clear that very many Jews rejected Jesus' messiahship (see Romans 9–11). Jesus had been crucified by his enemies, a fate which most Jews would have thought inconceivable for the messiah. If they did not believe in Jesus' resurrection, they could view him at best as a persecuted prophet, whose predictions of an imminent eschatological kingdom had failed to materialize. Only those Jewish followers who did believe in his resurrection could acknowledge him as God's agent and Christ, as the First Gospel does. They could also observe the success of the Gentile mission as evidence of the fulfilment of God's plan (e.g. Isa. 9.1-2, quoted in Mt. 4.15-16). Moreover, if the Gospel was written in the eighties, people could look back on the defeat of Jewish armies and the destruction of the temple in the war against Rome, 66–74 CE. Probably Mt. 22.7 and 23.37–24.2 refer to those events.

The Matthaean Jesus' symbolic action in the temple and his later prediction of the destruction of the temple (24.1-2) were, then, in line with scriptural prophetic actions and oracles. They depicted the fate of the Jewish people as a whole, without distinction. While blaming the leadership, they recognized that ordinary people suffered the consequences of their leaders' policies. Moreover, even the most ardent individualists in modern Western societies recognize the same connections. When rulers declare war, ordinary soldiers and civilians suffer and die, whether they agree with their leaders' decisions or not.

Nevertheless, modern Christians are less likely to see the failure of the Jewish war in 66–74 CE and the destruction of the temple as God's punishment for the Jewish rejection of Jesus. They can see other causes. Although the Jews of the first century BCE had won privileges from Rome which allowed them to practise their religious tradition, they came to see that Rome could not be trusted to keep its promises. Only the assassination of the emperor Gaius Caligula prevented the erection of his statue in the Jerusalem temple in 44 CE and a war which would undoubtedly have followed. In 68 CE, there was civil war in the Roman empire between rival claimants to the imperial throne. Jewish leaders from quite different groups, from the conservative Sadducees to the revolutionary Zealots, thought God had provided them with an opportunity to win their freedom. They were not to know that the Roman general sent to quell the revolt, Vespasian, would become emperor and re-establish Roman control. Moreover, the horror of the Jewish defeat did not mark the end of Judaism, but the beginning of renewal. Even the defeat of the second revolt in 135 CE did not lead Jews to abandon their faith. And Christians, too, soon came to experience the persecuting power of Rome.

There is, however, a reason why the Mattheaean narrative connects rejection of Jesus with the horrors and destruction of war. It presents Jesus as someone who preached against the use of retaliatory violence and whose life showed his practising what he preached. Only by suffering instead of inflicting violence could the cycle of violence which God abhorred come to an end. From the Matthaean perspective, any armed revolt, whether it ended in victory or defeat, was a sign of infidelity to the God whose agent Jesus was believed to be. Christians' suffering persecution, however, was not understood as God's punishment, but as the inevitable consequence of sinful power-structures. But in the fourth century CE, when the emperor Constantine became a patron of Christianity and Christian leaders began to exercise secular as well as religious influence, the problems which faced the Jewish leadership in the first century faced Christian leaders. And they behaved as some of their Jewish forebears had behaved, using violence not only against non-Christians but against Christians who were considered heretics.

To return to the Matthaean depiction of Jesus' action in the temple, it is difficult historically to locate the action ascribed to him. People could pay the temple tax when they visited Jerusalem, and since only Tyrian coinage was acceptable and people came from many different areas, money changers were necessary. Pilgrims also offered sacrifices, and only animals or birds without blemish were to be sacrificed according

to scriptural commands. Purchasing them in Jerusalem could ensure that
they were without blemish and not damaged on the journey. The less
wealthy usually offered pigeons, except at Passover, when lambs were
essential. But we do not know where money could be exchanged or
pigeons purchased. The most likely place was the Royal Portico, a
magnificent structure at the top of a flight of steps on the south-east side
of the temple, at one side of the court of Gentiles.[1]

Historians are puzzled by another aspect of the story. The temple
was a sacred place. People went through cleansing rituals before entering it. Worshipping there was an awesome experience. Moreover,
temple guards assured orderly conduct. If Jesus performed such an
outrageous action in the sacred temple, it is difficult to see how he could
have escaped from officials or from offended worshippers. The
Matthaean narrative does not explain how this could have happened. It
is more concerned with the theological significance of Jesus' action than
with any actual historical circumstances (cf. Mark 11.18). If Jesus did
perform such an action in the Royal Portico, it must have been on a
sufficiently small scale for him to avoid immediate arrest. The author and
original readers, however, must have been unaware of these difficulties,
since the story continues by relating further activities of Jesus in the
temple and in Jerusalem. It tells how the blind and lame came to Jesus in
the temple and he healed them (contrast Mark and Luke). It notes that
the scribes and chief priests saw the wonders which he did, and the
children crying, 'Hosanna to the son of David', but were only indignant.
They asked him if he heard what they were saying, to which he replied
'Yes' and asked, 'Have you never read, "Out of the mouths of babies
and sucklings did you prepare praise?"' (the Septuagint of Ps. 8.3). The
biblical quotation is taken as a sufficient justification for accepting their
confession of his messiahship, reference to which silenced Jesus' critics.
The account is brought to an end, not by the chief priests' ordering
Jesus' arrest, but by Jesus' leaving them, going out of the city to
Bethany and lodging there. Again, the theological significance for the
readers, rather than a depiction of historical realities, has determined the
form of the narrative. (This is the first mention of Bethany in the
Matthaean narrative. The place can plausibly be identified with modern
El Azariyeh, south-east of the Mount of Olives.)

The Withering of the Fig Tree: 21.18-22[2]
The Gospel according to Mark places its account of the temple incident
between the introduction and the conclusion of the story about the fig
tree's withering, suggesting that one incident is to be understood as an

---

1   E.P. Sanders, *Judaism: Practice and Belief 63 BCE–66 CE* (London: SCM
Press, 1992).
2   See Mk 11.12-14, 20-24; cf. the parable in Lk. 13.6-9.

interpretation of the other. The Matthaean version achieves the same end by placing one incident after the other and by describing the withering as instantaneous.

The narrative relates that, early in the morning, on his way to the city, Jesus was hungry. He saw a single fig tree by the way, but found nothing but leaves on it. Then he said to it, 'May there never be fruit from you', and the fig tree withered immediately (contrast Mark). The miracle is confirmed by noting that the disciples were amazed when they saw it and asked, 'How was the fig tree withered at once?' (contrast Mark), to which Jesus replied, 'Truly I say to you, if you have faith and do not doubt, not only will you do what has been done to this fig tree, but even if you say to this mountain, be taken up and thrown into the sea, it will happen. And whatever you ask in prayer, believing, you will receive'.

Unlike the prophets in Scripture (Moses, Elijah, Elisha), Jesus had not been depicted performing destructive miracles before this one. Only in the temple incident and in this miracle were his actions destructive rather than creative. And like the accounts of other nature miracles in the Gospel, which are never mentioned in summaries, this account seems to be symbolic. In Scripture a fruitless fig tree stands for a rebellious Israel (e.g. Jer. 8.13; 11.16; Hos. 9.10; Joel 1.7; Ezekiel 17). Like the account of Jesus' action in the temple, the account of the fig tree's withering represents God's destructive judgment against those who rejected his agent, Jesus. And it promises disciples that they too would perform such prophetic actions, if they had faith and did not doubt (cf. 17.19-21).

Matthew 21.23–22.46: A Series of Five Confrontations between Jesus and Jewish Leaders

This series of five confrontations between Jesus and Jewish leaders is set in the temple. The account of the first, between Jesus on the one hand and chief priests and elders (later, Pharisees are also mentioned) on the other, is by far the longest. It consists of the Jewish leaders' challenge to Jesus (21.23), his counter-challenge (21.24-25), their refusal to reply (21.25-27), and Jesus' pronouncements against them in three parables (21.28-32; 21.33-43; 22.1-14), which depict God's condemnation of their leadership and their replacement by Jesus' followers. The other accounts of confrontations, between disciples of the Pharisees with Herodians and Jesus over Roman taxation (22.15-22), between the Sadducees and Jesus over belief in resurrection (22.23-33), between a Pharisee and Jesus over the greatest commandment (22.34-40), and between Jesus and the Pharisees over Davidic sonship (22.41-46) present Jesus as victorious in argument.

First Confrontation: 21.23–22.1-14
Authority: 21.23-27.[1] Jesus' arrival in the temple and the fact that he was teaching there are noted. The first confrontation is then related. It is introduced by the chief priests and elders of the people going to him and saying, 'By what authority do you do these things, and who gave you this authority?' In the context, 'these things' could refer both to Jesus' teaching and to his actions on the previous day. Jesus' reply begins with a counter-question and a promise that he would reply if they did: 'The baptism of John, whence was it? From heaven or from human beings?' This leads to a report of a discussion among the chief priests and elders: 'If we say from heaven, he will say to us, why did you not believe him? And if we say from human beings, we fear the crowd, for all hold John as a prophet'. The contents of the discussion assume that the chief priests and elders had been unimpressed by John's ministry and implies that they had been wrong in their assessment (see 11.9-11). It also assumes that the crowd had recognized John as a prophet (see 11.9), in spite of a contrary impression created by 11.16-19, and it interprets the behaviour of the chief priests and elders as cowardly. Their reply, 'We do not know', allows Jesus' refusal to tell them by what authority he acted. Hence the story does not state what Jesus' authority was, but implies that it came from God, like John's, and that the Jewish leaders were wrong to oppose them.

Parable of the Two Sons: 21.28-32.[2] Jesus' refusal to answer the question leads immediately into his recounting a provocative parable. It opens with Jesus' challenge, 'What do you think?' The simple story of the two sons, one of whom refused his father's request to work in the vineyard, but who, later, relented and obeyed, while the other son accepted the request but did not obey it, gains its point from the context. Jesus was clearly condemning the chief priests and elders to whom the parable was addressed (21.23) as disobedient sons, sent to work in their father's vineyard (God's Israel) but failing to do so. These leaders were forced to answer Jesus' question, 'Which of the two did the will of the father?' with the reply, 'The first', a person with whom they could not identify. Jesus' next statement identifies the first son: 'Truly I say to you, tax collectors and prostitutes will go before you into the kingdom of God. For John came to you in the way of justice [see 3.15], and you did not believe him [see 3.7; 21.25], but tax collectors and prostitutes believed him. And when you saw [that], you did

1   See Mk 11.27-33; Lk. 20.1-8.
2   Cf. Lk. 7.29-30.

not later repent and believe him'. Tax collectors and prostitutes represent archetypal sinners. They had not specifically been mentioned as responding to John's preaching in the account in ch. 3, where only a general reference to people from Jerusalem, Judaea and the region of the Jordan is found (3.5). Rather, Jesus' ministry had been depicted attracting tax collectors and sinners (9.1-13). Now readers have to include tax collectors and prostitutes among the crowds who believed that John was a prophet. In spite of the leaders' refusal to answer the question about John's authority, then, an implied answer (from God) was used against them. In the narrative, the sweeping condemnation left them with no retort.

In the historical context of the time, however, the chief priests and elders could justifiably have pointed to their faithful adherence to God's will in safeguarding both the temple service required by Scripture and the security of the people against Roman oppression. Nothing of this, however, is allowed to intrude into the narrative, which caricatures Jewish leadership in order to provide a portrait which is antithetical to that of Jesus.

Parable of the Vineyard and the Tenants: 21.33-46.[1] Jesus' condemnation continued: 'Hear another parable'. The parabolic situation described in which the householder planted a vineyard, surrounded it with a fence (to keep out animals; Ps. 80.12-13), built a tower (for watchmen), let it out to farmers and went away from home, recalls the opening of Isaiah's song of the vineyard (Isa. 5.1-2). But the parable develops the theme of God's relations with Israel in criticism of chief priests and elders, who are represented by the farmers. The parable is clearly allegorical, referring to God's relations with Israel's leaders, rather than an accurate depiction of relations between an absentee landlord and his tenants in first-century Palestine. Hence, when the time for fruit came near (the time when God would judge his people's fruitfulness; contrast Mark and Luke), he (God) sent his servants (prophets) to the farmers (chief priests and elders and their predecessors) to receive his fruit (good works: 7.15-20; 12.33-37). The farmers, however, beat one servant, killed another and stoned another (Mark and Luke treat the fate of each servant separately). According to Scripture, Moses was in danger of being stoned, Elijah had to flee for his life, Jeremiah was persecuted, and, according to the second-century Jewish tradition in the *Ascension of Isaiah*, Isaiah was killed in the reign of Manasseh. These are taken to typify the fate of a prophet. Again the householder sent even more servants, but the farmers treated them likewise. The repetition implies God's forbearance. But afterwards, he sent his son to them, saying, 'They will respect my son' (that is, Jesus, the Christ, who was

1   See Mk 12.1-12; Lk. 20.9-19.

obedient and hence a true son of God). But the farmers saw the son and said, 'This is the heir. Come, let us kill him and let us have his inheritance'. And they took him and cast him out of the vineyard and killed him. This is the fate which the narrative will shortly describe happening to Jesus and which it had already described Jesus' predicting to his disciples. Readers are in a position, therefore, to understand the reference, and are encouraged to blame Jewish leaders, not Romans, for Jesus' execution. But the parable does not end there. It looks forward to the lord of the vineyard's advent and asks the question, 'When, therefore, the lord of the vineyard comes, what will he do to those farmers?' In this way, the chief priests and elders are led to supply the answer, 'He will kill the wicked people and will hand the vineyard to other farmers, who will repay him the fruits in their season' (see Ps. 1.3 and contrast Mark and Luke). The parable tells an allegorical story of God's rejection of the Jewish leadership and his handing it over to other leaders, Jesus' followers, who would repay God with good works.

The narrative continues with Jesus' response, 'Have you never read the Scriptures, the stone which the builder rejected, this became the head of the corner; this happens from the Lord and it is wonderful in our eyes?' (Septuagint of Ps. 118.22-23). The image has changed from vineyard to building and from son to cornerstone. Finally, the parable's insights are applied to Jesus' opponents: 'On account of this, I tell you, the kingdom of God will be taken from you and will be given to a people which bears its fruit'. 'The kingdom of God' refers to God's present rule in the world. The parable condemns Jewish leaders for forfeiting God's present kingdom and sees Jesus' followers as those who inherited it (contrast Mark and Luke. Mt. 24.44, found in some manuscripts seems to have been added on the basis of Lk. 20.18).

The reaction of those who heard the condemnations is noted: 'And the chief priests and Pharisees who heard his parables knew that he spoke about them [so confirming the readers' understanding]. And they sought to arrest him but feared the crowds, since they were holding him to be a prophet'. Their reaction to Jesus is described in parallel terms to those used earlier in connection with John (21.26).

Parable of the Marriage Feast: 22.1-14.[1] Another parable completes the condemnation. As often in ch. 13, this parable opens with, 'The kingdom of heaven may be likened to...' Readers can expect to learn something about the kingdom of heaven from the parable (the Lukan parable is different in many particulars and has a different setting and point). Like the last parable, this one is allegorical, and the allegorical significance militates against the story's realism. The king (God) prepared a wedding feast for his son (Jesus), and sent his servants (prophets) to

1   See Lk. 14.15-24.

call those who had been invited to the wedding, and they (the Jewish leaders) would not come. He sent other servants (more prophets) to persuade them: 'Behold, I have prepared my breakfast, my bulls and fatted calves are slain, and everything is ready. Come into the wedding'. The invitation highlights both God's forbearance and the delights that he had prepared for his guests. But, amazingly, those invited took no notice and went away, one to his own field, another to his shop. Worse, the rest laid hold of the servants, treated them insolently and killed them. At this, the king was angry and sent his troops to kill those murderers and to set their city on fire (see Isa. 5.24-25). This depiction of the destruction of Jerusalem as God's punishment for the obduracy of the Jewish leadership could refer either to its destruction by the Babylonians in the sixth century BCE or to its destruction by the Romans in 70 CE or to both. The whole series of events is assumed to have happened while the prepared feast awaited the arrival of the guests. The parable continues, 'Then he said to his servants, the feast is ready and those who were invited were unworthy. Go, therefore, by way of the main road [out of town] and whomever you find invite to the wedding. And those servants went out into the roads and gathered all whom they found, both evil and good. And the wedding feast was filled by those who reclined at table.' 'Those who were unworthy' represent the Jewish leadership. Those subsequently invited could represent post-exilic Jews, or Jews and Gentiles who joined the church. The parable does not end here, however, but continues with an explanation of what happened to the 'evil' who had come to the wedding with the 'good' (contrast Luke): 'When the king entered and looked at those who were reclining, he saw there a man who was not wearing a wedding garment, and said to him, friend, how did you enter without a wedding garment? And he was silenced. Then the king said to his helpers [angels], bind his feet and hands and throw him into outer darkness'. The scene represents God's final judgment, the man without the wedding garment the wicked who were ill prepared (cf. 7.21-23), the wedding feast the kingdom of heaven which the good would enjoy, and outer darkness Gehenna or Hades. The parable is concluded by a favourite Matthaean description, 'there will be weeping and gnashing of teeth', and by a warning, 'for many are called but few are chosen' (see 7.13-14).

In the context of the narrative, the parable warned the chief priests and Pharisees about exclusion from the eschatological kingdom which their rejection of God's invitation would bring. The parable depicts them as people who were more concerned with their own affairs than with God's. But readers and listeners, although they are encouraged by the parable to accept God's invitation, are also warned about the result of their failures (cf. 7.21).

In summary, the Matthaean Jesus' three parables condemned the

Jewish leadership for its failure to respond to John the Baptist's teaching, for its failure to repay God with Jewish good works which its leadership should have engendered, and for its failure to accept God's repeated invitations to his eschatological kingdom. In this way, its opposition to Jesus, God's agent, is construed as opposition to God and his purpose. Christians, unfortunately, have found little difficulty through the centuries in applying the criticisms to church leaders.

Second Confrontation: Paying Taxes to Caesar: 22.15-22[1]

The narrative depicts Pharisees' withdrawing to take counsel so that they might trap Jesus in his speech. The negative description reinforces readers' understanding that Pharisees were vicious enemies of Jesus. There follows a series of stories in which three awkward questions were addressed to Jesus. These represent the leaders' counter-attacks. The contest, however, is represented as unequal; Jesus' parables had provoked the leaders to self-condemnation or withdrawal, whereas the awkward questions, in spite of their ingenuity, would not silence Jesus.

The first of the questions is said to come from disciples of the Pharisees (contrast Mark and Luke) and the Herodians, that is, supporters of Herod the Great's descendants, whose presence was appropriate to the topic. Their question is prefaced by an expression of respect for Jesus, which readers had been led to endorse: 'Teacher, we know that you are true and that you teach the way of God in truth, for you have no regard for human position'. But this leads immediately to a question which would test Jesus' political loyalty: 'Tell us therefore what you think. Is it lawful to give poll-tax to Caesar or not?' Paying tax to the Roman emperor's representatives expressed Israel's subjugation and could be construed as disloyalty to the God of Israel. Jesus is said to have been aware of their evil intent and his reply includes an unmasking: 'Why do you test me, dissemblers?' He demands, 'Show me the coin for the poll-tax'. When they bring a denarion (a silver Roman coin), he asks, 'Whose likeness and inscription is this?' which forces the reply, 'Caesar's'. Jesus' final admonition, 'Therefore repay to Caesar the things that are Caesar's and to God the things that are God's' met with their amazement and withdrawal.

Jesus' reply allowed him to escape a charge of disloyalty to Rome without his actually advocating loyalty, but it highlights the problem rather than providing a solution because it defines neither 'the things that are Caesar's' nor 'the things that are God's', and nor does it consider circumstances in which they clash. Even if a coin bearing Caesar's image and inscription was in some sense Caesar's, the narrative teaches that the whole world is God's. It is not clear what readers were to make of this teaching. Perhaps the story discouraged open disloyalty to Rome,

1   See Mk 12.13-17; Lk. 20.20-26.

which a refusal to pay taxes would have demonstrated. Nevertheless, teaching in the rest of the narrative encourages dedication to God even in circumstances in which martyrdom was inevitable.

Readers who live in modern Western societies have less cause to resent paying taxes because they have some power in electing and dismissing a government and in influencing its policies. Even so, there is still room to oppose injustices, both in the systems of taxation and in the ways in which public money is used. If opposition takes the form of refusal to pay a tax, this may result in imprisonment. By contrast, in first-century societies within the Roman empire, people who wanted to avoid taxation had to become outlaws living on the fringes of society, and anyone who incited others to refuse payment would have been executed. The Gospel according to Matthew never suggests that followers of Jesus should cut themselves off from the rest of society by forming a separate clique without contact with the rest of the world.

Third Confrontation: The Sadducean Attempt to Ridicule Belief in Resurrection: 22.23-33[1]

With the failure of the attempt at entrapment, the narrative introduces the Sadducees to take their turn in questioning Jesus. They are described as people who did not believe in the resurrection. Jewish sources provide little information about Sadducean belief because, after the destruction of the temple in 70 CE and the later failure of the Bar Kochba Revolt in 135 CE, they ceased to play a prominent role in Jewish life. But Josephus provides a short summary of Sadducean beliefs for his Greek readers:

> The Sadducees, the second of the orders, do away with fate alto-gether, and remove God beyond not merely the commission but the very sight of evil. They maintain that man has the free choice of good and evil, and that it rests with each man's will whether he follows the one or the other. As for the persistence of the soul after death, penalties in the underworld, and rewards, they will have none of them (*War* 2.164-165. See also *Ant.* 18.6).

Later, in *Ant.* 13.297, he notes that,

> [Sadducees] hold that only those regulations should be considered valid which were written down [in Scripture], and that those which have been handed down by former generations need not be observed.

In the first century CE, the exact extent of Jewish Scriptures was not fixed. In particular, the book of Daniel, which unambiguously refers to resurrection from the dead (12.2-3), eventually found a place only in the third section of Jewish Scriptures, among the writings, not in the

---

1   See Mk 12.18-27; Lk. 20.27-40.

second section, among the prophets, as in Christian bibles. From Josephus' account of Sadducean belief, it appears that Sadducees did not accept Daniel as Scripture.

In the Matthaean narrative, the Sadducean challenge begins by referring to Moses' command that, if a man died without children, his brother should marry the wife and should raise up children for his dead brother (an allusion to Gen. 38.8 and Deut. 25.5-6). The challenge goes on to cite the case of seven brothers, the first of whom married a woman but died without children, so that she became the wife of the second brother, who died without children, and so on, through the seven brothers, until all of them and the wife were dead. In this context, the question is posed, 'At the resurrection, therefore, to which of the seven brothers will she be wife, for they all had her?' In effect, the case and the question scoff at belief in resurrection. Again, Jesus' reply silenced the Sadducees and astonished the crowd (22.33-34): 'You are straying, knowing neither the Scriptures nor the power of God. For at the resurrection they neither marry nor are given in marriage, but are like the angels in heaven. And about the resurrection of the dead, did you not read what was spoken by God, saying, I am the God of Abraham and the God of Isaac and the God of Jacob [Exod. 3.6, with minor variations from the Septuagint]. He is not the God of the dead but of the living'.

Jesus is not depicted trying to justify his assertion by quoting Daniel or any other part of Scripture which could be interpreted as referring directly to the resurrection of the dead. Instead the quotation comes from the Torah, that part of Scripture whose authority no Jew would have disputed. The quotation represents God's self-identification to Moses: he is the God of the patriarchs, Abraham, Isaac and Jacob. Jesus' next statement interprets the self-identification: 'He is not the God of the dead but of the living'. The implication seems to be not that the patri-archs were still alive but that, as the God of the living, God's power could raise the patriarchs from the dead. But no further questions about this difficult theological topic are attributed to the Sadducees.

The narrative will give more substance to belief in resurrection in its final chapter, which will relate the disappearance of Jesus' corpse from the tomb and his resurrection from the dead. An intimation of God's power to give life had already been provided by the earlier story of the dead girl's restoration to life (9.18-26), but that had been a miracle of resuscitation, a restoration back to an ordinary mortal existence that would end in another death. Jesus' reply to the Sadducean question makes it clear that resurrection would involve transformation as well as restoration to life: 'They neither marry nor are given in marriage, but are like the angels in heaven'. Such views are expressed in Jewish apoca-lyptic literature from the second century BCE to the second century CE, in which the resurrected righteous are depicted living in peace for ever and ever, their ordinary mortal lives transformed into immortal lives of glory. Two images are commonly used to intimate this transformation. Dan. 12.2, and other texts influenced by that work, liken the eternal life of the righteous to that of the stars:

> And many of those who sleep in the dust of the earth shall awake, some to everlasting life, and some to everlasting contempt. And those who are wise shall shine like the brightness of the firmament, and those who turn many to righteousness, like the stars for ever and ever (see also *1 En.* 104.2).

The stars were bodily creations which were thought to go on existing for ever, and as supposed sources of light they provided an effective image of the resurrected righteous. But other apocalyptic works compare the life of the resurrected to that of angels. Angels are described as somewhat like human beings, but more glorious (e.g. Dan. 3.25; 8.15-17; 9.21; 10.5-6, 12-21), and, as created beings who exist for ever, they had no need to beget children (e.g. *1 En.* 62.13-16; *2 Bar.* 51.5). *2 Bar.* 51.10 combines the images of angels and stars:

> For they [the righteous] will live in the heights of that world [that is, the world to come] and they will be like the angels and be equal to the stars (see also *1 En.* 104.2, 4).

The Matthaean Jesus took over this imagery. It is not clear that, historically, Sadducees would have been impressed by it, since they did not accept the Jewish writings concerned as authoritative.

Fourth Confrontation: Which Command is the Greatest? 22.34-40[1]

This section is linked to the preceding one by the statement, 'When the Pharisees heard that he had silenced the Sadducees, they gathered together'. Their antagonism is then made known to the readers in the introduction to their question: 'And one of them asked, testing him' (contrast Mark's introduction and ending). The question then tests both Jesus' knowledge and his insight: 'Teacher, which commandment in the law is the greatest?' Since all of the commandments were understood to be God's, they all voiced God's purpose. Jesus' reply, 'You shall love the Lord your God with your whole heart and with your whole life and with your whole understanding; this is the greatest and first commandment. And the second is like it, you shall love your neighbour as yourself. On these two commandments hang the whole law and the prophets', echoes Deut. 6.5 and quotes Lev. 19.18. First-century Jews commonly summarized the twin aspects of the law as human piety towards God and love of one another (e.g. Philo, *Spec. Leg.* 2.63; *Rer. Div. Her.* 168-73; Josephus, *Ant.* 9.16; 10.50; 18.117; *Apion* 2.146, 291), and

---

1   See Mk 12.28-34; Lk. 10.25-28.

Josephus explained the relationship between the two:

> For Moses did not make religion a department of virtue, but the various virtues—I mean justice, temperance, fortitude, and mutual harmony in all things between members of the community—departments of religion. Religion governs all our actions and occupations and speech (*Apion* 2.171).

Moreover, all Jews regularly recalled Deut. 6.4-9 (the 'Shema') morning and evening (*m. Ber.* 1.1-3; Josephus, *Ant.* 4.212-13). In other words, Jesus' answer is just the kind of answer with which no Jew would have found fault, and, in the narrative, no further question is put to him.[1] By implication, then, Jesus had silenced both the Sadducees and the Pharisees, who were taken to be the whole of Jewish leadership (e.g. 3.7; 16.1, 6, 11, 12).

Fifth Confrontation: Why does David Call his Son Lord? 22.41-46[2]

Opponents' silence allowed Jesus to put a question to the Pharisees: 'While the Pharisees gathered together, Jesus asked them a question' (contrast the introduction and conclusion in Mark). The question concerns the descent of the Christ: 'What do you think about the Christ? Whose son is he?' They, of course, replied, 'David's' (contrast Mark and Luke). But Jesus' next statement alludes to Ps. 110.1 and Ps. 8.6, attributed to David, as part of a further question: 'How is it then that David, inspired by the spirit, called him lord, saying, the Lord [God] said to my lord [the Christ], sit at my right, until I put your enemies under your feet? If David therefore called him lord, how is he his son?' Fathers did not normally address their sons as lord or master, rather the reverse. The narrative ends by noting, 'And no one was able to answer him a word nor did anyone any longer dare question him from that day'.

But readers of the narrative had been prepared from its beginning to answer this question. Jesus is understood to be the Christ, and the messianic descendant of David (1.1–2.12; 9.27; 12.23; 15.22; 20.30-31; 21.9, 15), yet Jesus' humility made him a better messianic agent of God than David was. Hence it was appropriate for David to call Jesus, the Christ, his successor, 'lord'.

1   See Sanders, *Jewish Law*, pp. 68-72, 90.
2   See Mk 12.35-37; Lk. 20.41-44.

Matthew 23.1-39: Jesus' Discourse of Criticisms and Woes

The narrative depiction of Jesus' success in argument leads into a further discourse, first addressed to the crowds and his disciples (23.1-12), but then issuing in a series of seven prophetic woes addressed to scribes and Pharisees (23.13-36, without parallel in Mark). The narrative had linked scribes and Pharisees earlier (12.38; 15.1) and here associates them again (contrast Mark and Luke). Historically, the two groups were not identical. The Pharisees were mainly lay people, though some priests seem to have belonged, who were concerned about obeying the commandments, loving God and fellow human beings. The scribes were lay people but were particularly learned in the law and its interpretation, and so could teach others. Not all scribes were Pharisees and not all Pharisees were scribes.

Criticisms: 23.1-12[1]
The teaching addressed to crowds and disciples begins by according scribes and Pharisees authority: 'The scribes and Pharisees have taken their place on Moses' seat. Therefore do and keep whatever they tell you' (no parallel in Mark and Luke). In other words, insofar as the scribes and Pharisees taught what Moses taught in the law, their teaching was to be followed. It would agree with that of the Matthaean Jesus (e.g. 5.17; 22.34-40). But this instruction is immediately followed by a description of scribes and Pharisees as dissemblers: 'But do not do as they do; for they teach but do not practise' (no parallels in Mark and Luke). This is one meaning of 'dissembler' which the teaching goes on to illustrate. 'They bind heavy burdens and put them on people's shoulders, but they themselves do not want to move them with their finger. They do all their deeds to be seen by people, for they make their phylacteries broad [for phylacteries see Exod. 13.9, 16; Deut. 6.8] and their tassels long [for tassels see Num. 15.38; Deut. 22.12; and see the references to people's touching the tassels of Jesus' garment in Mt. 9.20; 14.36. No parallel to Mt. 23.5 in Mark and Luke], and they love the chief places at suppers and the first seat in the synagogues and greetings in the market place and to be called rabbi [my master] by people' (cf. 6.1-16; 7.15-23). The characterization of their burden as heavy is the opposite of the characterization of Jesus' burden as light (11.28-30). Their behaviour to others is described as unmerciful. The 'heavy burdens' are defined by what follows: their courting honour from other people. And this makes sense as the opposite of the humility which the Gospel attributes to Jesus and which it seeks to encourage among his followers

---

1   See Mk 12.38-40; Lk. 20.45-47.

(e.g. 20.20-28). The accusations take for granted that scribes and Pharisees belonged to an alien and despised religious group, and open the way for Jesus' positive teaching: 'But you shall not be called rabbi, for you have one teacher and you are all brothers. And none of you shall be called father on earth, for you have one heavenly Father. Neither be called masters, for you have one master, the Christ [no parallel in Mark and Luke]. And the greatest among you shall be your servant. And whoever exalts himself will be humbled, and whoever humbles himself will be exalted' (see Lk. 14.11). This teaching provides further concrete examples to illustrate the humility and service which earlier teaching had encouraged followers to emulate. It recognizes the Christ as master, as the previous section had depicted David's acknowledgment of his lordship, yet even the master exemplified the humble life of a servant (11.29; 20.28; 23.12). It is a pity that 'you are all brothers' does not include 'sisters'.

That the Matthaean accusations against scribes and Pharisees are unfair caricatures is clear from their own writings. Jews in the first century who pondered the teachings of their sacred Scriptures gained the same insights that Christians did. The danger of hypocrisy which preached and did not practise was well recognized. For example, Simeon, the first century CE scribe, is quoted in *m. Ab.* 1.17: 'Not the expounding of the law is the chief thing but the doing of it'. And the need for whole-hearted dedication to God was emphasized: 'Be not like slaves that minister to the master for the sake of receiving a bounty, but be like slaves that minister to the master not for the sake of receiving a bounty; and let the fear of heaven be with you' (Simon the Just, third century BCE, *m. Ab.* 1.3). Moreover, they had learnt through bitter experience that the rich and powerful who were honoured by society were not to be trusted. They could distinguish the righteous from the powerful and accord respect to the former. In first-century Jewish society, unlike first-century Roman society, influence could be exercised by an economically humble person who was honoured for his just life and teaching. For example, the advice of the first-century BCE scribe, Shemaiah, is quoted in *m. Ab.* 1.10: 'Love labour and hate mastery and seek not acquaintance with the ruling power'. In the historical context of first-century Palestine, therefore, the Matthaean Jesus' positive teaching reflects something of the egalitarian ethos of Pharisaic and scribal teaching. Some forms of later church institutions, on the other hand, reflect the ethos of those criticized in the narrative as hypocrites. Church institutions have usually mirrored the power structures of the societies in which they have functioned. But the teachings of Scripture, including those in the First Gospel, have also inspired Christians to criticize and reform both their own institutions and the institutions of the wider societies to which they have belonged. Western democracy owes as much to Jewish and Christian Scriptures as it does to classical Greek literature.

Seven Woes Against Hypocrites: 23.13-36[1]

The particular examples of scribal and Pharisaic hypocrisy in the seven woes are equally polemical. The teaching attributed to the scribes and Pharisees in the third woe (23.16-18) is contradicted by Jewish sources. The criticism in the fourth woe (23.23), that they tithed small produce while neglecting the weightier matters of the law, justice, mercy and faith, and that in the fifth and sixth woes, that they were concerned with outward purity while being extortionate and lawless (23.25, 27), are without warrant. Moreover, the epithets used of them, 'sons of Gehenna', 'blind guides', 'blind fools', 'snakes', a 'brood of serpents', provide examples of what Jesus had forbidden in the Sermon on the Mount (5.22). Indeed, the whole tenor of the chapter provides a counter-example to earlier teaching about reconciliation and generosity. Paul, in his epistle to the Romans, expresses his grief at the rejection of Jesus' messiahship by so many of his Jewish contemporaries and looks forward to their eventual acceptance of Jesus (Romans 9–11). The Gospel according to Matthew caricatures Jewish piety in order to depict and illustrate the corrupting influence of hypocrisy. Modern Christians have to reject and regret the caricature and read the chapter as a discourse against the kind of hypocrisy to which the positive teaching of the Gospel was prone.

Each of Jesus' prophetic woes (cf. Isa. 5.8-23; Zech. 11.17; Jer. 23.1) is directly addressed to the scribes and Pharisees of the narrative as hypocrites, and then goes on to illustrate the hypocrisy. The first criticizes them as follows: 'Because you shut the kingdom of heaven against people, for you are neither entering it nor allowing those who are entering it to go in' (cf. Lk. 11.52). From the perspective of the narrative, no more stringent criticism could have been made. According to the Gospel, God was about to transform the world into the kingdom of heaven but hypocrites were excluding both themselves and others (cf. 21.33-41). By contrast, the narrative had earlier assigned to Peter and the other disciples the role of opening the kingdom to others (16.19; 18.18), and at the end of the narrative they will be told to open it to Gentiles (28.19-20). (Mt. 23.14, which appears in some manuscripts, is a scribal interpolation from Mk 12.40; Lk. 20.47.)

The second woe criticizes them because they are 'crossing sea and land to make one convert, and when it happens, you make him twice as much a son of Gehenna as yourselves' (no parallel in Luke). The criticism takes for granted the missionary efforts of scribes and Pharisees towards Gentiles, but, as hypocrites, their very zeal and success

1   See Lk. 11.37-52.

becomes a source of further condemnation.

The third woe (no parallel in Luke) varies the introductory formula to, 'Woe to you, blind guides, who say...' It picks up the description of Pharisees from 15.14. Their teaching is then quoted: 'Whoever swears by the temple, it is nothing. But whoever swears by the gold in the temple, it is binding'. Jesus' comments on this teaching are then introduced with, 'Fools and blind people', and his criticism is presented as a question which ridicules the teaching: 'For which is greater, the gold or the temple which sanctifies the gold?' The same point is made again: 'And whoever swears by the altar, it is nothing; but whoever swears by the gift upon it, it is binding. Blind people, for which is greater, the gift or the altar which sanctifies the gift?' This time inferences are drawn: 'Therefore, he who swears by the altar swears by it and by everything upon it; and he who swears by the temple swears by it and by everything housed in it; and he who swears by heaven swears by the throne of God and by him who sits upon it'.

In first-century Palestine, it was the poor who might find that only an oath could secure a loan at times of severe distress, because they could offer no other forms of security. But if their situation did not improve and they could not repay the loan as promised, they would be in difficulties not only with their neighbours but with God. Hence, it was not unreasonable for poor people to swear oaths by something less sacred than the name of God or the temple, but still sufficiently impressive to guarantee the loan. Earlier, in the Sermon on the Mount, after Jesus' prohibition of swearing, further teaching had met the difficulty by insisting that others should give, not lend, to those in need (5.33-37, 42). Moreover, what evidence we have from scribal discussions about the practice of substituting words in vows and oaths suggests that it was as much discouraged by scribes as it was by the Matthaean Jesus (see *m. Ned.* 1.1-3). The teaching in Mt. 23.16 and 18, therefore, seems to be unjustly attributed to scribes and Pharisees.

The fourth woe returns to the usual introductory formula. The criticism accuses them of tithing small produce—mint, dill and cumin— but neglecting the weightier matters of the law, justice, mercy and faith (cf. Mic. 6.8). The law required that people should give a tenth of their produce as tithes for the support of the priests, the Levites, the city of Jerusalem and the poor (Lev. 27.30-32; Num. 18.21-32; Deut. 14.22-29). Perhaps the rhetoric suggests that most people did not include herbs among produce to be tithed since they are not mentioned in the law.[1] The Matthaean teaching does not advocate the abolition of tithing, even tithing herbs, but says, 'these you ought to have done [justice, mercy and faith] while not neglecting the others' (tithing produce including herbs). Tithing, after all, was one of many expressions of justice, mercy

1   See Sanders, *Jewish Law*, pp. 43-48.

and faith. The rhetoric and the context in which it occurs, however, suggest that living a humble and even more generous life was to be understood as a better expression of justice, mercy and faith (e.g. 23.8-11; 19.16-30; 5.3-48). A hyperbolic metaphor ridicules those who neglect these weightier expressions: 'Blind guides who strain out a gnat and swallow a camel' (no parallel in Luke). We are familiar with a tendency to be punctilious over small matters while neglecting centrally important religious and social issues. But there is no evidence that scribes and Pharisees encouraged such a tendency and much to the contrary. For example, Simon the Just is quoted as follows: 'By three things is the world sustained: by the law, by the temple and by deeds of loving-kindness' (*m. Ab.* 1.2). Or Jose ben Johanan (second century BCE) is quoted as follows: 'Let your house be opened wide and let the needy be members of your household' (*m. Ab.* 1.5). Moreover, neither Matthaean teaching nor scribal teaching made the mistake of suggesting that 'lighter' matters should be neglected. The Matthaean text includes 'while not neglecting the other' and Judah the Patriarch, to whom the compilation of the Mishnah is attributed, taught: 'Be heedful of a light precept as of a weighty one' (*m. Ab.* 2.1). We are equally familiar with a tendency to pursue important issues to the neglect of minor ones.

The fifth woe has the usual introductory formula. Hypocrites are criticized for cleansing the outside of the cup or dish, while inside they are full of extortion and rapacity. The first part of the statement is to be taken literally. People did cleanse the outside and the inside of cups and dishes to remove impurity (Lev. 11.31-32). But the second part is figurative. The food we expect them to contain is replaced by the unjust method of acquiring the food, extortion and rapacity. Extortion is particularly condemned in the law, according to which nothing should be lent to brothers at interest (Deut. 23.19). This law has always been taken seriously in Judaism and Islam, but has been largely ignored in Christianity. The prophetic books also condemn extortion (e.g. Isa. 3.14-15; Amos 5.11; 8.4-6). Once again, however, the teaching does not abrogate the requirement to cleanse cups and dishes, but continues: 'You [singular] blind Pharisee; first cleanse the inside of the cup [of examples of extortion and rapacity] so that its outside may also be clean' (contrast Lk. 11.41). Again there is no evidence that first-century scribes and Pharisees were rapacious extortioners.

The sixth woe, with the same introductory formula, likens hypocrites to whitewashed tombs, which appear beautiful outside, but inside are full of dead people's bones and every uncleanness. Contact with the dead caused the most serious form of impurity, which required a seven-day ritual for its removal when people wanted to enter the sacred temple (Numbers 19). Tombs were whitewashed not to increase their beauty but to warn people of the danger. Likening people to whitewashed tombs, therefore, was an even more powerful image of hypocrisy in the first century than it is today in Western societies. The application of the metaphor 'so you also appear to people as outwardly just, but inside you are full of hypocrisy and lawlessness' doubles the impact of the message. Once more, however, there is no evidence that scribes and Pharisees were 'lawless'; quite the contrary, as the Mishnah bears witness.

The final woe, with the same introductory formula, sees the hypocritical potential in even pious activities: 'You build the tombs of the prophets and adorn the sepulchres of the just, and you say, if we had lived in the days of our fathers, we would not have shared in the blood of the prophets', that is, taken part in their murders (cf. Lk. 11.47-48 and contrast Lk. 11.44). Honouring those who had been unjustly killed in the past could be thought to discourage a repetition of injustice, but the Matthaean teaching draws the opposite inference: 'So you bear witness to yourselves that you are sons of those who killed the prophets. And you, fill up the measure of your fathers'. The rhetoric assumes the truth of the saying 'like father, like son'. A warning follows in the form of a rhetorical question: 'Snakes, you brood of serpents, how will you flee from the judgment of Gehenna?' (see the Baptist's preaching in Mt. 3.7 and Jesus' in 12.34). The image of snakes as deceivers seems to derive from the story in Genesis 3. The threat of Gehenna implies that the insidious nature of hypocrisy would provide no cover at the final judgment. Even before the final judgment, however, their deeds would declare their sonship, because they would persecute Jesus' followers: 'On account of this, behold I am sending you [contrast Lk. 11.49] prophets and wise people and scribes [Jesus' disciples had been depicted as prophets: 5.11-12; 10.5-25; wise people, 10.16; and scribes, 13.52], some you will kill and crucify and flog in your synagogues and pursue from city to city' (see 10.17, 23). The text assumes that scribes and Pharisees would be responsible for persecuting Christian missionaries.

What evidence is there that this happened during the early years of the Christian movement? Paul admits that he had persecuted Jesus' followers before his call (Gal. 1.13; 1 Cor. 15.9), but Acts indicates that his authority came from the high priest (Acts 9.1-2). Paul himself, however, was a Pharisee (Phil. 3.5). Could this fact have been known to the writers and readers of the Gospel? If so, perhaps the accusations against scribes and Pharisees in Matthew 23 represent a generalization of that single instance. Later, Paul mentions that he had been flogged in synagogues (2 Cor. 11.24), but Pharisees did not run synagogues in the first two centuries CE. Acts depicts missionaries driven from cities by Jewish opponents (Acts 8.1; 14.5-6), but does not hold scribes and Pharisees responsible. Acts also describes the martyrdom of Stephen, but that incident is best understood as a mob's stoning of a man who was thought to have denigrated the temple (Acts 7.54-60). Acts attributes responsibility for the execution of James, son of Zebedee, to Herod

Agrippa (Acts 12.2). Josephus's account of the martyrdom of James, the brother of Jesus, and other Christians in Jerusalem attributes the responsibility to the high priest Ananus, and points out that other Jews complained to the authorities, so that Ananus was deposed (*Ant.* 20.200-203). From the evidence we have, therefore, it appears that some Christian missionaries suffered persecution at the hands of some Jews, but the only Pharisee involved in these persecutions was Paul, whose authority came from the high priest. Acts even depicts Pharisees as defenders of Christians (Acts 5.33-39; 23.6-9). The accusations against all scribes and Pharisees in Mt. 23.29-36, therefore, are not justified by the evidence available.

Curiously, Mt. 23.34 includes a reference to crucifixion, a form of execution which only Romans could inflict in the first-century Graeco-Roman world. Probably it is mentioned in this list because Jesus was crucified and his disciples were to follow him in taking up their cross (16.24). Perhaps the original readers of the narrative knew about the emperor Nero's persecution of Christians in Rome, when they were blamed for the fire in 64 CE, and were executed in hideous ways, including crucifixion (Tacitus, *Annals* 15.44.2-8).

The condemnation concludes, 'So all the just blood poured out upon the earth shall come upon you, from the blood of Abel [Gen. 4.8-10] to the blood of Zechariah the son of Barachiah, whom you killed between the sanctuary and the altar. Truly I say to you all these things will come upon this generation' (cf. Lk. 11.51). 'The blood of Zechariah' seems to refer to the Zechariah who was stoned (2 Chron. 24.2-23), but he is identified with the prophet Zechariah the son of Barachiah (Zech. 1.1). The expression 'blood upon you' refers to the guilt of shedding innocent blood, a guilt which God would punish (see later 27.25; and see Lev. 20.9; Deut. 21.8-9; 22.8). The prophesy presupposes that violence issues in violence, that a people that behaves violently towards others will suffer violence. Perhaps the prophecy refers to the Jewish defeat in the war against Rome in 66–74 CE (see 23.37-39). Tactfully, the narrative says nothing about the violence of the Roman empire, gained by military conquest and sustained by military occupation and slavery.

Readers of this chapter are left in no doubt that hypocrisy separates people from the God to whom they pretend to be dedicated. The narrative's positive teaching about devotion to God in purity of heart is the opposite of hypocritical devotion, which completely undermines it. This chapter, addressed in the story to scribes and Pharisees, is addressed in the narrative to Christian readers, and warns them against a piety which is selfserving and which issues in acts of violence against other people.

The narrative had earlier sought to encourage readers to express in their lives a justice which imitated God's generosity, even towards enemies and persecutors (5.43-48), yet in this chapter it is unjust in its caricature of scribes and Pharisees. Only in recent years, however, have people come to realize that justice includes a just appreciation of alien religious traditions. Polemical caricatures always highlight what is considered to be worse in other traditions and set it against what is thought best in the tradition advocated. Moreover, Christians know that in their own history the Gospel's caricature has been used as an excuse to denigrate and persecute Jews, actions which express the hypocrisy this chapter condemns.

Jesus' Lament over Jerusalem: 23.37-39[1]

The tone of the narrative changes from that of withering denunciation to that of regret with the account of Jesus' lament over Jerusalem. Jerusalem is still depicted negatively, as the city that killed the prophets and stoned those who had been sent to it (from God), but now it is made clear that Jesus, God's agent, had wanted its inhabitants to embrace a different destiny: 'How often did I want to gather your children, as a hen gathers her chicks under her wings'. This is the only metaphor in the Gospel which draws attention to a mother's rather than a father's care for children. But the desire had not met with an appropriate response: 'And you would not'. An abrupt change of image follows: 'Behold your house is left to you desolate [cf. Jer. 22.5]. For I say to you, from now on you will not see me until you say, blessed is he who comes in the name of the Lord' (see Ps. 118.26). This lament is placed earlier in the Lukan narrative (13.34-35) so that it is fulfilled at Jesus' entry into Jerusalem when people greeted him with those words (Lk. 19.38). But the First Gospel places it after Jesus' entry into Jerusalem (21.1-11) and just before the discourse about the eschatological events, so that it looks forward to his return at the eschatological judgment. Since 'your house is left to you desolate' echoes Jeremiah's words about God's destruction of Jerusalem because of the people's violence, the Matthaean narrative probably understands the words to refer to the destruction of Jerusalem in 70 CE (see 22.7).

This long discourse, together with the even longer discourse which will follow in the next two chapters, slows down the tempo of the narrative. Direct speech takes about the same amount of time to read or hear as it would have taken to speak, whereas the depiction of events, especially in summaries, takes much less time to read than they would have taken to enact. This slowing of the tempo through discourses provides time for readers to reflect on Jesus' teaching. Moreover, by characterizing scribes and Pharisees as hypocrites who commit acts of violence, their responsibility for Jesus' death is implied, while Roman responsibility is ignored, in spite of the mention of crucifixion, as it had been ignored in Jesus' prophecies about his future martyrdom. In this

1   See Lk. 13.34-35.

way, readers are predisposed to understand the events to be described in chs. 26 and 27 as a depiction of violence against an innocent Jesus caused by Jewish hypocrisy alone. No doubt two factors influenced this presentation. The first is that most Jews had not become followers of Jesus. This is explained polemically: it was caused by hypocrisy. The second is that Christians had to go on living in the Roman empire. If their own documents had clearly depicted Pilate's reasons for crucifying Jesus, they would have encouraged other Roman governors to follow Pilate's example in crucifying Jesus' adherents. By depicting Pilate as a weak governor, who was swayed by vicious and envious Jewish leaders, they discourage other Roman governors from following his example.

We who are fortunate enough to live in democratic societies are nevertheless not unaware of the connection between the hypocrisy of our leaders and the sufferings of the innocent, within our own societies and in the rest of the world. But nor do we ourselves easily escape the charge of hypocrisy: it is difficult to avoid involvement in the extortionate and rapacious ethos of our economic system.

Matthew 24–25: Jesus' Discourse About the Future and the Final Judgment

The Matthaean Jesus' last discourse, about the future and the final judgment, looks beyond the events which will be described in the final chapters, Jesus' arrest, trial, crucifixion and resurrection, and so guides readers to understand them in the light of God's purpose to transform the world into the kingdom of heaven. Unlike such discourses in apocalyptic literature (e.g. Daniel, *1 Enoch*, *2 Baruch*), the Matthaean discourse does not relate what Jesus saw on a heavenly journey or in dreams. Rather, it takes the form of prophetic speech about the future, although the contents of the speech include references to the final eschatological judgment, the subject of apocalyptic literature (e.g. Daniel 7).

Introduction: 24.1-2[1]
The introduction marks a change in location and audience from the public teaching inside the temple, addressed to crowds and Jewish leaders, to the private teaching outside the temple on the Mount of Olives, addressed to disciples alone: 'Jesus went out from the temple and was going away, when his disciples came to point out the buildings of the temple' (contrast Luke). Herod's rebuilt temple was an awesome sight, an enormous and beautiful structure, built with huge stones. Even

1   See Mk 13.1-2; Lk. 21.5-6.

what remains today gives evidence of its magnificence. 'But Jesus asked them, "Do you see all these things? Truly I tell you, there shall not be left here one stone upon another that shall not be pulled down."' This unambiguous prophecy of the temple's destruction helps to interpret the earlier story of Jesus' prophetic action in the temple (21.12-17). Since the temple was understood to be a holy place where the sacrifices ordained by God were performed, its destruction would have to be construed as indicating something fundamentally important about God's purpose for the world. Like the prophetic interpretation of the temple's destruction in 586 BCE, this second destruction could suggest both judgment and the prelude to God's new act of salvation. These twin themes are explored in the rest of Jesus' discourse. Some scholars have suggested that the form of Jesus' prophecy in the Synoptic Gospels about the destruction of the temple has been influenced by the subsequent event of 70 CE Had that been so, however, we should expect the description to correspond more closely to what actually happened. The temple was in fact destroyed by fire (Josephus, *War* 7.1), and, as can be seen, many stones still remain on one another. 'Not one stone upon another which shall not be pulled down' (see Hag. 2.15) is not a depiction of what happened but a dramatic intimation of destruction. It is a prophecy of what violence brings in its wake.

Warnings not to be Led Astray: 24.3-14[1]
It is not surprising that Jesus' disciples (contrast Mark's Peter, James, John and Andrew, and Luke's public teaching) should be described asking him privately about his teaching. Jesus is pictured sitting on the Mount of Olives, across the valley from the temple, when his disciples urged, 'Tell us when shall these things be and what is the sign of your coming and the end of the age?' The question links the destruction of the temple with Jesus' earlier teaching about the advent of the son of man (10.23; 13.41-43; 19.28) and the end of the age (13.49; contrast Mark and Luke). Jesus' initial reply, however, is a series of warnings beginning 'see that no one leads you astray'. The ways in which they could be led astray are then listed. There would be many who would come in Jesus' name claiming to be the Christ (contrast Mark and Luke), there would be wars and rumours of wars, but the disciples should not be alarmed since these 'must' happen (see Dan. 2.28), that is, this would all be part of the working out of God's purpose, though the end would not be yet (see Dan. 11.27). Nations and kingdoms would arise against one another, and there would be famines (contrast Mark) and disturbances in various places. But all these things were to be understood as only the beginning of 'birth pains'. This traditional language of 'birth pains' preceding God's renewal (e.g. Hos. 13.13; Mic. 4.9; Isa. 13.8; 26.17; Ezek.

1   See Mk 13.3-13; Lk. 21.7-19.

7.5-9) fits well with the Matthaean term for the new world, 'rebirth' (19.28). This section, therefore, suggests that the *parousia* or coming of the son of man, Jesus, would not follow immediately after the destruction of the temple.

The predictions of persecutions that had been addressed to the disciples in the missionary discourse (10.5-42) are now repeated. 'They will hand you over to affliction [see Dan. 12.1] and they will kill you' (see 10.28; 21.35; 22.6; 23.34, 37), and 'you shall be hated by all nations on account of my name'. Not only persecutions from Jewish leaders but also from Gentiles are clearly in view. Moreover, this would cause many followers offence (13.21), so that they would hand one another over and hate one another (10.21-22, 34-36). The false prophets and the increase in lawlessness would affect many followers whose love would grow cold (13.21). There is no suggestion in this discourse that persecution would be good for the Christian community. It realistically depicts the betrayals and hatred that would follow such evils. But the disciples and readers are encouraged to remain faithful: 'This person who remains to the end will be saved' (10.22). In the context, clearly this includes salvation beyond death (see 16.24-26). Finally, an answer to the disciples' question about when the end would come is provided: 'This good news about the kingdom will be preached throughout the whole inhabited earth for a witness to all the nations, and then the end will come' (see 13.38). The earlier mission of the disciples had been restricted to Israel (10.5-6), but before the eschatological judgment, their mission would extend to all nations (28.19). This is in keeping with Jewish prophetic and apocalyptic expectations about the involvement of all the nations in God's judgment.

Let the Reader Understand: 24.15-28[1]
Although the whole narrative is directed to readers and listeners, this section contains the only explicit reference to the reader: 'When you see the abomination of desolation which was spoken through the prophet Daniel standing in the holy place, let the reader understand' (see Dan. 12.9-11 and 9.27; 11.31. Contrast Luke). The event referred to in Daniel's prophecy was probably the desecration of the temple in 168 BCE (1 Macc. 1.54; 2 Macc. 6.2), yet the prophecies are set at the time of the earlier destruction in 586 BCE (Dan. 1.1-2). What had happened in the past as the prelude to God's deliverance could be expected in the future. Moreover, the temple was desecrated in 70 CE both by the Jewish defenders and by the Roman army, so perhaps the reader was supposed to understand the prophecy as a reference to those events (see 23.38; 24.2). If so, the depiction of events following after the destruction of the temple would make sense to a Christian community

1   See Mk 13.14-23; Lk. 21.20-24.

which continued to exist and still looked forward to the final eschato-logical judgment.

The discourse continues with advice to people who would suffer the persecutions just described: let people in Judaea flee to the mountains, let someone on a roof not go down to take possessions from his house, let someone in a field not turn back to take his cloak (see 1 Macc. 2.28). One woe is addressed to women who would be pregnant or feeding young children. The discourse urges disciples to pray that their flight not be in winter or on the Sabbath (when flight would be more difficult). This advice conjures up the horror of the events, and countenances flight from persecutions, whenever possible (see 10.23). Moreover, the events would be even worse than those in the past: 'For then there shall be great affliction like none that has happened from the beginning of the world until now, no, and never will be [see Dan. 12.1]. And if those days were not cut short, no flesh [that is, vulnerable human being] would be saved; but those days will be cut short on account of those who are called'. The discourse could not have made it clearer that persecution and martyrdom would be the fate of Jesus' followers in an unjust world (see 10.16-39; 16.24-26; 20.22-28), but it also suggests that God would not allow the violence to continue for ever.

Again the discourse returns to the theme of the disciples' fidelity in the face of people who would try to lead them astray: 'Then if someone says to you, behold here is the Christ, or here, do not believe. For many false Christs and false prophets will arise, and they will give great signs and wonders in order to lead astray, if possible, even those who are called'. About such things, they have been warned: 'Behold, I have told you beforehand', and the teaching is repeated: 'Therefore, if they say to you, behold he is in the desert, do not go out; behold he is in the chambers, do not believe'. There is no need to believe in these false prophetic figures because the eschatological events would be unmistak-able: 'For as the lightning goes out from the east and shines as far as the west, so will be the coming of the son of man. Where the corpse is, there will the vultures assemble' (contrast Mark and see Lk. 17.24, 37). The coming of the son of man at the end of the age would be as unmis-takable as lightning flashing across the sky. But to what does the proverbial final statement refer? It could be a rather gruesome image of the unmistakable advent of the son of man. But it is more likely to be an image of those who would go after false prophets: 'Where the corpse [the false prophet] is, there will the vultures [unjust people] assemble'.

The Sign of the Son of Man: 24.29-31[1]

The advent of the son of man and the eschatological judgment would be unmistakable because it would involve the transformation of the

1   See Mk 13.24-27; Lk. 21.25-28.

whole cosmos. 'Immediately after the affliction of those days, the sun will be darkened, and the moon will not give its light, and the stars will fall from heaven, and the powers of the heavens will be shaken' echoes Isa. 13.10 and 34.4. In 'and then will appear the sign of the son of man, and then will all the tribes of the earth mourn' (see Zech. 12.10, 14), the son of man is described arriving with an ensign like a warrior (e.g. Isa. 49.22), imagery which fits with the reference to a loud trumpet in 24.31 (e.g. Isa. 18.3; Jer. 4.21). 'And they will see the son of man coming on the clouds of heaven with power and great glory' echoes the vision of 'one like a son of man' in Dan. 7.13-14. 'And he shall send his angels with a loud trumpet and they will gather his elect from the four winds, from one end of heaven to the other' (see. 13.41 and Deut. 30.4). At last the discourse looks beyond the horrors of persecution to the advent of the son of man and the gathering of those who were called and remained faithful.

Parable of the Fig Tree: 24.32-35[1]

The common experience of recognizing the nearness of summer from the new leaves on a fig tree is applied to the disciples' future experience: 'so also you, when you see all these things, you know that he is near, at the gates'. Again the image is that of the arrival of a warrior. Moreover, further encouragement to remain faithful is given by the assurance, 'Truly I tell you, this generation will not pass away until all these things happen. Heaven and earth will pass away, but my statements will never pass away'. Within the story, this assurance is addressed to the disciples, but something like fifty years had passed between the time of the story and the time when the narrative was written, years in which many but not all of the disciples' generation must have died. Nevertheless, the assurance stands, giving hope to the readers that the advent of the son of man would happen in the very near future (see 16.28). Jesus' teachings, however, are understood to have an eternal significance.

Ignorance of the Exact Day or Hour when the Son of Man would Come: 24.36-44[2]

In spite of this assurance, however, disciples and readers are warned that no-one, not even the angels of heaven, would know the exact day or hour of the son of man's advent. Only the Father (God) would know (cf. 20.23). This ignorance is compared to people's ignorance at the time of Noah, before the flood (Genesis 6–9; contrast Mark). The flood took them unawares and so would the advent of the son of man. The story of Noah and the flood had influenced the description of the eschatological events in Jewish apocalyptic writings (e.g. *1 En.* 6–11).

1   See Mk 13.28-31; Lk. 21.29-33.
2   See Mk 13.32-37; Lk. 17.26-30, 34-36.

The effect is dramatically described: 'Then two men will be in a field, one is taken and one left. Two women will be grinding at a mill, one is taken and one left' (cf. Luke and contrast Mark). The implication of the teaching is then brought out: 'Watch, therefore, because you do not know on which day your lord is coming'. The expectation of the imminence of the son of man's advent, together with ignorance of its exact timing, implies that Jesus' followers would remain alert, and not find themselves unprepared. This message will be reinforced by the parables which follow.

The first parable (contrast Mark and see Lk. 12.39-40), introduced by 'Know this', likens the disciples' and readers' position to that of a householder who, had he known at what hour of the night the thief would come, would have watched and not let his house be broken into. The message is made explicit: 'On account of this, you also are to be ready, for the son of man is coming at an hour you do not know'. Boldly likening the son of man to a thief in the night serves the purpose of emphasizing his unexpected time of arrival. Disciples were to live their lives in expectation of God's imminent judgment through his human agent. This expectation was to make them steadfast in conforming their lives to Jesus'.

Who is the Faithful and Wise Servant? 24.45-51[1]

In this section, the responsibility of leaders in the community seems to be in view (see 13.24-30, 36-43), and the son of man is likened, less offensively, to the lord of a household. The introductory question, 'Who is the faithful and wise servant whom the lord has set over his household to give them food in season?' (see Ps. 104.27) distinguishes those who minister from those to whom they minister. A faithful and wise servant is conceived as one who gives what others need. A blessing is pronounced on the servant who, 'when his lord comes, will find him doing so'. This faithfulness would lead to future responsibility: 'Truly I say to you, he will set him over all his possessions' (see 19.28). But this hope of blessing is followed immediately by an implied warning: 'And if that wicked servant says in his heart, my lord is lingering, and he begins to beat his fellow servants, and to eat and drink with the drunken, the lord of that servant will come on a day he does not expect and at an hour he does not know,and will cut him to pieces and put his lot with the dissemblers. There shall be weeping and gnashing of teeth' (contrast Luke). In other words, those whose leadership expressed hypocrisy, condemned in the seven woes of the previous chapter, would be destroyed at the final judgment.

1   See Lk. 12.41-46.

Parable of the Ten Virgins: 25.1-13

The parable, which appears nowhere else in the New Testament, illustrates the need to remain watchful (25.13; see Mark 13.33). It begins, 'the kingdom of heaven will be compared to ten virgins'. This implies that something will be learnt about the kingdom of heaven from the whole story which follows, not that the kingdom is like the ten virgins themselves. All ten virgins took their lamps and went out to meet the bridegroom, but five were foolish and did not take oil with them. When the bridegroom tarried, the virgins grew drowsy and were sleeping. But in the middle of the night, they were summoned to go and meet him. All the virgins rose and trimmed their lamps, but the foolish had to ask the wise for oil, a request which the wise refused because they had only enough oil for their own lamps. While the foolish were away buying oil, the bridegroom arrived, the wise virgins entered the wedding with him and the door was shut. Later the foolish virgins returned and cried, 'Lord, lord, open to us', but he replied, 'Truly I do not know you'. The extraordinary circumstance of the bridegroom's arrival in the middle of the night highlights the unexpected timing of the son of man's arrival. The conclusion, 'Watch, therefore, because you do not know the day nor the hour' recalls 24.36 and 44. In fact the whole parable is reminiscent of earlier teaching. The wedding recalls the parable in 22.1-14; the bridegroom recalls 9.15-16; the lingering recalls the parable in 24.48; the cry of the foolish and their lord's reply recalls 7.21-23; the lamps recall the lamps and good works of 5.14-16; and the depiction of the wise recalls 10.16, 7.24-25 and 24.45. The conclusion which emphasizes the need to remain watchful is to be taken in the broadest sense. The story itself suggests less that people should remain awake (both wise and foolish virgins were sleeping), than that they should be watchful in the sense of being prepared to meet the bridegroom (the son of man) whenever he might arrive. Like the wise and faithful servant of the previous parable, the wise virgins behaved appropriately during their lord's absence. Those who did not were excluded from the wedding (the kingdom of heaven).

In both these parables and in the one to follow, the situation of Jesus' followers between the time of his resurrection and the final judgment is conceived as an experience of Jesus' absence. In other sections of the narrative his continuing presence is mentioned: in 28.20, 'Behold I am with you always till the end of the age', or in 18.20, 'For where two or three are gathered together in my name, there am I in the midst of them'. This second reference, together with the references in 25.40, 45, 10.40 and 18.5, make it clear that Jesus' presence in the world after his resurrection is a presence through his agents, his followers. Hence the need for them to remain faithful.

Parable of the Talents: 25.14-30[1]

This parable also describes the behaviour of servants in their master's absence, and the repercussions when their master returned (see 24.45-51). The more usual introduction is replaced by the simple comparison: 'For as...', referring back to the lesson in 25.13: 'Watch, for you know neither the day nor the hour'. This time the story concerns the servants' use of their master's goods during his absence. Five talents, two talents and one talent were huge amounts of silver, since a talent weighed between fifty and eighty pounds. Each servant received an amount according to his ability (cf. Mk 13.34 and contrast Luke). In his master's absence, the servant with five talents traded and gained another five, the one with two talents gained two more, but the servant with one buried it in the ground. After a long time, the master returned to settle accounts. The servant who had gained five talents was commended as good and faithful and, because he had been faithful in a few matters, his master promised to set him over many, and invited him to enter into his joy. The conversation is repeated with the servant who had gained two talents. But the servant who had received one talent which he had buried in the ground addressed his master, 'Lord, I knew that you are a hard man, reaping where you did not sow and gathering where you did not scatter, and I was frightened and went and hid your talent in the ground. See, you have what is yours'. This servant, however, was addressed as evil and lazy. His description of his master's hardness is repeated in the master's rhetorical question and then an inference is drawn: 'You ought therefore to have given my silver to bankers, and when I came I would have received my own with interest'. Then the master pronounced judgment against the servant: 'Therefore take the talent from him and give it to him who has ten talents, for to everyone who has shall more be given, and he will have abundance, and from him who has not, even what he has will be taken away from him [see 13.12]. And throw the useless servant into outer darkness. There shall be weeping and gnashing of teeth' (see 24.51). In the description of five talents as 'a few things', in the invitation to the faithful servant to enter into his master's joy, and in the command to throw the useless servant into outer darkness, the allegorical significance of the parable obscures its realism. On the other hand, the realistic portrait of the rich master's greed serves a purpose: it provides a context in which the creative responsibility of faithful servants makes sense. They were not to be passive recipients of bounty but active participants in fulfilling their master's mission (see 18.23-35). The force of the parable, with its doubling of the master's praise to the faithful servants, but its ending with details about the unfaithful servant's fate, offers both encouragement and warning. Given the depiction of persecutions and disturbances

1   Cf. Lk. 19.11-27; Mk 13.34-37.

in the previous chapter, whether these were actually experienced by readers or formed part of their expectations, fifty years or so must have seemed to them like a long time (contrast the different details in the Lukan version).

These parables help to give a sense of positive purpose to the period between Jesus' resurrection and the final judgment. They encourage people to remain faithful during Jesus' absence, to live in such a way that they would always be ready to meet their lord whenever he arrived, and they emphasize the responsibilities of leaders to care for followers and creatively to continue Jesus' mission in the world. Persecutions and hatred were not to be taken as indications that Jesus' mission had failed, or that his followers were rejected by God, but as the inevitable expression of evil in a violent world which God was about to transform into the kingdom of heaven.

The Son of Man's Judgment: 25.31-46

There are no Gospel parallels to this impressive depiction of the son of man's judgment. The son of man is pictured coming in glory with all the angels (cf. 13.41, 49; 24.30-31). Then he would sit upon the throne of his glory (19.28), and all the nations would be gathered before him (see 24.14). As in the judgment scene in Daniel 7, all peoples would be involved in the final judgment. And the judgment would bring division, like that of a shepherd dividing sheep from goats (13.49). The sheep would stand at his right and the goats at his left. Then the son of man, now described as a king, would address each in turn. To those at his right he would say, 'Come, beloved of my Father, inherit the kingdom prepared for you from the foundation of the world' (13.43). This eschatological kingdom is understood to be the fulfilment of God's purpose for humanity. The explanation of the parable of the wheat and the weeds had ended at this point (13.36-43), but the king's discourse in ch. 25 continues with an explanation of the decision: 'For I was hungry and you gave me to eat, I was thirsty and you gave me to drink, I was a stranger and you took me in, naked and you clothed me, I was sick and you visited me, I was in prison and you came to me' (see 10.40-42; Isa. 58.7). But the explanation fails to make sense if the son of man is identified simply with Jesus, since the people addressed had done none of these things for him. Hence the just (those at the right; see 13.43), earlier called sheep, would ask when they did all these things for him. The repetition of each of the instances reinforces their importance. The king's final answer is, 'Inasmuch as you did it to one of the least of these my brothers, you did it to me'. The representative role of the son of man, which had been intimated in earlier references, is here brought into focus. Jesus was the son of man as the representative of a way of life dedicated to God's purpose, a way which never met violence with violence, but suffered violence in an unjust world. Those who followed him are understood to be faithful sons of their heavenly Father, brothers of Jesus (see 5.3-48. Christian women have to correct the male orientation of the writing by adding 'and sisters'). Those who responded to injustice by meeting the needs of the vulnerable and persecuted and by associating with them are called the just. The people addressed as sheep, therefore, were those who had for the moment escaped the persecutions and afflictions which their fellows had suffered, but who had helped those who were suffering (see 10.11-23, 40-42). Perhaps readers should infer that generally it was missionaries and leaders rather than ordinary followers who suffered persecution. These ordinary followers' expressions of justice, moreover, had been unselfconscious (see 6.3). They had not behaved justly in order to gain a reward. The assurance of rewards in God's kingdom which had been repeatedly given were not to be understood as bribes for good behaviour. Rather unselfish and unselfconscious devotion to God's people who suffered would be rewarded at the final judgment (see 7.21). Hence both groups, sheep and goats, are pictured as surprised by their acceptance or rejection. Even self-concern for future vindication by God is treated as a kind of hypocrisy (6.3).

This message is so important that the whole conversation between the king and the just is repeated in the negative between the king and the unjust. The king would say to those on his left, 'Go from me, you cursed, into the eternal fire prepared for the slanderer and his angels (13.41-42, 49-50; 3.12; see Dan. 7.11). The unjust, then, would depart to a place that had not been prepared for them from the foundation of the world. Again an explanation of the decision is given: 'For I was hungry and you did not give me to eat, I was thirsty and you did not give me to drink, I was a stranger and you did not take me in, naked and you did not clothe me, sick and in prison and you did not visit me'. Again the list of instances is repeated in the unjust's question 'When?' and again the king's reply expresses identification with the vulnerable and persecuted, those who followed his way of life: 'Inasmuch as you did not do it to one of the least of these, you did not do it to me'. The scene ends: 'And these shall go into eternal punishment, but the just into eternal life'.

Is there a contradiction in Matthaean theology? On the one hand, the narrative pictures God as a generous Father who gives to good and bad alike (5.45), and it encourages people to follow God's example (5.48). It also encourages people to acknowledge their own receipt of God's mercy in showing mercy to others (6.12, 14-15; 18.21-35). Then, in the depiction of the final judgment, those who had acted mercifully would enter the kingdom of heaven (25.34-40, 46). On the other hand, those who had acted unmercifully, God would exclude at the final judgment (18.34; 25.41-46). Can these two visions, of God's mercy towards wicked people in the present, but of his exclusion of the unmerciful at the final judgment, be reconciled? In one sense, they can.

Those who were merciful shared God's purpose and hence belonged to his kingdom, while the unmerciful had cut themselves off from God and his purpose, like the lawless in 7.21-23 and the foolish virgins in 25.11-12. They would go, not to the place prepared for them from the foundation of the world, but to the place prepared for the slanderer. The kingdom of heaven would include no form of evil, and those whose lives expressed evil could find no place in it. The narrative, therefore, emphasizes the importance of people's mortal lives. Their devotion and commitments in the present world would determine their fate at the final judgment. There would be no second chance in a second life. Their mortal lives are understood to express what they truly are. While they were alive, they could respond to God's mercy or turn away from him, but death would be real and final. The final judgment is conceived as the recognition of whether they had shared God's purpose or not. And the judgment would be carried out, appropriately, by the son of man, the representative of a human way of life dedicated to God. Sheep would be divided from goats on the basis of whether people had served the needs or neglected the needs of those who lived out God's purpose.

The last two discourses, about hypocrisy in ch. 23 and about future sufferings and final vindication in chs. 24 and 25, describe God's judgment on two ways of life. Both were religious ways of life; a way of life which denied the existence of the Creator God is not even countenanced. The contrast is between the way which only seems to express devotion to God but in fact is an expression of regard for social esteem and self-esteem, and the way which is so entirely devoted to God and his purpose that any form of self-concern is excluded. The second way is shown not only to bring no honour in an unjust world, but to bring persecution. Afflictions and even martyrdom would be the prelude to God's vindication of the just. And the narrative will describe Jesus' martyrdom in its final chapters. The discourses encourage followers of Jesus to continue in his way, looking forward to God's transformation of the present unjust world into his eschatological kingdom. The warnings and assurances would have encouraged first-century readers to remain faithful.

But can these discourses any longer encourage or warn followers of Jesus who can look back on nearly two thousand years of history in which the just and merciful have repeatedly encountered derision, persecution and martyrdom? Does the fact that the Matthaean Jesus was wrong about the imminence of the eschatological transformation suggest that he was also wrong about the way of life he followed and advocated, even wrong in his belief in the Creator God? Without belief in the Creator God's vindication, Jesus' way of life might still be appealing but it would be tragic. The Matthaean narrative, however, does not advocate a tragic way of life, for two reasons. First, it asserts that God raised Jesus from the dead after his crucifixion. Secondly, this event is seen to give hope to his followers. In the first century, Jesus' resurrection was understood by Christians to be the beginning of the transformation of the world which would therefore follow shortly (e.g. 1 Cor. 15.20-28).

People living at the end of the twentieth century can imagine only too readily the world's imminent destruction. They live at a time in which human beings could bring it about. A war in which nuclear or biological weapons were used could destroy life on earth. And even if this were avoided, the rape of the earth's resources and the pollution which modern lifestyles create could destroy all forms of life. We can envisage a future even more horrific than that depicted in Mt. 24.6-28. And the complicated causes which could bring this about are deeply rooted in the exploitative ethos of modern societies. Christians and other religious groups who assert that the world is God's creation have little time in which to fight against and try to change the aims and objectives of the societies in which they live. The sense of urgency is as great for them as it was for first-century Christians. But modern Christians do not see these possible ends of the world as the necessary prelude to God's eschatological kingdom, although they do share with the Gospel according to Matthew the understanding that they represent the working out of human violence. They can also share its concern to convince people that God calls them to live merciful lives like Jesus', but they also have to join with others, some of whom do not even believe in the Creator God, in their efforts to alter the actions of modern societies.

Today, Jesus' resurrection is still the basis of Christian hope for the future, but the final judgment is no longer expected in the immediate future. Modern Christians expect to die before a final transformation. But recognition of their mortality gives them a sense of the importance of their present lives and opportunities which is not entirely dissimilar to the sense given to early Christians by their expectation of an imminent judgment. The timing of neither event, individual death or eschatological transformation, can be known beforehand. Twentieth-century Christians, like their predecessors, can live each day as if it were their last. Nevertheless, belief in the future kingdom of heaven embraces natural and social as well as personal ends. The vision of the kingdom of heaven inspires Christians to work for the creation of more merciful and just communities for as long as the world continues to exist. Belief in the possibility of post-mortem eternal life does not decrease but increases the importance of that work.

Matthew 26–27: Jesus' Condemnation and Crucifixion

The disparate episodes depicted in these chapters are unified by four themes. The first suggests that Jesus was rejected, suffered and died as God's faithful and obedient son and as God's Christ. The frequent references to the son of God, the Christ and the king of the Jews repeatedly remind the reader of this Matthaean belief, and the repetitions are necessary because Jesus' fate was so unlike that of David, and so much more like that of a prophet. The second is that everything which happened was in accordance with God's purpose. This is exemplified by the many quotations from and allusions to Scripture, and by the scene in Gethsemane. The third is that Jesus consciously accepted his destiny. This had already been suggested, both by Jesus' earlier predictions of what awaited him in Jerusalem and by his descriptions of the fate of prophets. It is also highlighted by Jesus' statements in Gethsemane. His suffering and execution were not to be construed as a tragic accident, but as his conscious fulfilment of God's purpose. The fourth is that Jesus suffered and died as an innocent martyr. Already the depiction of his ministry had made it clear that he was guilty of no crime for which he should have suffered the penalty of execution. In chs. 26 and 27 Judas's confession of sin, Pilate's wife's dream, and Pilate's washing his hands dramatically reinforce the perception of Jesus' innocence. The narrative seeks to convince readers of the theological and human significance of Jesus' suffering and death.

But it does so by recounting history. Inescapable historical problems are raised for modern readers by the account. Four versions of the events, each of them different from the others, have come down to us in the Gospels. Moreover, evidence from Jewish sources about the period cast doubt on the historical accuracy of the portrait of Pilate and of the nocturnal trial by a sanhedrin (in Matthew and Mark but not in Luke and John). Details about these matters will be discussed in what follows.

Jesus' Prediction and the Plot to Kill Him: 26.1-5[1]

The formulaic reference to the completion of Jesus' discourses, and Jesus' prediction that after two days the Passover would arrive when the son of man would be handed over to be crucified, renew the sense that Jesus himself had determined to face martyrdom. The detail 'after two days' means that the event would happen on the third day, the day on which something decisive could be expected to happen (cf. Gen. 22.4; Exod. 19.15-16). The scene shift, to the gathering of the chief

1   See Mk 14.1-2; Lk. 22.1-2; Jn 11.45-53.

priests and elders of the people in the courtyard of the high priest Caiaphas's house, where they plotted to arrest Jesus by stealth and kill him, is understood in the light of Jesus' statement. It creates the impression that these Jewish leaders were unconsciously fulfilling God's purpose, without absolving them from the responsibility for the injustice of their plans. This is the point brought out even more clearly by the Johannine recounting of the council meeting, set earlier in that Gospel's narrative (Jn 11.47-53). And the Johannine account gives a clearer sense of the political difficulties which popular charismatics could cause chief priests. The high priest and his associates in Jerusalem were constantly required to safeguard Jewish religious interests against Roman infringements without provoking Rome into military action. During the pilgrim festivals, when thousands of Jews gathered in Jerusalem, the prefect moved from Caesarea where he normally lived to Jerusalem with troop reinforcements so that he would be present to quell any Jewish enthusiasm for freedom. The feast of Passover celebrated the exodus of Israelite slaves from Egypt and naturally encouraged Jewish expectations of God's deliverance from oppression. A charismatic preacher who urged people to expect God's imminent transformation of the world would be seen as politically dangerous by Rome, because such an expectation would imply that Roman rule was limited, and Jewish leaders in Jerusalem might justifiably be concerned about uncontrollable crowd reactions, which could result in Roman military retaliation and widespread slaughter. The First Gospel pictures Jesus' recent teaching about the imminent judgment as private, given to the disciples alone. But the discourse in chs. 24–25 only develops more explicitly teaching about the kingdom which had been given openly to crowds, according to earlier parts of the narrative (e.g. 4.17; 13.1-35). Moreover, Judas the betrayer was one of the disciples. In addition, the expectation of an imminent kingdom implies that someone would be king. Even an implied claim to kingship in the future would be politically significant in the present. If God had sent his Christ to lead people into his eschatological kingdom, many people might respond by throwing off the Roman yoke. These considerations help to make sense of the chief priests' and elders' concern, according to the Matthaean account: 'Not at the feast, so that there may not be a riot among the people'. The concern suggests that crowds might be expected to defend Jesus.

Only the First and Fourth Gospels name Caiaphas as the high priest in their accounts of Jesus' execution in Jerusalem. Luke refers to the high priesthoods of Annas and Caiaphas in an introduction (Lk. 3.2). Caiaphas was high priest in approximately 18–36 CE.

An Anointing of Jesus: 26.6-13[1]

This account of an incident set at Bethany near Jerusalem is placed in the context of a plot against Jesus' life (a similar but in many respects different account of an anointing is placed earlier in the Lukan narrative: Lk. 7.36-50. The Johannine account is set slightly earlier, before Jesus' entry into Jerusalem, and it identifies the woman concerned as Mary, sister to Martha and Lazarus: Jn 12.1-8). In Matthew, the house is identified as that of Simon the leper, but he plays no part in the action and is never mentioned again. Perhaps the fact that he was a leper and therefore an outcast is intended to remind readers that Jesus' fate would be similar. But the story relates that it was an unnamed (contrast John) woman who came with an alabaster flask of costly aromatic ointment ('myrrh' is a Semitic loanword, and the ointment was used as a perfume, worn by the rich or used in the preparation of a corpse for burial), and she began to pour it over Jesus' head (contrast Luke and John) while he was reclining. The disciples (contrast Mark and John) are shown expressing indignation: 'Why this waste? For this [ointment] could have been sold for a large sum to be given to the poor'. Their concern for the poor was warranted by earlier teaching of Jesus (e.g. 19.21). But Jesus is depicted opposing their insight: 'Why do you cause the woman trouble? For she did a good deed for me. For the poor you have with you always, but me you do not have always. For in pouring this ointment on my body, she prepared me for burial. Truly I say to you, wherever this good news is preached, even what she did will be told as a memorial to her'. In the context of the whole narrative, 'the poor you have with you always' implies no complacency towards the needs of the poor (see 5.42; 19.21), but suggests that the woman's action was even more important than meeting their needs, because it was an unrepeatable preparation for Jesus' burial. The action is understood as prophetic; it was a preparation for burial before Jesus was dead. No doubt the anointing of his head would also have reminded readers that he was the anointed one, the Christ (see 1 Sam. 16.1-13; 2 Kgs 9.1-13), but they are prevented from understanding that kingship in triumphalist terms by Jesus' explicit reference to burial. Finally, the significance of Jesus' death is indicated by the mention of the worldwide preaching of the good news, when the woman's action would not be forgotten. Even the dominant androcentric perspective of the narrative has not precluded this attribution of a prophetic action to a woman.

Judas's Agreement of Terms for Betrayal: 26.14-16[2]

The narrative shifts to a recounting of Judas' action in furthering the chief priests' plot against Jesus. He is introduced as one of Jesus' twelve

1 See Mk 14.3-9; Jn 12.1-8.
2 See Mk 14.10-11; Lk. 22.3-6.

disciples and is distinguished by a second name, Iscarioth, which probably means 'from Kerioth'. The narrative relates that he went to the
chief priests with the question, 'What do you want to give me if I hand
him over to you?', which suggests greed as a motive for Judas' betrayal
(contrast Mark and Luke). Their settling to pay thirty silver pieces
(contrast Mark and Luke) is reminiscent of Zech. 11.12, according to
which thirty silver pieces paid off the shepherd and left the sheep to
destruction (see later, Mt. 26.31). The narrative ends on a threatening
note: 'From then he began to seek an opportunity to betray him'.

Judas's betrayal comes as no surprise at this stage in the narrative.
When he was first introduced to the readers, he had been identified as
the one who betrayed Jesus (10.4). Moreover, Jesus had warned his
disciples about betrayal in contexts in which their experiences were
seen to mirror his (10.21-25; 24.10). But the narrative never specifies
exactly what Judas betrayed. From the Matthaean description of subsequent events, readers can infer three possibilities. His leading officers
to Gethsemane to arrest Jesus suggests that he betrayed a time and
place for arrest away from the crowds (see 26.4). His identifying Jesus
with a kiss suggests that he showed them whom to arrest. But the question about kingship at Jesus' trials suggests that he betrayed Jesus'
acceptance of the title 'Christ'.

Jesus' Passover Meal with his Disciples: 26.17-30[1]
The Matthaean and Markan accounts describe the preparation for the
supper and the supper itself, at which Jesus predicted that one of his
disciples would betray him, and interpet the significance of eating bread
and drinking wine. The Johannine account, which dates the supper on
the evening before the Passover, includes a parallel to the prophecy of
betrayal, together with an account of Jesus' washing the disciples feet,
and Jesus' long farewell discourses. The Lukan account includes parallels to all the Markan and Matthaean sections, in a different order and
with differences in detail, together with further teaching of Jesus. Paul
reminds Corinthian Christians about what Jesus said and did 'on the
night that he was betrayed' (1 Cor. 11.23-25).

None of the Gospels includes any reference to the necessary
cleansing rituals through which all Jews had to go before entering the
temple to offer the sacrifice of the Passover Lamb.[2] If the meal was a
Passover meal, one of the disciples or Jesus would have gone through
those rituals. It was noted earlier that nothing had been said about such
matters in the account of Jesus' first entry into the temple (Mt. 21.12ff.
and parallels). But the omission is even more startling at this point since
other preparations for the supper are detailed.

1   See Mk 14.12-26; Lk. 22.7-23; Jn 13.21-30.
2   E.P. Sanders, personal communication.

'On the first day of unleavened bread' marks the progress of time since 26.2, 'after two days the Passover happens'. The narrative takes for granted readers' knowledge that Passover, when the Passover lambs were sacrificed in the temple, led into the seven-day feast of unleavened bread, which began that evening. Such knowledge could be gained from Scripture (e.g. Exod. 12.1-20). The story relates that when the disciples asked where Jesus wished to eat the Passover meal, he instructed them to go to a certain person, whose name is not given, and say, 'The teacher says, "My time is at hand; I will keep the Passover at your house with my disciples"'. Jesus' speech reminds readers that his death was near. In this way, and in this context, the disciples are pictured preparing for the Passover. The Markan and Lukan versions provide more details about the disciples' finding the room, which suggest even more strongly that Jesus had made secret arrangements, in order to avoid arrest at that time.

Only this introduction suggests that Jesus' last supper was a Passover meal. No detail in the account which follows makes any further connection. At Passover meals Jews ate the lamb which had been sacrificed, together with unleavened bread, but no lamb is mentioned, and the bread is not described as unleavened. Since we know from Paul's first letter to the Corinthians that Christians met together to eat bread and drink wine over which Jesus' words were pronounced, it is likely that Christian practice is reflected in the Gospel accounts of the supper. This suggestion helps to explain the differences in the wording of Jesus' statements in each of the four accounts: each reflects developments of the tradition in each of the Christian communities. The connection with Passover in the Synoptics' introductions, however, serves a useful theological purpose. Passover celebrated the rescue of Israelite slaves from Egypt. The Matthaean Jesus' statements at the meal interpret Jesus' death in terms of God's rescue of people from sin (cf. 1 Cor. 5.7).

The Matthaean account notes that, in the evening, Jesus reclined at table with the twelve, and that, while he was eating, he told them, 'One of you will betray me'. The disciples' reaction is said to be one of sorrow rather than indignation, and each is depicted asking 'Is it I, lord?' None is sure of his fidelity. Jesus' reply, 'He who dipped his hand in the dish with me will betray me', does not specify which of the disciples would betray him, since all had shared the meal, but it highlights the meanness of the betrayal by someone so close (contrast John). Jesus' statement, 'The son of man goes as it is written concerning him, but woe to that person by whom the son of man is betrayed; it would be well for him if that person had not been born' asserts that Jesus' death fulfilled God's purpose, expressed in Scripture (though no particular text is alluded to here), but that this did not free the betrayer from ethical responsibility. At this point, Judas 'who was to betray him' asks,

'Surely it is not I, rabbi?', to which Jesus replies, 'You said so' (no synoptic parallel). Readers are in a better position to understand this conversation than disciples within the story were. Readers have been told that Judas was the betrayer and about Judas' visit to the chief priests. His question, then, can be understood either as a desperate attempt to resist betraying Jesus after all, or as a cynical pretence. Either way, Jesus' reply implies that deeds should match words.

The Matthaean account moves on to describe Jesus' blessings of bread and wine. It was and is customary for Jews to express their gratitude to God by saying blessings over bread whenever they eat, and over wine whenever that forms part of the meal, but the Matthaean Jesus' blessings relate to his imminent death. He took bread, blessed and broke it, and gave it to his disciples with the words, 'Take, eat, this is my body'. Blessing and breaking bread identified as his body points to his martyrdom. The disciples eating the blessed and broken bread identified as his body means that they made his life and death their own, and were to live and die in conformity with him. All four accounts include Jesus' words 'this is my body', but the Pauline account adds 'which is for you. Do this in remembrance of me'. The possible meanings of the terms 'for you' and 'remembrance' are topics for expositions of Pauline theology. The Matthaean depiction may imply that the Matthaean community, like the Pauline, repeated Jesus' words at community meals.

Secondly, Jesus took and blessed the cup (containing the wine, implied but not stated; see 26.29), and gave it to the disciples with the words, 'Drink from this, all of you [contrast Mark], for this is my blood of the covenant which is poured out for many for the forgiveness of sins' (the Markan account does not include 'for the forgiveness of sins' and the Pauline account avoids the direct identification of wine with blood: 'This cup is the new covenant in my blood. Do this, as often as you drink it, in remembrance of me'. Lk. 22.19b-20 seems to be interpolated from 1 Cor. 11.25). The Matthaean words interpret the wine (implied) as Jesus' blood, establishing a covenant relationship between God and Jesus' followers (see Exodus 24; Jer. 31.31-34). 'Poured out for many for the forgiveness of sins' interprets Jesus' death as a sacrifice for the forgiveness of sins (see Leviticus 7; Isa. 53.12). The disciples' drinking means that they made his life and death their own and were to live and die as he did (see 20.22-28) in expressing their covenant relationship with God who had forgiven their sins (see 18.21-35).

In the first century CE, all religions in the Mediterranean world and the Near East centred on animal sacrifice, and Judaism was no exception. In the temple, animal sacrifices were offered to God daily, as expressions of thanksgiving. Individual Jews went to the temple to have particular sacrifices offered for the removal of uncleanness, for example, that occasioned by childbirth or by contact with the dead, or as an expression of their repentance for sins. At Passover, the sacrifice of lambs commemorated God's rescue of Israelite slaves from Egypt, though the lambs were not thought to be sacrifices for sins. But Scripture eschewed human sacrifice and commanded that a lamb should be offered instead of a human being. In the account of Passover in Exodus 12–13, the sacrificed lambs were understood to take the place of first-born Israelites.

It is difficult for most people who live in modern Western societies to imagine the awesome experience of animal sacrifice, since few have witnessed animal sacrifices, which are still performed in some contemporary religious traditions, and few have ever taken part in the slaughter of animals for meat. Most modern Westerners are inclined to view the practice with distaste or revulsion. But in the second century, when it was clear to Greeks and Romans that Christians did not participate in animal sacrifices, and yet were not Jews (who no longer performed sacrifices because their temple had been destroyed), they were considered to be atheists.

Since animal sacrifices are unknown in modern Judaism and Christianity, the word 'sacrifice' is commonly used in many modern languages only in a metaphorical sense: the surrender to God or to other human beings of some object of possession, the destruction or surrender of something valued or desired for the sake of something having a higher or more pressing claim. Similarly, the term 'victim' is used metaphorically of a person sacrificed to the will of another. For example, in English, we might say, 'he sacrificed his career for the sake of his family' or 'the unemployed were the victims of governmental fiscal policies'. Amongst religious people, 'sacrifice' in this metaphorical sense can still be understood in a religious context as a sacrifice of human expectations for the sake of God's purpose. For example, we could say, 'she sacrificed marriage to devote her life to God's service'. But religious people no longer describe human beings as God's victims, since 'victim' has connotations of the abuse of power which no one would want to attribute to God's agency.

When the Gospel according to Matthew interprets Jesus' death as a covenant sacrifice and as a sacrifice for the forgiveness of sins, should readers understand the language as metaphorical? Since actual death was involved, not merely the giving up of a promising career, the Matthaean use of sacrificial language was more appropriate than most modern uses. In modern usage, were death to be involved, we should have to further define 'sacrifice' to make this clear; for example, 'she made the ultimate sacrifice'. Nevertheless, Matthaean usage is also metaphorical. It does not imply that Jesus was killed according to biblical sacrificial customs and offered on the altar in the temple as a sacrifice for people's sins or as a covenant sacrifice. On the contrary, it interprets his dishonourable death by crucifixion outside Jerusalem as a sacrifice which brought a covenant community into being and which expressed God's forgiveness of sins. Moreover, there is no suggestion that Jesus' death made other people's sacrificial deaths unnecessary. The disciples were to eat and drink and in this dramatic way make his life and death their own (cf. 20.20-28). They too had to live in a way which would witness to God's forgiveness of sins, and they too could expect to suffer a martyr's death. They were to sacrifice their lives as servants and sons of God. Like Jesus, they were to suffer violence instead of inflicting it. This seems to be the Matthaean meaning. Later, Christians developed sacrificial language in a variety of ways which affected eucharistic beliefs and practices and which led to sectarian divisions.

The Matthaean Jesus' concluding remarks about wine look beyond the immediate future to the time when God would establish his kingdom: 'And I tell you, from now on, I shall never drink from this fruit of the vine until that day when I drink it new in the kingdom of my Father'. Jesus' death, which was about to be described, was to be seen as an essential part of God's purpose, as a necessary prerequisite for entry into the eschatological kingdom. The image of drinking wine in the kingdom intimates its joyous nature (cf. the images of feasts, e.g. 22.2, 25.10). The account of the supper is brought to a close with, 'And they sang a hymn and went out to the Mount of Olives'.

Jesus' Prediction of the Disciples' Scattering: 26.31-35[1]

The contents of the next recounted prediction of Jesus are even more disheartening than his earlier prediction of a disciple's betrayal, since it involves all the disciples: 'All of you will be offended at me in this night, for it is written, I shall strike the shepherd and the sheep of the flock will be scattered' (an allusion to Zech. 13.7; see Mt. 26.15). Some relief for disciples and readers from this disastrous prospect is provided by the allusion to Scripture which includes even desertion within God's purpose. Moreover, the prediction is followed by a command: 'But after I am raised, I will go before you into Galilee'. This implies that neither the disciples' flight nor Jesus' death would be the end of the story. Peter's response: 'Though all are offended at you, yet I shall not be offended' represents an appropriate expression of faith, but it leads only to another of Jesus' predictions: 'Truly I say to you, in this night, before the cock crows [Mark includes 'twice'], you will deny me three times'. Again, Peter's reply, 'Even if I must die with you, I shall never deny you' encapsulates a true understanding of discipleship, and all of the disciples are said to have joined Peter in his assertion. The Lukan and Johannine versions mention Peter's subsequent return to Jesus after his denial, but the Matthaean version leaves readers to discover what would happen only by reading on.

1   See Mk 14.27-31; Lk. 22.31-34; Jn 13.36-38.

Jesus' Prayer in Gethsemane: 26.36-46[1]

The name Gethsemane means 'oil valley' and indicates a particular part of the Mount of Olives, overlooking Jerusalem. The name is not mentioned in other literature from the period, and must have been handed down in Christian tradition because it was the place where Jesus was arrested. The narrative relates that Jesus told his disciples, 'Sit here while I go there to pray'. There are some earlier references to Jesus' praying and to his instructions to followers about prayer (14.23; 19.13; 24.20). He even provided disciples with an exemplary prayer (6.5-15). Only in this story, in which his words echo his exemplary prayer, and in 11.25-26, are the words of Jesus' own prayers recounted. Both prayers represent Jesus' response to his rejection by his contemporaries and his devotion to God.

Before Jesus' praying is described in ch. 26, readers are told that he took Peter and the two sons of Zebedee and began to express sorrow and great distress. Readers are reminded of the earlier account when these three disciples had accompanied Jesus on the mount of transfiguration, after his first prediction of his execution. On that occasion, they had recognized God's endorsement of Jesus' destiny, with all its implications for their own way of life. On this second occasion, Jesus' instructions encourage them to watch with him: 'My life is very sorrowful, even to death [see Ps. 42.5, 6, 11; 43.5]; remain here and watch with me'. Once again readers are allowed to share their experience. The account continues: 'Jesus went forward a little and fell on his face, praying and saying, "My Father, if it is possible, let this cup pass from me. Nevertheless, not what I will but what you will"'. The metaphor of the cup, taken from Scripture (e.g. Ps. 11.6; 75.8; Jer. 25.15-28; Isa. 51.17), had already been used in connection with Jesus' death in 20.22-23 and 26.27-28. The depiction of Jesus' distress and prayer movingly capture his natural shrinking from public execution by torture, while emphasizing his determination to remain faithful to God's purpose. The Matthaean and Markan narratives do nothing to hide the terror and pain of martyrdom, as the Lukan and Johannine accounts do.

The narrative then relates that, in spite of Jesus' distress and in spite of his instructions to the three disciples, when he rejoined them he found them sleeping. His rhetorical question to Peter, 'So were you [plural] not able to watch with me one hour?', and his further instruction, 'Watch and pray that you do not enter into a test' [see 6.13; contrast Mark and Luke, 'The spirit is ready but the flesh is weak'] again stresses human frailty at a time of danger, and the difficulties the disciples were already encountering with their earlier promise not to fall away. They were to pray not to put God to the test or not to fail God's testing of them (see 6.13). A second time, Jesus' prayer is recounted: 'My Father, if

1   See Mk 14.32-42; Lk. 22.39-46.

this cannot pass unless I drink it, let your will be done' (see 6.10 and contrast Mark and Luke). It expresses Jesus' resolve to fulfil God's purpose even in suffering and death. But again, on his return to the three disciples, he found them sleeping, 'for their eyes were heavy' (contrast Luke). This time he did not wake them but went and prayed again with the same prayer. The contrast between Jesus' praying and the disciples' sleeping provides readers with an example and counter-example of how to behave when they have to meet persecution. It suggests that only God can help frail humanity to meet the crisis without falling away. The scene ends with Jesus' final rally to the disciples: 'Do you sleep on now and take your rest? Behold the hour has drawn near and the son of man is delivered into the hands of sinners. Arise, let us go; behold my betrayer has drawn near' (contrast Luke). Jesus is described going to meet his enemies in fulfilment of God's purpose, but those who were responsible for his death are nevertheless called 'sinners'.

The Fulfilment of Jesus' Prophecy about the Betrayer, and Jesus' Arrest: 26.47-56[1]

Judas' departure from the other disciples had not been noted earlier (Jn 13.30 supplies the information). Again readers are told that he was one of the twelve. His story provides a dramatic warning against betrayal. The narrative tells that he came while Jesus was speaking, and brought with him a large crowd armed with swords and wooden clubs. They are said to have come from the chief priests and elders of the people. In the Synoptic Gospels, Jesus' arrest is made the responsibility of the Jewish leaders. According to the Fourth Gospel, Roman soldiers were involved (18.3, 12), but their presence would have ensured that Jesus be taken directly to Pilate rather than to the high priest. If Jesus was first questioned by the high priest and his advisers, it makes better historical sense to present his arrest as their responsibility. They could have sent their own officers who patrolled the temple to keep order. The reference to swords and clubs suggests their expectation of resistance. At this point, the narrative mentions that the betrayer gave them a sign: 'The one I shall kiss is the man. Sieze him'. Immediately, he went to Jesus, greeted him as 'rabbi' and kissed him. Jesus reacted, either with a command—'Friend, do what you are here for'—suggesting acceptance of his fate, or with an exclamation—'Friend, what a deed you are here for'—suggesting abhorrence of betrayal. Then the crowds put their hands on Jesus and siezed him.

But the narrative continues by relating that one of Jesus' companions took his sword and struck a servant of the high priest, cutting off his ear (the Fourth Gospel attributes the action to Peter and names the servant;

1   See Mk 14.43-50; Lk. 22.47-53; Jn 18.3-12.

the Third Gospel includes a reference to Jesus' healing the servant). Jesus, however, is described as immediately condemning the action: 'Put your sword into its place. For all who take the sword will perish by the sword. Or do you suppose that I am not able to call on my Father, and that he will at once supply more than twelve legions of angels? How then are the Scriptures to be fulfilled that it must happen so?' (contrast Mark and Luke). The incident and Jesus' condemnation dramatically exemplify his teaching against meeting violence with violence (5.38-48), and remind the audience in the story and readers of the narrative that what happened to Jesus was part of God's purpose. The reference to twelve legions of angels (the same as the number of disciples) is reminiscent of stories in 2 Maccabees (e.g. 3.24-39). The opportunity to concretize earlier teaching appears to have obscured historical reality. Had any of Jesus' disciples been armed and resisted Jesus' arrest, it is impossible to explain how he escaped arrest with him or immediate execution.

Jesus is pictured making the same points again in his address to the crowds: 'Did you come with swords and clubs to take me, as against a bandit? Day by day I sat in the temple teaching and you did not sieze me. But all of this happened so that the writings of the prophets might be fulfilled'. No quotations or allusions are provided here, but earlier quotations will be supplemented by more in the following depiction of Jesus' crucifixion. Moreover, Jesus' earlier allusion to Zech. 13.7 in his prophecy about the disciples' scattering is shown as fulfilled: 'Then all the disciples left him and fled'. In the context, their cowardice is to be understood as the result of their failure to pray (26.36-46).

Jesus before a Jewish Council: 26.57-68[1]

The narrative relates that those who arrested Jesus brought him to Caiaphas the high priest, where scribes and elders were assembled, apparently during the night. The Johannine account includes a condemnation by the high priest and his council before Jesus' arrest and in his absence (11.47-53), and pictures Jesus' questioning by a high priest, Annas, after his arrest (18.13, 19-24). There are historical uncertainties about the nature and function of the assembly, called a sanhedrin (from the Greek *sunedrion*) or council in Mt. 26.59 (see Mk 14.55; Lk. 22.66; Jn 11.47). The Mishnah, written about 225 CE, contains a whole tractate on the sanhedrin, which describes the authority of the 'greater sanhedrin of one and seventy', and of the 'lesser sanhedrin of three and twenty'. The numbers are justified from Scripture and so is their authority, but it is difficult to know whether the contents of the tractate reflect historical reality, and if so which period, or prescribe what should happen. It is unlikely that the tractate reflects what actually

1   See Mk 14.53-65; Lk. 22.54-55, 63-71; Jn 18.13-14, 19-24.

happened before the destruction of the temple in 70 CE. In the early
years of the first century no doubt the high priest consulted advisers in
matters of religious and political importance. Among his advisers could
have been chief priests, scribes and elders. The Fourth Gospel, but not
the Synoptics, mentions Pharisees (11.47). It is noteworthy that,
although the Synoptics picture Pharisees among Jesus' opponents in the
earlier parts of their narratives, they are never mentioned after Jesus'
arrest (except in the Matthaean story about the setting of a guard at the
tomb). Whatever the membership of an assembly when Caiaphas was
high priest, we would certainly be wrong in thinking of a sanhedrin as a
legally constituted body of elected representatives, like present-day city
councils in Western democracies. The Fourth Gospel describes a meeting of *a* council, rather than *the* council. The Synoptics refer to 'the
chief priests and the whole council' which does not imply the council's
formal standing. Scholars have debated whether it would have been
possible to assemble a council at night to consider charges against Jesus,
as Matthew and Mark, but not Luke and John, depict the proceedings.
Historically, this seems unlikely. But both Matthew and Mark juxtapose
the account of Jesus' appearance before the high priest with that of
Peter's denial in the courtyard outside. It was part of the tradition of
Peter's denial that it happened at night, before the cock crowed (Mt.
26.34, 74-75 and parallels in all the Gospels). The juxtaposition deter-
mines the timing of Jesus' appearance before the high priest at night. It
seems that a useful teaching purpose has overruled a historical purpose.

Immediately after the Matthaean reference to Jesus' appearance
before the high priest and the assembly of scribes and elders, the scene
shifts to Peter, who had followed Jesus from afar, entered the court of
the high priest and was sitting with the guards to see the end. The
narrative seems to imply that the assembly met within the high priest's
house. Readers are given a picture of Jesus within and Peter outside, in
the courtyard. As in the earlier story of Peter's walking on the sea
(14.28-29), he is initially pictured as more courageous than his fellow
disciples.

At this point, the spotlight shifts back to the chief priests and the
whole council, who were seeking false witnesses against Jesus, so that
they might put him to death. Many false witnesses came forward but
they were, apparently, unconvincing. But afterwards, two people came
forward and said, 'This man said, "I am able to destroy the temple of
God and to build it in three days"' (contrast Mark and note that Luke
and John do not mention this charge). It is remarkable that Judas, the
betrayer, is not represented as a witness against Jesus, although the
agreement of at least two witnesses would have been necessary to
sustain a capital charge (see Deut. 17.6-7; 19.15), so his witness alone
would not have been sufficient. In the context of the Matthaean narrative, the quoted accusation was false because, although Jesus' action in

the temple had symbolized destruction (21.12-13), his lament over Jerusalem had implied destruction (23.38), and he had prophesied its destruction to his disciples (24.2), he had been describing God's action, not his own, and had said nothing about rebuilding it. (The Fourth Gospel accepts the statement as Jesus' and interprets it as a reference to 'the temple of his body': Jn 2.19, 21). Undoubtedly, Jesus' action in the temple would have been offensive to all pious Jews, but it is not included among the charges at the hearing. The narrative guides the readers' response by picturing the Jewish leaders' seeking false testimony and by calling the quoted testimony false. When the high priest required an answer to the testimony, however, Jesus is pictured remaining silent (see Isa. 42.1-4, quoted in Mt. 12.18-21).

Nevertheless, the high priest is said to have demanded an answer to a further question: 'I adjure you by the living God that you tell us if you are the Christ, the son of God' (contrast John, which states that Annas questioned Jesus in general about his disciples and his teaching). In this way the major theme of chs. 26 and 27 is introduced. 'Christ' and 'son of God' are used as synonyms. But nothing had prepared readers to expect this question from the high priest. No witnesses had been described testifying to Jesus' claim to be the Christ, in spite of the fact that the narrative had depicted crowds' greeting him as son of David in Jerusalem (20.29, 31; 21.9, 15). It is the reader who can recognize that the high priest's question echoes Peter's confession (16.16). It is, moreover, this accusation which makes historical sense of Jesus' crucifixion by the Romans. According to all the Gospels' descriptions of Jesus' crucifixion, the charge that he or others claimed that he was the king of the Jews was written on his cross. Such a supposed claim would have been enough to make Jesus a danger to political security in Palestine, and would have constituted sufficient cause for his execution by crucifixion on the orders of the Roman prefect.

But the reply attributed to Jesus in the First Gospel is evasive: 'You say' or 'those are your words' (contrast Mark). The reply continues, however, with words reminiscent of his earlier teaching to the disciples in private (24.29-31): 'Nevertheless, I say to you, hereafter you will see the son of man seated at the right hand of power and coming on the clouds of heaven' (see also Dan. 7.13-14, 18, 22, 27; Ps. 110.1; Mt. 25.31-46). The prophecy sets Jesus' dialogue with the high priest in the larger context of God's imminent eschatological judgment and implies that the roles of the high priest and Jesus would be reversed. The high priest's reaction is described as tearing his robes, a sign of outrage (2 Kgs 18.37), and declaring, 'he reviled [God]. Why do we still need witnesses? See now you heard his slander. What do you think?', to which the assembly replied, 'He is worthy of death'. How are readers to interpret this charge, 'worthy of death'? Scripture required that someone who cursed God should suffer the death penalty (Lev. 24.10-23). But Lev. 24.16 uses the phrase 'specify the name [of God]' and later Jews interpreted this to mean that only people who explicitly cursed the name of God were guilty (*m. Sanh.* 7.5). Neither in the Leviticus passage, nor elsewhere in the Pentateuch, however, does the Septuagint use the vague Greek word *blasphemein*, to slander or revile, or *blasphemia*, slander, which are used by the high priest in the synoptic accounts. These Greek words are most often used in contexts in which people, not God, were slandered. In Ezek. 35.12-13 and 1 Macc. 2.6, however, they are found in contexts in which it was God who was slandered.[1] In what sense could Jesus' statement, 'You will see the son of man seated at the right hand of power [God] and coming on the clouds of heaven' slander God? Jesus had not claimed in his address to the high priest that he was that son of man, although readers would make that identification. The prophecy implied that God was about to transform the world into his eschatological kingdom by means of a human agent within the lifetime of the high priest ('You will see'). The high priest seems to be depicted interpreting the prophecy as false and hence as a slander against God. Readers had already been made aware of the Sadducees' mockery of belief in the resurrection (22.23-33). According to Deut. 13.5, a false prophet should be put to death. It is the Deuteronomic command which makes sense of the high priest's interpretation and the assembly's decision: 'He is worthy of death'.

Nevertheless, the decision raises historical problems. Jesus and his followers were not the only Jews who expected an eschatological judgment. Both Essenes and Pharisees shared that expectation. In the first century, however, chief priests and elders did not persecute Essenes and Pharisees for their belief. Perhaps what distinguished John the Baptist and Jesus from those other Jewish groups was that they expected God to act in the very near future, and that crowds of people believed them. John the Baptist had been killed by Herod Antipas' order, and now Jesus was reckoned worthy of death.

The Matthaean scene ends, 'Then they spat in his face and struck him; and some slapped him saying, prophesy to us, Christ, who struck you?' (contrast Mark and Luke and see Isa. 50.6). This abuse and mockery of Jesus' ability to prophesy confirms the interpretation that he was condemned as a false prophet. But the repetition of the word 'Christ', in spite of the fact that he had not affirmed the claim, suggests that he was also condemned as a messianic pretender.

The Matthaean account of Jesus' questioning by the high priest and his advisers, then, is neither nonsensical nor historically inconceivable, but it is historically unverifiable. Not only does it differ in detail from the accounts in the other Gospels, but there are also the difficulties that none of Jesus' followers was present, and that they had no opportunity

1   See Sanders, *Jewish Law*, pp. 57-67.

to learn anything about the proceedings from Jesus himself. Given the general probability, however, that the high priest would have questioned a Jewish religious leader in order to advise Pilate, the Matthaean account provides plausible reasons for their wishing to see him executed. Someone who could sway crowds with a vision of God's imminent judgment and who was thought by some people to be the messiah posed a political threat to the stability of Palestine. The high priest would have wanted to discourage any movement which could have led to Roman troops' killing many Jews, and the Roman prefect would have been anxious to prevent disturbances in his territory. Nevertheless, the main purpose of the Matthaean narrative was to create understanding in its Christian readers, and it creates the understanding that Jesus was executed as the Christ, the prophet and the son of man by people who did not believe that he was those things.

Peter's Denial of his Association with Jesus: 26.69-75[1]

The story of Peter's threefold denial of his association with Jesus serves as a warning to readers. Peter had been courageous enough to follow Jesus after his arrest, but, when faced with dangers to himself, he lied in his denials (cf. 14.30). The four versions in the Gospels differ in detail but agree in presenting three occasions when Peter denied his association with Jesus in answers to questions from bystanders. According to the Matthaean version, he was questioned by two serving girls, first in the courtyard and then in the gateway, and finally by a group who heard his previous denial. The questioners identified Jesus as a Galilean or as Jesus of Nazareth, and the final group suggested that Peter's speech betrayed his association. Peter's denials arose in intensity: 'I do not understand what you say', then with an oath, 'I do not know the person', and finally he began to curse and swear 'I do not know the person'. The narrative notes that immediately the cock crowed and that Peter remembered Jesus' statement, 'Before the cock crows, you will deny me three times' (see 26.34). Peter's reaction is to go out and weep bitterly, but there is no suggestion that he retracted his denials (cf. 10.33; 13.21; and contrast 14.31-32). Peter's three denials mirror his three lost chances to pray in Gethsemane.

Jesus is taken to Pilate: 27.1-2[2]

The crowing of the cock had marked the dawn, and the narrative returns to the activities of the Jewish leaders: 'Early in the morning, all the chief priests and elders of the people took counsel to put him to death, and they bound him and brought him and handed him over to Pilate the governor' (only Matthew explains that Pilate was the gover-

1   See Mk 14.66-72; Lk. 22.56-62; Jn 18.15-18, 25-27.
2   See Mk 15.1; Lk. 23.1; Jn 18.28-32.

nor). The text seems to imply, without a full explanation, that only the Roman governor had the power to execute offenders (see Jn 18.31). We are not in a position to be quite certain, however, whether the high priest had power independently to effect the execution of offenders during the twenties and thirties of the first century. Some evidence suggests that he did. For example, he certainly had power independently to effect the execution of Gentiles who dared to enter the inner courts of the temple (Josephus, *Ant*. 15.417, and note the archaeological evidence cited in the LCL edition). Moreover, Acts' account of Stephen's stoning (Acts 6.8–8.1) relates that the stoning was carried out after a hearing by the high priest and his advisers. Nevertheless, the account is open to the interpretation that the stoning was an expression of revulsion at Stephen's denigration of the temple, rather than a legal execution. The reason for suggesting this interpretation is provided by Josephus, whose account of the execution of James, the brother of Jesus, and of other Christians in Jerusalem at the instigation of the high priest Ananus makes clear that Ananus acted illegally, taking advantage of the absence of the Roman governor (*Ant*. 20.200). Other Jews complained to King Agrippa and to the new Roman governor, with the result that Ananus was deposed from the high priesthood. This evidence supports the view that the high priest had no legal power to order Jesus' execution. Whatever the power of the high priest, however, if Pilate became aware of a messianic claim on Jesus' behalf, Jesus' execution would have been his responsibility.

Judas's Suicide: 27.3-10[1]

In contrast to the account of Peter's remorse at denying Jesus, the account about Judas' realization that Jesus had been condemned relates that Judas both repented and tried to undo his part in the proceedings. He returned the money to the chief priests and elders, saying, 'I sinned in betraying innocent blood'. But his action failed to save Jesus, meeting only with dismissal: 'What is that to us? You see to it'. Judas then threw the money into the temple, and departed and hanged himself (contrast Acts 1.18). The story impresses readers with the assertion of Jesus' innocence, with the powerlessness of Judas to prevent the consequences of his betrayal and his despairing suicide, and with the complacency of the Jewish leadership, who had already found reasons for Jesus' execution. The story discourages Christian readers from betraying others. But the narrative does not immediately return to the subject of Jesus' appearance before Pilate. Instead it recounts what happened to the money. It tells that, since the money could not become part of the temple treasure, the priests bought the potter's field in which to bury foreigners. It notes that 'that field is called the field of blood to this day', that is, to the day

1   Cf. Acts 1.18-19.

when the narrative was written. Stories which explain a contemporary name in this way are common in Scripture (e.g. Gen. 26.33; 35.20; Josh. 4.9; Ezek. 20.29). It seems unlikely that the original readers would have been familiar with the named field, since Jerusalem had been ravaged in the war of 66–74 CE, but the reference helps to authenticate the story. Acts 1.19 also calls the field 'the field of blood' but offers another explanation of the name. Further support for the Matthaean account is supplied by a quotation from Scripture, which is said to have been fulfilled: 'Then was fulfilled what was spoken through Jeremiah the prophet, saying, and they took the thirty silver coins, the price of him on whom a price had been set by some of the sons of Israel, and they gave them for the potter's field, as the Lord directed me' (Jer. 18.2; 19.1, 4, 11; 32.6-9; and see Zech. 11.12-13). Most of the details of the citation come from Zechariah, including the amount of silver, which was thrown into the treasury according to the Syriac version, or to the potter according to the Hebrew version, or to the smelting furnace according to the Septuagint. The text is no more than an allusion to the Jeremiah passages, with details from Zechariah, but it creates the impression that God's purpose encompassed even the repercussions of betrayal.

Jesus is Questioned by Pilate: 27.11-14[1]

The most remarkable features of this account of Jesus' trial before Pilate are its brevity and its lack of details. The story opens by noting that Jesus stood before the governor and then reports the governor's question, 'Are you the king of the Jews?' Why Pilate asked the question is not explained. Readers are not even encouraged to infer that he had been briefed by the high priest. Jesus' reply, 'You say so', is an evasion, but nothing is said about the question's being repeated. Instead there is a general statement about unspecified accusations from the chief priests and elders (contrast Luke), to whom Jesus answered nothing, so that Pilate asked, 'Do you not hear how many things [unspecified] they testify against you?' And the narrative relates that, when Jesus gave no reply, Pilate was exceedingly amazed. The account may have been influenced by Isa. 42.1-4 and 53.7. It hardly represents accurate knowledge of the proceedings of a trial before a Roman governor. Its brevity, the vagueness of the accusations, apart from Pilate's initial question about Jesus' kingship, the acceptance of Jesus' silence and the absence of a sentence serve to mask the fact that Pilate must have condemned Jesus to death by crucifixion as a messianic pretender. That Jesus alone was tried, while his disciples were allowed to go free, implies that he was not thought to be a guerilla leader with armed confederates.

1   See Mk 15.2-5; Lk. 23.3-5; Jn 18.33-38.

Otherwise his disciples would have been killed with him.[1]

The nature of the narrative and the portrait of Pilate in this and subsequent Matthaean scenes suggests an apologetic motive. Pilate is represented as an ineffectual governor, too easily swayed, against his own convictions, by the local population. Since Christians had to live in the Roman world, it would have been too dangerous for them to specify the reasons for Pilate's sentencing Jesus to crucifixion, a sentence which other governors could have used against Jesus' followers. But in the historical context of the time, had Pilate known that Jesus was thought to be the Christ, he would have had no compunction in having him executed for sedition, and the detail that Jesus was crucified with the claim to be king of the Jews written on the cross implies that this is what happened. Nor did the Gospels' obscuring the matter succeed in endearing Christians to the Romans. Tacitus, the first-century Roman historian, in recounting Nero's persecution of Christians in Rome, explains that 'Christ, from whom the name [Christians] had its origin, suffered the extreme penalty during the reign of Tiberius at the hands of one of our procurators, Pontius Pilate, and a deadly superstitition, thus checked for the moment, again broke out, not only in Judaea, the first source of the evil, but also in the city [Rome]' (*Annals* 15.44.2-8). Moreover, both Philo and Josephus, first-century Jewish writers, provide portraits of Pilate which emphasise his decisiveness, severity and cruelty (Philo, *Leg. Gai.* 28.299-305; Josephus, *War* 2.167-77). He appears not to be the kind of man to be impressed by a poor provincial's dignified silence.

Nevertheless, Christian readers, to whom the narrative is directed, could gain insight from the depiction of Jesus' behaviour at his trial. Like the servant in Isaiah's prophecies, he did not wrangle with his accusers.

The Governor's Passover Custom: 27.15-26[2]

The next scene is introduced by a reference to the governor's custom of releasing a prisoner to the crowd at Passover time (Matthew calls it the governor's custom, Mark Pilate's personal custom, John a Jewish custom, and Luke mentions no custom but simply depicts the crowd's asking for Barabbas' release). There are no other references to such a custom in contemporary literature, Jewish or Roman, but since Passover celebrated the release of Israelite slaves from Egypt, it is not impossible that a Roman governor might release a prisoner at such a time, as a sop to the crowds, although it is surprising that Josephus never mentions it. In the Matthaean account, Barabbas is introduced with, 'And they had then a notorious prisoner called Barabbas' (Mark and Luke specify his crimes). Barabbas is a patronym meaning 'son of

1   See Sanders, *Jesus and Judaism*, ch. 11.
2   See Mk 15.6-15; Lk. 23.13-25; Jn 18.39–19.16.

Abba', and 'Abba' itself means 'father'. Some manuscripts of Matthew supply the personal name Jesus, which is not found in other accounts. If the reading is accepted, and if it accurately records the name, it suggests that the crowd chose between two prisoners with the same name, since Pilate's question to the crowd which had gathered would read, 'Whom do you want me to release to you, Jesus Barabbas or Jesus who is called Christ?' (contrast Mark). The narrative then explains the question by giving information about Pilate's private thoughts: 'For he knew that out of envy they had handed him over'. The explanation guides readers to condemn the Jewish leadership accordingly.

The First Gospel, without parallel in the others, also provides another explanation for Pilate's desire to release Jesus: 'And while he was sitting on the judgment seat, his wife sent to him saying, "have nothing to do with that just man, for I suffered many things today in a dream on his account"'. Not since the stories about Jesus' birth and infancy had dreams been mentioned. In those earlier accounts, dreams had been understood as warnings from God to avoid dangerous mistakes. Pilate's wife's dream serves the same purpose. This time, however, the danger was not avoided. The story graphically reminds readers of Jesus' innocence (Luke achieves the same end by recounting Jesus' appearance before Herod).

The narrative then relates that, apparently during this interlude, the chief priests and elders persuaded the crowds to ask for Barabbas and destroy Jesus. Earlier, readers had been told that the crowds had been so impressed by Jesus that they had hailed him as son of David. Some explanation of their change of allegiance is therefore necessary. The responsibility is placed with the Jewish leadership. Hence, when Pilate again asks, 'Which of the two do you want me to release to you?', they call for Barabbas. Moreover, when Pilate goes on to ask, 'Then what shall I do with Jesus who is called Christ?' all the crowds respond, 'Let him be crucified'. Readers are left in no doubt that Jesus was crucified as the Christ, his true status from the narrative's perspective. This is the first time in the story of Jesus' ministry in Jerusalem that the manner of his death is mentioned. Crucifixion was a horrific form of execution, a slow death by torture in public, inflicted by Romans against provincials whom they found guilty of sedition. Hundreds of Jewish insurgents were crucified around the walls of Jerusalem during the Roman siege in 70 CE. This public torment warned others not to revolt against Rome.

Nevertheless, the reply attributed to Pilate suggests Jesus' innocence: 'Why, what evil has he done?' In the context of the unspecified accusations from Jewish leaders and of Pilate's own question about his kingship, none of which had been answered, the question hardly makes sense in the historical context, but it prompts readers to supply the answer 'None'. The crowds, however, are depicted crying the more, 'Let him be crucified'. The account of Pilate's next action (no synoptic parallels) reinforces the theme of Jesus' innocence, but it is set in the context of menace: 'And when Pilate saw that he was gaining nothing but rather a riot was beginning, he took water and washed his hands before the crowd saying, "I am innocent of this man's blood; you see to it" '. The dramatic action and its interpretation absolve Pilate from responsibility (see Deut. 21.1-9). The whole people is then shown accepting the responsibility which Pilate refused: 'His blood be upon us and upon our children' (no synoptic parallels). The narrative clearly guides readers to see Jesus' execution as the sole responsibility of the Jews and not the Romans. Moreover, the guilt incurred is understood by the narrative to lead to God's punishment in the destruction of Jerusalem (23.35-39). Historically, however, there can be no doubt that the Romans were responsible for Jesus' execution. Had Pilate really handed him over to the Jews for execution, he would have been stoned, not crucified by Roman soldiers. The apologetic motive behind the narrative has to be recognized to make sense of what happened. In laying the blame on Jews, however, the narrative was not inciting readers to take revenge on their Jewish contemporaries. Earlier teaching had excluded such behaviour (5.43-48). We cannot hold the narrative responsible for the vicious persecutions of Jews by Christians in pogroms at Easter when Christians had gained power.

The scene is brought to a close by the statement, 'Then he released Barabbas to them, but Jesus he had scourged and handed him over to be crucified'. Scourging and torture were customarily the prelude to Roman crucifixion (e.g. Josephus, *War* 5.449). The narrative shows that what Jesus had predicted was fulfilled (20.17-19).

Soldiers' Mockery of the King of the Jews: 27.27-31[1]
That the soldiers of the governor took Jesus into the praetorium (a Latin loanword indicating the governor's residence), where the whole cohort (normally 600 men) gathered before him, demonstrates, despite everything said to the contrary, that responsibility for Jesus' crucifixion was Roman. Whether Pilate's residence in Jerusalem was Herod's palace or the Antonia fortress is uncertain. The narrative relates that Jesus was stripped and dressed in a scarlet cloak (contrast Mark's purple; scarlet was the colour of the troops' cloaks), with a plaited crown of thorns on his head and a reed in his right hand (contrast details in Mark, Luke and John; Luke sets the scene at Herod's residence). In other words, he was mockingly dressed as a king. Hence the soldiers' falling on their knees before him and mocking him: 'Hail king of the Jews'. But this play-acting was also accompanied by their spitting upon him as a gesture of contempt and their taking the reed and beating his head (contrast John). The story not only invites readers' sympathy for Jesus' sufferings

1   See Mk 15.16-20; Jn 19.2-3.

but again reminds them that he was truly king. It ends with the restoration of Jesus' garments and their leading him away to be crucified.

Jesus' Crucifixion: 27.32-44[1]

'As they were going out, they found a man from Cyrene called Simon and forced this person to carry his cross.' It was customary for prisoners to carry their own crosses (Plutarch, *Morals* 554, and see the Johannine account), but perhaps someone else was forced to do so if the prisoner was too weak after the scourging. Simon of Cyrene is never mentioned again (Mark calls Simon the father of Alexander and Rufus, as if the sons were known to the Markan community). Cyrene was a district in north Africa, and the detail about his place of origin implies that either he had come from there as a pilgrim to the festival or had moved to Palestine (Mark and Luke mention that he had come in from the countryside). The narrative continues, 'And they came to the place called Golgotha, which means the place of the skull'. The place cannot be identified with certainty; it must have been outside the city. The name suggests that it was either a rocky prominence shaped like a skull or a place of execution. The account notes that, before Jesus was crucified, he was given wine mixed with gall (see Ps. 69.21; Mark has 'wine mixed with myrrh', a concoction which probably deadened pain), but that when he tasted it, he did not want to drink it. Nevertheless, the allusion to the psalm which describes the sufferings of a just person reminds readers that God allowed the sufferings of the innocent. 'And they crucified him and divided his garments, casting a lot' (see Ps. 22.18. Mark mentions that he was crucified at the third hour, 9am) alludes to a second psalm about the sufferings of the just. 'And they were sitting and keeping watch over him there. And above his head was written the charge against him, this is Jesus the king of the Jews.' The notice warns others about the fate awaiting any claimant to kingship in a Roman province, but yet again reminds readers that Jesus died as the Christ. The narrative then notes that two bandits were crucified each side of Jesus.

The reactions of passers-by are then depicted: they were 'shaking their heads and saying, "You who would destroy the temple and rebuild it in three days, save yourself; if you are a son of God, come down from the cross"'. 'If you are a son of God' echoes the words of the slanderer in the story of Jesus' tests (4.3, 6) and helps readers to understand the suggestion as a test of Jesus' fidelity. Similarly, the chief priests, scribes and elders are described joining in the abuse by saying: 'He saved others, himself he cannot save. He is the king of Israel, let him now come down from the cross and we shall believe in him. He has trusted in God, let him rescue him now if he wants him, for he said, "I

1   See Mk 15.21-32; Lk. 23.26-43; Jn 19.17-27.

am a son of God"' (see Wis. 2.6-20; 5.4-5; Ps. 22.7-9; Lam. 2.15). Again, this is to be construed as a test from those who did not believe that the Christ could suffer violence. Even the bandits crucified with Jesus are pictured reviling him in the same way (contrast Luke).

The narrative highlights the way in which Jesus was surrounded in his torment by agents of the slanderer (contrast Luke and John). The statement that he had saved others, as the narrative had described, suggests to readers that he could have saved himself (cf. 26.53) but that he remained faithful to God's purpose, expressed in the psalms and wisdom writings. Readers could find no easy comfort in this scene.

The Death of Jesus: 27.45-56[1]

In spite of the narrative's failure to mention the time when Jesus' crucifixion began (compare Mark's 'the third hour'), it now mentions that there was darkness over all the land from the sixth to the ninth hour (from noon till 3pm). Scriptural references suggest that the darkness at noon signalled God's judgment against injustice (Amos 8.9-10; Exod. 10.22). Up to this point in the account of Jesus' crucifixion, the narrative had focused on people other than Jesus, but now his only words from the cross are recounted: 'About the ninth hour, Jesus cried out in a loud voice, "Eli, Eli, lama sabachthani?", which means, "My God, my God, why did you abandon me?"' (contrast Luke and John). The words come from Ps. 22.1 and poignantly express a sense of abandonment to suffering and death inflicted by enemies. Like the psalmist, Jesus had been scorned, despised and mocked by everyone. The cry offers no consolation to readers since it implies that God had truly let Jesus suffer and die (see 26.39). It was necessary for the text to quote the Hebrew of the psalm (Mark seems to quote the Aramaic, but the Matthaean version better explains what follows), so that the bystanders' misunderstanding would be comprehensible. Some of them are depicted saying, 'This man is calling for Elijah', but readers had already learned that Elijah had come (John the Baptist) and that they did to him whatever they wanted (17.12), that is, that he too had suffered martyrdom (14.3-12). The action of the crowd, then, is seen to express a false hope: 'one of them ran and took a sponge, and filled it with vinegar (see Ps. 69.21) and put it on a spear to enable him to drink. And the rest was saying, "Let us see if Elijah comes to save him"'. Immediately, however, the narrative records Jesus' death: 'But Jesus again cried in a loud voice [see Ps. 22.2, 5] and gave up his spirit'.

This stark and harrowing depiction of Jesus' death is followed by the recounting of a series of extraordinary events which indicate the human and theological significance of his death. First the curtain of the temple (see Exod. 26.31-35; Lev. 21.23; 24.3; the curtain veiled the Holy

1   See Mk 15.33-41; Lk. 22.44-49; Jn 19.28-30.

of Holies) was torn in two from top to bottom. This graphic intimation of the temple's profanation reminds readers of Jesus' prophecy about the temple's destruction (24.2) and of the accusations made against him by the false witnesses (26.61), which were repeated by people who passed by the cross (27.40). It represents God's endorsement of Jesus' fidelity and God's warning to his enemies. But in the Matthaean version, that event was also accompanied by the splitting of rocks so that 'the tombs were opened and many bodies of saints who were dead arose [see Ezek. 37.7, 12-13] and, after his [Jesus'] resurrection, went out from the tombs and entered the holy city and appeared to many'. Jesus' predictions of his suffering and death had also included predictions of his resurrection. The narrative here looks beyond the time of his death to his resurrection and pictures the saints who had died as martyrs in the past (see Dan. 7.18; 12.1-3) as fellow witnesses, restored from the tombs when Jesus' contemporaries had abandoned or rejected him. The narrative gives hope to the readers that those who died a martyr's death would be resurrected.

The words of the Gentile centurion and those who were with him guarding Jesus, were, then, an expression of their terror at the earthquake and the things that had happened (contrast Mark): 'Truly this man was a son of God' (contrast Luke and John). As in the infancy story, Gentiles are presented as people who recognized Jesus' significance when Jewish leaders had rejected him (2.1-18).

The narrative then indicates that Jesus was not quite bereft of followers when he died: 'Many women who had followed him from Galilee to serve him were watching from afar, among whom was Mary Magdalene, and Mary the mother of James and Joseph (that is, Jesus' mother; see 13.55), and the mother of the sons of Zebedee (see 20.20. These women must be understood to have been amongst those who gathered in Galilee to go to Judaea: 17.22; 19.1). Mark names Mary Magdalene, Mary the mother of James the younger and Joseph (that is, Jesus' mother; see Mark 6.3) and Salome. Luke includes no names. John names Mary the wife of Clopas, Mary Magdalene, and mentions Jesus' mother and his mother's sister. These women, then, were witnesses of Jesus' death. Some of them will also be mentioned as witnesses of his burial and resurrection. In the absence of Jesus' disciples, the narrative allows them to play the important part of confirming that the Jesus who was crucified and buried was the Jesus who was raised from the dead.

The Burial of Jesus' Corpse: 27.57-61[1]

The narrative introduces a new character as the person who was responsible for Jesus' burial: 'When it was evening, there came a rich person from Arimathaea [apparently a place in Judaea] whose name

1   See Mk 15.42-47; Lk. 23.50-56; Jn 19.38-42.

was Joseph, and who was himself a disciple of Jesus'. All the Gospels attribute Jesus' burial to Joseph (only the Fourth Gospel associates Nicodemus with him), but the Markan and Lukan accounts explain his action by noting that he was a member of the council and was looking for the kingdom of God. The Matthaean version does not describe him as a member of the council, makes him a rich man (see Isa. 53.9), and calls him a disciple (also John), although he was not one of the twelve. To him is given the task of asking Pilate for Jesus' body, again indicating Pilate's responsibility for Jesus' execution, a request which Pilate granted (cf. 14.12). Then he took it and wrapped it in a pure linen garment (contrast John) and laid it in his (contrast Mark and Luke; see Isa. 53.9) new grave which he had hewn from the rock, and he rolled a great stone to the door of the grave and departed. Such tombs, hewn from the rock with stones covering the entrance, have been excavated outside Jerusalem. The narrative leaves the readers in no doubt that Jesus really had died and was buried. Once more, it notes the presence of women, Mary Magdalene and the other Mary, who were sitting opposite the tomb. In this way, the correct identity of the tomb is ensured.

The need for a comparative stranger to perform the service of burial is partly explained by the flight of Jesus' eleven disciples, and by his family's Galilean origin. The Matthaean narrative, however, is formed to remind readers of the suffering servant's fate: 'And they made his grave with the wicked and with a rich man in his death, although he had done no violence, and there was no deceit in his mouth' (Isa. 53.9).

Setting a Guard at the Tomb: 27.62-66

Only the First Gospel recounts this story and what followed from it (28.11-15). 'Next day, that is after the preparation' seems to refer to the Sabbath, since 'the preparation' was the day before the Sabbath. 'The chief priests and the Pharisees gathered before Pilate [this is the first mention of Pharisees since ch. 23] saying, "Lord, we remember that that deceiver said while living, 'After three days I am to be raised'"' (see 12.40 addressed to scribes and Pharisees). Jesus' claim is the reason for a request: 'Therefore, order that a guard be set at the tomb till the third day, lest his disciples come and steal him and say to the crowd, "He is raised from the dead", and the last deceit will be worse than the first'. Pilate is said to have acceded to the request: 'Take a guard; go and set the guard as you know [how]'. The narrative notes that they secured the tomb by sealing the stone and setting the guard (see Dan. 6.17).

The story serves three purposes. It shows that Jewish leaders viewed Jesus as someone who had led people astray, and viewed his disciples as deceivers too. Thus their failure to believe in Jesus' resurrection is explained. Secondly, it allows the presence of spectators at the tomb, Roman soldiers who had been presented as more sympathetic to Jesus' claims than the Jewish leaders (27.54). Thirdly, it alerts readers to a possible but false explanation of the empty tomb which will be described in the account which follows.

Looking back over this series of scenes as a historian, they seem to provide sufficient if not straightforward evidence to conclude that Jesus was crucified by the Romans as a claimant to kingship who threatened Roman power by raising hopes among the Jewish population. But even the Roman authorities could distinguish a charismatic preacher from a guerilla leader. Hence, it makes historical sense that only Jesus was crucified and his disciples were allowed to go free. As in the case of John the Baptist, the authorities could assume that once a prophetic figure was dead, any following would disappear. We can be less sure of the role of Jewish authorities in these events. It is likely that the high priest and his advisers would have been alarmed by Jesus' preaching about an imminent kingdom, by his dramatic action in the temple, and by any suggestion that he was regarded as the Christ, since they too would have realized the political implications of these beliefs, and would have wanted to save the Jewish population from enthusiastically embracing them, with their likely effects of rioting and Roman military reprisals. In this context, Jesus' appearance before the high priest, as a prelude to his trial before Pilate, makes historical sense. But Pilate must have been responsible for Jesus' execution by crucifixion, and even the Matthaean narrative makes it clear that his soldiers carried out the sentence. The details of the Matthaean hearing before the high priest are not implausible but, historically, they could rest at best on hearsay or a likely reconstruction. Details about Jesus' trial before Pilate are significantly lacking and the portrait of Pilate as a dithering incompetent who was outwitted by Jewish leaders must be reckoned unhistorical, not only because it conflicts with accounts in Philo and Josephus, but also because such a governor could not have retained his position for ten years as Pilate did (26–36 CE). Details about Jesus' crucifixion, Simon's carrying his cross, Jesus' isolation in suffering and death, his cry of abandonment and its misunderstanding by those who heard, and Joseph's arranging his burial, are all historically probable. Other details which echo Amos 8.9-10, Psalms 22 and 69 and Isaiah 42 and 53 serve to make sense of Jesus' suffering and death as the expression of God's purpose for human beings. Some accounts of incidents—Judas's suicide, Pilate's wife's dream, the setting of the guard at the tomb—which are found only in the First Gospel, have to be reckoned as historically improbable, as inventions which serve rhetorical rather than historical purposes. The whole narrative combines history and theology in order to convince readers that Jesus was the prophet and Christ promised by God in Scripture, that his sufferings and death were those of a just and obedient son of God, and that they were exemplary for readers, encouraging them to take up their cross and follow Jesus.

Matthew 28: Jesus' Resurrection From the Dead

The narrative had shown that Jesus' prophecies about his future death in Jerusalem had been fulfilled, but those prophecies had also included references to his resurrection from the dead 'on the third day'. Readers had been reminded about his resurrection at the moment of his death, in the description of the saints' coming out of the tombs (27.51-53). The final chapter of the narrative focuses both on the fact of Jesus' resurrection and on the significance of his resurrection for other people.

Jesus' Tomb found Empty: 28.1-10[1]

'Late in the night of the Sabbath, at the dawning of the first day of the week, Mary Magdalene and the other Mary came to see the grave' (Mark and Luke give the women the alternative purpose of going to anoint the corpse. Mark names Mary Magdalene, Mary the mother of James, and Salome: Luke names Mary Magdalene, Mary the mother of James, and Joanna, with other women; John names Mary Magdalene). The events to be described, then, take place 'on the third day' after Jesus' death. 'And behold there was a great earthquake, for an angel of the Lord descended from heaven and came and rolled away the stone and was sitting upon it. And his appearance was like lightning and his clothing white as snow' (contrast the other Gospels, and see 27.51-53 and Dan. 10.6). The angel is understood to be a messenger from God, but unlike the angels appearing in dreams to Joseph (1.20; 2.13, 19), this angel is not described as coming in a dream and nor did he warn about historical dangers. Rather he appeared in order to interpret a past event as an eschatological reality. The description of the guards' reaction intensifies the awesomeness of the appearance: 'Those who were keeping watch were shaken by fear and became like the dead' (no parallels in the other Gospels; see Dan. 10.7-9). These 'outsiders', therefore, were made aware of God's action and responded with terror. But the angel reassured the women, 'Do not be afraid, for I know that you are seeking Jesus who was crucified'. The speech also highlights the reality of Jesus' death by crucifixion, but continues by announcing Jesus' resurrection from the dead, inviting the women to recognize that the tomb was empty: 'He is not here, for he is raised as he said. Come, see the place where he was lying'.

The form of the narrative guides readers to understand that belief in Jesus' resurrection was not based on the wishful thinking of credulous women but was inspired by God. That the tomb was empty is recognized, however, as no proof of Jesus' resurrection. That fact is

1   See Mk 16.1-8; Lk. 24.1-12; Jn 20.1-10.

open to the interpretation, for example, that the disciples had stolen the corpse, as the earlier narrative about the setting of the guard had shown. However unlikely such an interpretation had been made to appear by the account of the sealing of the stone and the setting of the guard, that or an alternative common-sense explanation was still more likely than that God had raised Jesus from the dead. The narrative does nothing to hide the extraordinary novelty of God's raising Jesus, and it emphasizes that belief in his resurrection came from God's inspiration.

All the Gospels record, with varying details, that women (in John only Mary Magdalene) found the grave empty. This implies that resurrection was understood to involve bodily transformation. Resurrection was not the survival of Jesus' soul after his physical death, but the transformation of his corpse into a new bodily life. It assumes an anthropology which did not separate soul and body, and which conceived post-mortem existence as bodily existence. Moreover, bodily resurrection implies personal, individual survival after death, not the post-mortem survival of an undifferentiated humanity. It is understood as God's vindication of a just and obedient person. Nevertheless, the narrative distinguishes resurrection from resuscitation. The little girl who had been resuscitated (9.18-26) came back from the dead to live a normal, historical, mortal existence. It would have made sense to ask about her where she lived and when she died a second time. But it would not make sense to ask about the resurrected Jesus, 'what was his address', or 'when did he die a second time?' Bodily resurrection gave a different kind of personal existence. In the Matthaean account, Jesus' corpse had disappeared while the tomb was sealed and guarded. Moreover, Jesus' post-mortem existence was conceived as eternal. It was the beginning of God's eschatological transformation of the world. On the historical level, there was the ambiguous evidence of the grave's emptiness, which faith interpreted as evidence of an eschatological reality. Acceptance of God's raising Jesus from the dead is presented as a matter of faith inspired by God. And only those who believed that Jesus was God's agent during the historical ministry are described by the Gospels as those who believed God had raised him. Those who rejected him during his ministry also rejected belief in his resurrection (28.11-15); so, at least, suggest the Gospels. They do not encompass the case of Paul, who was a persecutor of Christians but who became a Christian missionary to Gentiles in response to what he described as God's revelation of his son and God's call to become a missionary (Gal. 1.12-17).

In the Matthaean narrative, the angel's message continues with instructions about what the women should do: 'Go quickly and tell his disciples that he is raised from the dead and that, behold, he goes before you into Galilee; there you will see him. Behold, I told you'. Hence the women became the first human messengers of Jesus' resurrection. They had witnessed his death by crucifixion, his burial, the emptiness of his

grave, and they had been given the divine message to make his resurrection known to his disciples, who had deserted him. They were in a
position to know that it was the Jesus who had been crucified and
buried who was raised from the dead.

The narrative notes their immediate obedience: 'And they departed
quickly from the grave with fear and great joy and were running to
report to the disciples' (contrast Mark). But it goes on to recount their
meeting with Jesus himself: 'And behold Jesus met them saying, "Hail",
and they went up and took hold of his feet and did obeisance'
(contrast Mark and Luke). Their response is appropriate to a meeting
with the Christ who had been raised from the dead. It expresses the
significance of his resurrection for them; he was their master who had
shown them the way to live and to die in obedience to the God who
vindicated the just after death. The gesture of holding his feet indicates
that the women were determined to prevent Jesus' departure (compare
the woman's holding Elisha's feet, 2 Kgs 4.27, and see Jn 20.17). Perhaps,
therefore, 'they took hold of his feet' should not be taken literally but as
an idiomatic expression of their desire to keep him with them. The narrative gives no indication of the resurrected Jesus' appearance, but
rather draws attention to his words: 'Then Jesus said to them, "Do not
be afraid. Go and tell my brothers to go into Galilee, and there they shall
see me"' (contrast Luke and John). The content of Jesus' message is the
same as the angel's, but he refers to his disciples (see 28.16) as brothers.
In spite of the disciples' desertion and Peter's denial, therefore, they are
still reckoned to be sons of their heavenly Father, brothers of Jesus.
Moreover, Jesus' command to go and tell the disciples implies that the
women should not hold onto Jesus but should act as his agents.

Why does the narrative relate the story in this form, which centres on
the women's reactions and Jesus' message? We should recognize the
difficulty of conveying to readers the reality and significance of Jesus'
resurrection at the end of an account of his historical ministry. That
reality was unlike normal historical events, and the narrative had to
intimate the difference. But Scripture had also recounted extraordinary
meetings. For example, Genesis 18–19 tells the story of Abraham and
Lot's meeting with God's angelic messengers and receiving their
messages. According to Matthew, Jesus had taught that those who were
resurrected would be like angels (22.30). Hence the stories of the resurrected Jesus' meetings with his followers take scriptural stories of meetings with angelic visitors as models.

Jesus' message to the disciples is a message of reconciliation, but the
narrative provides no message for the women themselves, apart from
the command not to be afraid and to go to the disciples. Their story is
told, however, to epitomize the appropriate response of every reader
to inspired belief in Jesus' resurrection. The women were not commissioned in the manner in which the disciples would be (28.19-20), but

their role represents the part to be played by every follower of Jesus, whereas the disciples' role represents the part to be played by missionary leaders. That the two representations are divided between women and men, however, should not lead to the inference that only men could become prophetic leaders and missionaries among Jesus' followers. The unnamed woman who had anointed Jesus for burial (26.6-13) had performed a prophetic act. Even in the patriarchal world of the first century, women became missionaries and leaders in Pauline churches (e.g. 1 Cor. 1.11; 11.5; Romans 16).

The Bribing of the Guard: 28.11-15

The aftermath of the Matthaean story about the setting of the guard is now recounted: 'While they [the women] were going, behold some of the guard went into the city and reported to the chief priests all the things that had happened. And when they had assembled the elders and had taken counsel, they gave sufficient silver to the soldiers, saying, "Say his disciples came at night and stole him while we were sleeping; and if the governor hears about this, we shall persuade him and see that you have no trouble"'. Readers are not told exactly what the soldiers reported. They could infer that they were able to report the arrival of the women, the earthquake, the angel's appearance, and, presumably, the opening of the tomb which was found to be empty. The Jewish leaders, on the basis of such a story, would be disinclined to suppose that God had vindicated a man whom they judged had led people astray. Nevertheless, the references to the necessary bribing and to the reassurance that Pilate could be dissuaded from taking action (soldiers who slept on guard normally suffered the death penalty) reinforces the readers' understanding that Jesus had indeed been raised from the dead. The narrative concludes by noting, 'And they took the silver and did as they were instructed. And this statement is reported among Jews to this day'. As in the account of the naming of the field of blood (27.8), the form of the story serves the purpose of explaining the origin of something which still persisted at the time when the narrative was written. It indicates that Jews who did not become Jesus' followers could account for his grave's being empty by the assertion that his disciples removed his corpse. Moreover, the fact that nothing is recounted about an effort by opponents to find Jesus' corpse further reinforces belief in resurrection. Although the emptiness of the tomb was no proof of his resurrection, the production of his corpse while it was still recognizable would have been a disproof. As in the narrative about Jesus' historical ministry, so in this narrative about his resurrection, opponents are used as unwilling and perverted witnesses to the truths the narrative seeks to convey to readers.

The Resurrected Jesus' Commission to his Disciples: 28.16-20[1]

The narrative takes for granted that the women delivered their message to Jesus' disciples and simply notes that 'the eleven disciples went into Galilee to the mountain to which Jesus had commanded them'. In Jesus' instructions to the women, however, no mountain had been mentioned. No doubt a mountain setting was considered appropriate for an extraordinary meeting and commissioning (see 17.1), and it may also have served to remind readers of the slanderer's test, when he showed Jesus the kingdoms of the world from a very high mountain (4.8-10). This story will relate that all authority had been given to Jesus by God after he had rejected satanic rule and had suffered death by crucifixion (28.18). The setting in Galilee (contrast Luke and John 20; cf. John 21) is appropriate because Galilee had been associated with God's deliverance of Gentiles (4.12-16) and the disciples would be instructed to make disciples of all nations (28.19). That the 'eleven disciples' are specifically mentioned excludes the possibility of including either Judas or Joseph of Arimathaea. Only those disciples who had been with Jesus during his historical ministry, who had received his instructions, and who had survived the events in Jerusalem, in however cowardly a fashion, are presented as recipients of Jesus' commission.

The narrative continues: 'And when they saw him, they did obeisance to him, but they doubted' (cf. Jn 20.24-29). Throughout the Gospel, the disciples had been depicted as people of little faith, and the theme is continued to the end. Since belief included fidelity to God, even when encountering persecution and martyrdom, their doubt is unsurprising. The Jesus whom God had vindicated was the Jesus who had been crucified, and they had been told to take up their cross and follow him (16.24-26). Their obeisance, however, like the obeisance of the women, is a recognition of Jesus' status as their master. Once more, the description of this meeting centres on Jesus' words: 'And Jesus came and spoke to them saying, "All authority in heaven and on earth is given to me"'. The human being Jesus, like the 'one like a son of man' in Daniel's vision, had been given all authority by God (Dan. 7.14). He would act as God's agent in the eschatological judgment (25.31-46) because his life, death and resurrection had become the pattern for human fidelity to God. On the basis of this authority Jesus' words continue with a command to the disciples: 'Go therefore and make disciples of all nations'. During the account of Jesus' historical ministry, the disciples had been commanded to engage in a mission to Israel alone (10.5-6), but now that Jesus had been raised from the dead and the final eschatological judgment was in view, they were to extend their mission to all the peoples of the earth. The command makes sense in the

1   See Mk 16.14-18; Lk. 24.36-49; Jn 20.19-23; Acts 1.6-8.

context of scriptural expectations (e.g. Dan. 7.14; Gen. 12.3; 22.18; see Mt. 1.1-17).

What this world mission would involve is then spelt out. First, the disciples were to baptize people 'in the name of the Father and of the Son and of the Holy Spirit'. Since Jesus had been depicted as a law-abiding Jew, readers might have expected that the command to make disciples of all nations would have included a reference to circumcision. But the Gospel never mentions circumcision. It assumes that baptism had replaced circumcision as the rite of entry into the covenant community and ignores the early disputes among Christians about the terms on which Gentiles should enter the church (e.g. Galatians 2; Acts 15). This baptism was to be 'in the name of the Father', that is, in the name of the Creator God whose fatherly care had been stressed throughout the narrative, and whom people had been encouraged to imitate by following his merciful example (e.g. 5.43-48; 6.14-15; 18.21-35). Baptism was also to be in the name of the Son, that is, in the name of the human being Jesus, whose sonship had been depicted as exemplary for other human beings. And baptism was to be in the name of the Holy Spirit, that is, in the name of God's spirit which had inspired the prophets and Jesus, and would inspire Jesus' followers. Hence the Baptist's prediction about Jesus' baptism is seen to be fulfilled (3.11-12).

In modern church practice, when people are baptized in the name of the Father and of the Son and of the Holy Spirit, the understanding of the formula includes the Matthaean meaning but goes beyond it. In the centuries which succeeded the writing of the First Gospel, Christian philosophers discussed the question *how* a human being's life, death and resurrection could give knowledge of the transcendent God. Gradually they formulated answers to this question which recognized on the one hand God's transcendence and on the other hand Jesus' humanity. In the Creed of Nicaea (325 CE), they formulated the doctrine of the Trinity:

> We believe in one God, the Father Almighty, Creator of all things, visible and invisible; and in one Lord, Jesus Christ, the Son of God, only-begotten from the Father, that is, from the being of the Father, God from God, Light from Light, true God from true God, begotten not made, consubstantial with the Father, through whom all things were made ...Who for us people and for our salvation, came down and was incarnate, was made man, suffered and rose again the third day, ascended into heaven, and is coming to judge the living and the dead; and in the Holy Spirit.

Since this creed failed to safeguard the recognition of God's transcendence and of Jesus' humanity during the following century, however, in 461 CE the Calcedonian Definition of the Faith sought to do so more effectively:

> We all unanimously teach that our Lord Jesus Christ is to us one
> and the same Son, the selfsame perfect in Godhead, the selfsame
> perfect in manhood; truly God and truly man; the selfsame of a
> rational soul and body; consubstantial with the Father according to
> the Godhead, the selfsame consubstantial with us according to the
> manhood; like us in all things, sin apart; before the ages begotten of
> the Father as to the Godhead, but in the last days, the selfsame, for
> us and for our salvation, [born] of Mary the Virgin *Theotokos* as to
> the manhood; one and the same Christ, Son, Lord, Only-begotten;
> acknowledged in two natures unconfusedly, unchangeably, indivis-
> ibly, inseparably; the differences of the natures being in no way
> removed because of the union, but rather the property of each
> nature being preserved, and [both] concurring into one *prosopon*
> and one *hypostasis*; not as though he were parted and divided into
> two *prosopa*, but one and the selfsame Son and only-begotten God,
> *Logos*, Lord, Jesus Christ.

The modern practice of baptism in Western churches acknowledges
belief in these credal statements. But first-century writers like the author
of the First Gospel had not puzzled about these issues. They had
learned from Scripture that human beings were to imitate the Creator
God's justice and mercy in obedience to his purpose, and that those
who did so were called God's sons in a metaphorical sense (e.g. Exod.
4.22). The Matthaean narrative takes up this metaphor and encourages
everyone to acknowledge that sonship by living in wholehearted dedication to and dependence on the Creator God who is their Father, as
Jesus had done (e.g. 5.43-48).

The Matthaean instructions continue, 'teaching them [those baptized]
to observe all that I commanded you', that is, all of Jesus' teaching
which had been given in detail in the earlier parts of the narrative. The
emphasis on keeping Jesus' commands is typical of that earlier teaching
(e.g. 6.14-15; 7.21-23; 18.21-35). What is demanded of Jesus' followers is
not passive acceptance of what he had achieved, but active participation in his way of life.

Finally, the resurrected Jesus is depicted offering the disciples reassurance in view of the eschatological judgment: 'And behold, I am with
you always, to the end of the age' (cf. 18.19-20). Nevertheless, his presence with his disciples would be unlike his presence with them during
his historical ministry. Some of the parables even picture this period
before the end of the age as a time in which Jesus is absent (24.45-51;
25.1-13, 15-30). Moreover, in the judgment scene in 25.31-46, Jesus'
presence is conceived in terms of his identification with those who suffered hardships. In other words, Jesus' presence in the world was to be
found in those followers whose lives conformed to his, who had eaten
the broken bread which was his body and had drunk the wine which
was his blood, who had made his life their own. They were to become
God's sons in the manner in which he was God's son, to become Jesus'

brothers and sisters, continuing his mission, inspired by God's spirit as he was. Hence the narrative ends by making their responsibilities known to them. In spite of the disciples' failures this scene of vindication and reconciliation, and the promise of God's spirit, provide a foundation for the mission of Jesus' covenant community. They look beyond the present of the disciples and of the readers to the whole task of Jesus' followers before the imminent end of the age.

The Matthaean narrative about Jesus' resurrection has therefore achieved a number of goals. It has made clear that resurrection involved personal post-mortem survival through bodily transformation for an immortal individual existence, brought about by the Creator God in vindication of Jesus' fidelity. But this vindication included vindication of Jesus' way of life, implying that all people should follow in his way in obedience to the Creator's God's purpose. This way of life, advocated by the Matthaean narrative, provides a particular answer to the problem of evil in the world, especially the ethical evil of people's injustice and violence. It assures those who refuse to meet violence with violence but who follow a way which inevitably involves suffering that God will vindicate them in a post-mortem eternal life. The Gospels according to Luke and John, which both set resurrection stories in Jerusalem (Lk. 24.36-49; Jn 20.19-29), achieve the same aims through different details. Clearly, traditions about meetings with the resurrected Jesus had reached no fixed form by the time the Gospels were written (cf. 1 Cor. 15.1-11 and the additions to Mark 16). Each Gospel conveys the reality of Jesus' resurrection and its significance in stories which form a suitable climax to its particular theological and ethical themes.

Appendix

Quotations From Scripture in the Gospel According to Matthew

We would expect authors who write in Greek to quote Scripture in its Greek version, the Septuagint, as Paul does in his epistles. This is often the case in the Gospel according to Matthew (see list 1). Sometimes there are slight differences between the Matthaean quotation and the Septuagint text which has come down to us (see list 2). These differences may be explained in one of three ways: the text of the Septuagint known to the author differed from that which has come down to us, or the author quoted from memory with slight inaccuracies, or the author altered the text of the Septuagint so that it fitted more smoothly into the context of the Gospel. Where the quotations differ markedly from our Septuagint (see list 3), the variation may be explained in one of two ways: the Matthaean text is an allusion to scriptural passages rather than a quotation, or the author's text of the Septuagint was different from ours.

List 1. Quotations which exactly conform to the Septuagint text which has come down to us

Matthew 1.23 = Isa. 8.8

    3.3 = Isa. 40.3 (= Mk 1.3)

    4.4 = Deut. 8.3

    4.6 = Psalm 91, the first part of v. 11 and v. 12

    4.7 = Deut. 6.16

    5.21 = Exod. 20.15

    5.27 = Exod. 20.13

    5.38 = Exod. 21.24

    5.43 and 22.39 = Lev. 19.18

    9.13 and 12.7 = Hos. 6.6

    12.40 = Jon. 1.17

    13.14-15 = Isa. 6.9-10

    15.4 = Exod. 20.12

    19.4 = Gen. 1.27

    19.18-19 = Exod. 20.12-16 (except that the order is different) and
        Lev. 19.18.

    21.5 = Isa. 62.11

21.9 and 23.39 = Ps. 118.26 (Matthew prefaces and follows the quotation in 21.9 with a transliteration of the Hebrew *hosanna*, as does Mk 11.9. The Septuagint translates the Hebrew into Greek).

21.13 = Isa. 56.7 (Matthew omits 'for all the nations' from Isaiah and from Mk 11.17).

21.13 = Jer. 7.11 (= Mk 11.17)

21.16 = Ps. 8.3

21.42 = Ps. 118.22-23 (= Mk 12.10-11)

22.32 = Exod. 3.6, 15

List 2. Quotations which differ in minor respects from the Septuagint which has come down to us

Matthew 1.23, Isa. 7.14

2.15, Hos. 11.1

2.18, Jer. 31.15

4.10, Deut. 6.13

4.15-16, Isa. 9.1-2

10.35, Mic. 7.6

15.4, Exod. 21.17

15.8-9, Isa. 29.13

18.16, Deut. 19.15

19.5, Gen. 2.24

21.5, Zech. 9.9

22.44, Ps. 110.1

27.46, Ps. 22.1 (Matthew also differs from Mk 15.34).

List 3. Quotations which differ markedly from the Septuagint which has come down to us

Matthew 2.6, Mic. 5.2

5.31, Deut. 24.1. See also Mt. 19.7 which also differs from Deut. 24.1, and from Mt. 5.31 and from Mk 10.4.

5.33, Lev. 19.12, Num. 30.2, Deut. 23.21

5.43, nowhere in Scripture.

8.17, Isa. 53.4

11.10, Mal. 3.1 (Matthew's text agrees with Mk 1.2 but adds 'before you').

12.18-21, Isa. 42.1-4

13.35, Ps. 78.2

22.24, Gen. 38.8, Deut. 25.5

22.37, Deut. 6.5 (Matthew also differs from Mk 12.29-30).

24.30 and 26.64, Dan. 7.13 (Matthew is also different from Mk 13.26 and Mk 14.62).

27.9-10, Zech. 11.12-13, Jer. 32.6-9

Bibliography

Bauer, D.R., *The Structure of Matthew's Gospel: A Study in Literary Design* (JSNTSup, 31; Bible and Literature Series, 15; Sheffield: JSOT Press, 1988).

Davies, W.D., and D. Allison, *Matthew* (3 vols.; ICC; Edinburgh: T. & T. Clark, 1988, 1991, forthcoming).

Edwards, R.A., *Matthew's Story of Jesus* (Philadelphia: Fortress Press, 1985).

Gundry, R.H., *Matthew: A Commentary on his Literary and Theological Art* (Grand Rapids: Eerdmans, 1982).

Howell, D.B., *Matthew's Inclusive Story* (JSNTSup, 42; Sheffield: JSOT Press, 1989).

Iser, W., *The Act of Reading: A Theory of Aesthetic Response* (Baltimore: John Hopkins University Press, 1978).

Luz, U., *Matthew 1–7* (Minneapolis: Augsburg–Fortress, 1989; ET Edinburgh: T. & T. Clark, 1990).

Norris, C., *What's Wrong with Post-Modernism?* (London: Harvester Wheatsheaf, 1991).

Rivkin, E., *What Crucified Jesus?* (London: SCM Press, 1986).

Sanders, E.P., *Jewish Law from Jesus to the Mishnah* (London: SCM Press; Philadelphia: Trinity Press International, 1990).

—*Judaism: Practice and Belief, 63BCE–66CE* (London: SCM Press; Philadelphia: Trinity Press International, 1992).

—*Jesus and Judaism* (London: SCM Press, 1985).

Suleiman, S.R., and I. Grosman (eds.), *The Reader in the Text* (Princeton, NJ: Princeton University Press, 1980).

Tompkins, J.P., *Reader-Response Criticism* (Baltimore: Johns Hopkins University Press, 1980).

Vermes, G., *Jesus the Jew* (London: Collins, 1973).

—*The Religion of Jesus the Jew* (London: SCM Press, 1993).

Index of References

Old Testament

Apocrypha

New Testament

Index of Modern Authors